本书由中国联合国教科文组织全国委员会秘书处、联合国教科文组织驻华代表处提供支持

面向 2030

中国教育扶贫实践

联合国教科文组织国际农村教育研究与培训中心 / 编

社会科学文献出版社
SOCIAL SCIENCES ACADEMIC PRESS (CHINA)

图书在版编目(CIP)数据

面向2030：中国教育扶贫实践 / 联合国教科文组织
国际农村教育研究与培训中心编. -- 北京：社会科学文
献出版社，2023.6
ISBN 978-7-5228-1764-4

Ⅰ.①面… Ⅱ.①联… Ⅲ.①教育－扶贫－研究－中
国 Ⅳ.①G52

中国国家版本馆CIP数据核字（2023）第076355号

面向2030：中国教育扶贫实践

编　　者 / 联合国教科文组织国际农村教育研究与培训中心

出 版 人 / 王利民
组稿编辑 / 任文武
责任编辑 / 郭　峰
文稿编辑 / 程亚欣
责任印制 / 王京美

出　　版 / 社会科学文献出版社·城市和绿色发展分社（010）59367143
　　　　　　地址：北京市北三环中路甲29号院华龙大厦　邮编：100029
　　　　　　网址：www.ssap.com.cn
发　　行 / 社会科学文献出版社（010）59367028
印　　装 / 三河市东方印刷有限公司

规　　格 / 开　本：787mm×1092mm　1/16
　　　　　　印　张：14.5　字　数：261千字
版　　次 / 2023年6月第1版　2023年6月第1次印刷
书　　号 / ISBN 978-7-5228-1764-4
定　　价 / 98.00元

读者服务电话：4008918866

序

　　贫困是人类社会的顽疾，是全世界面临的共同挑战。消除贫困是人类孜孜以求的梦想，人类发展史就是与贫困不懈斗争的历史。2015 年，《2030 年可持续发展议程》在联合国大会第七十届会议上被通过，消除贫困被列为首要目标。自《2030 年可持续发展议程》实施以来，国际社会携手努力，不断取得进展。然而，困难和挑战依然严峻，新冠肺炎疫情的暴发更是加剧了全球各地的贫困状况。联合国发布的《2021 年可持续发展目标报告》显示，2020 年全球陷入贫困的人口数量增加 1.2 亿左右，极端贫困率由 2019 年的 8.4% 升至 9.5%，预计 2030 年全球将仍有 7% 的人口生活在极端贫困中。鉴于此，采取更大力度、更富创新性的减贫举措，努力实现消除贫困目标迫在眉睫。

　　1949 年中华人民共和国成立后，中国开展了大规模社会主义建设，致力于为摆脱贫困、改善人民生活而奋斗。1978 年实行改革开放以来，中国进行了大规模、有计划、有组织的扶贫开发工作，减贫进程加快推进，贫困人口大幅度减少。按照中国现行贫困标准计算，1978 年中国农村贫困人口数量约 7.7 亿，农村贫困发生率高达 97.5%；经过 30 多年努力，到 2012 年，农村贫困人口数量下降至 9899 万，贫困发生率降为 10.2%，扶贫工作取得显著成效。但剩余的贫困人口大部分生活在生态环境脆弱、自然灾害频发、交通不便、基础设施和社会事业发展滞后的 14 个集中连片特困地区，是脱贫难度最大的地方，脱贫工作任务异常艰巨。2012 年以来，中国把脱贫攻坚摆在治国理政的突出位置，把实施精准脱贫、开展脱贫攻坚、消除绝对贫困作为全面建成小康社会的底线任务。习近平亲自动员部署，全国各级政府全面动员，组织实施了人类历史上规模空前、力度最大、惠及人口最多的脱贫攻坚战。虽然突如其来的新冠肺炎疫情给脱贫工作带来了新的困难和挑战，但中国政府没有动摇决心和目标，更加坚定地动员一切可用资源，上下一心，向着消除绝对贫困的目标发起总攻。2021年2月25日，习近平在全国脱贫攻坚总结表彰大会上庄严宣告，脱贫攻坚战取得了全面胜利，中国完成了消除绝对贫困的艰巨任务。中国现行标准下9899万农村贫困人口全部脱贫，832个贫困县全部摘帽，12.8万个贫困村全部出列，区域性整体贫困得到解决，困扰中华民族几千年的绝对贫困问题得到历史性解决，创造了彪炳史册的人间奇迹。中国为全球减贫事业做出了重大贡献：1978年以来，按照现行贫困标准计算，中国7.7亿农村贫困人口全部脱贫；按照世界银行国际贫困标准，中国减贫人口占同期全球减贫人口70%以上。特别是在全球贫困状况依然严峻、一些国家贫富分化加剧的背景下，中国提前10年实现《2030年可持续发展议程》减贫目标，同时积极参与国际减贫合作，成为世界减贫事业的倡导者、推动者和贡献者。

教育是人类传承文明和知识、培养年轻一代、创造美好生活的根本途径。作为联合国《2030年可持续发展议程》的第4项目标，让全民享有包容、公平而有质量的终身学习机会，其既是17项目标的组成部分，也是实现其他目标的关键基础，尤其与消除贫困目标紧密相关。普及公平而有质量的教育可以防止贫困代际传递，从根本上消灭贫困。而贫困是普及公平而有质量教育的最大障碍，消灭贫困将极大推动《教育2030议程》目标的实现。然而，我们看到《教育2030议程》的实施并不理想，当前全球仍有超过2亿儿童失学，只有60%的学生能够完成高中教育，按照目前的进展情况，全球将无法在2030年实现既定发展目标。2020年，突如其来的新冠肺炎疫情给全球发展带来冲击，全球贫困人口总量在数十年来首次出现增加，7100多万人陷入极端贫困，超过190个国家的学校暂时关闭，5亿多学生无法进行远程教育学习。显而易见，将教育和减贫相结合，既解决扶贫教育事业发展之困，也通过提供教育扶持贫困人口从而增强其自身内生发展能力，是加快推进教育和减贫事业发展、实现2030年可持续发展目标的重要途径。

中国在与贫困做斗争的过程中，始终坚持"治贫先治愚、扶贫先扶智"，持续发挥教育的基础性、先导性和全局性作用，建立了一整套上下联动、统筹协调的教育脱贫攻坚领导决策体系、责任落实体系、政策制度体系、投入保障体系、考核评估体系、对口联系机制等，为打赢教育脱贫攻坚战提供了坚强支撑，也为后续全面推进乡村振兴积累了宝贵经验。同时中国也在促进《教育2030议程》目标的实现上取得了显著成就，其中，备受瞩目的是贫困家庭学生辍学问题得到历史性解决，实现动态清零，贫困学生实现应助尽助，贫困地区各级各类学校发生了格局性变化，一大批贫困家庭的孩子或家庭成员通过教育、培训掌握了就业技能，找到了有尊严的工作，带动家庭走出贫困，为阻断贫困代际传递奠定了坚实基础。

为了通过富有成效的实践经验，更好推动教育和减贫事业联动发展，促进《2030年可持续发展议程》特别是其目标1和目标4的实现，在中华人民共和国教育部、中国联合国教科文组织全国委员会以及联合国教科文组织北京办事处的支持下，联合国教科文组织国际农村教育研究与培训中心从中国教育脱贫攻坚的丰富实践中挖掘整理了一批教育减贫的经典案例与全球分享。

本书共分为三章，第一章从国际视角综述发展教育与减贫的关系，以及当前全球实现联合国可持续发展目标的情况，特别是目标1和目标4。

第二章概况介绍中国实施教育减贫的历史情况，重点介绍2012年以来，中国实施精准脱贫、开展脱贫攻坚的情况，包括总体战略、政策框架、教育精准脱贫的具体战略、实施精神，以及取得的显著成效。

第三章选取一批中国教育减贫典型案例，从五个方面介绍中国教育精准扶贫政策与措施：第一，确保教育的普及性和公平性，确保贫困地区学生有平等的受教育机会。第二，提高质量，确保贫困地区学生完成学业，学到必要的技能。第三，技术赋能帮助贫困家庭直接脱贫。第四，普通高等学校与职业院校帮助贫困地区发展产业及经济。第五，多渠道共同推动教育脱贫。

我们认为中国在教育减贫实践中探索形成的经验，既属于中国也属于世界，可以为国际上致力于教育减贫的人们提供借鉴。但需要强调的是，世界各国国情不同、所处发展阶段不同，减贫标准、方式方法、路径手段也必然会不同。要真正有效地实现教育减贫，还应立足本国本地实际情况和自身积累的有效经验，充分发挥本国本地比较优势。编者期待与各国相关机构加强教育减贫交流合作，携手推进实现联合国 2030 年可持续发展目标，为构建没有贫困、共同发展的人类命运共同体做出更大贡献。

联合国教科文组织

国际农村教育研究与培训中心

2022 年 11 月

目　录

第一章　贫困、减贫与教育的国际背景

第二章　中国教育精准扶贫的行动与成效

第三章　中国教育减贫的实践案例

第一章

贫困、减贫与教育的国际背景

一　贫困的概念

贫困是一个复杂的概念，最初主要指物质生活的贫困，但随着多年来人们对贫困认识的深入，贫困的内容与标准也在不断发展变化。如根据不同的划分标准，贫困可以被分为相对贫困、绝对贫困，生存型、温饱型和发展型贫困等。牛津大学曾提出了多维贫困指数（Multidimensional Poverty Index, MPI）[①]，包括健康（营养状况、儿童死亡率）、教育（儿童入学率、受教育程度）和生活水平（饮用水、电、日常生活使用燃料、室内空间面积、环境卫生和耐用消费品）三个维度，用以衡量个体的贫困属性及贫困程度，并对单纯依靠收入评估贫困进行补充。

近年来，贫困逐渐成为一个包括经济、社会、政治、环境等的多层面概念，其意味着选择和机会的匮乏、尊严和人权的侵犯，尤其是能力和技能的缺失。联合国开发计划署发布的《2019年人类发展报告》

---

① Alkire, S., Santos, M. E., "Multidimensional Poverty Index," 2010, www.ophi.org.uk.

（Human Development Report 2019）进一步扩展了能力的概念，并将其分为基本能力和强化能力（见图1-1）。报告认为，尽管人的基本能力对其自身生存很重要，但仅具备基本能力还不够，强化能力对人类寻求有尊严的生活有着不可或缺的作用。该报告还认为，强调由基本能力向强化能力的转变，提高人的能力和技能是社会解决贫困问题与实现可持续发展目标的需要。

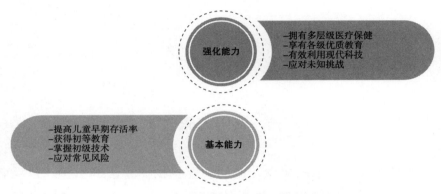

图1-1　人类发展：从基本能力到强化能力

资料来源：联合国开发计划署《2019年人类发展报告》。

二　教育、能力提升与减贫

教育是人们获得能力提升技能最基本、最重要的渠道，受教育权的缺失既是贫困的主要表现，也是导致长期贫困的重要原因。普及教育是积累人力资本和消除贫困的关键途径，保障受教育权是消除社会排斥的重要方式，也是实现人的全面发展和社会的可持续发展的重要基础。受教育权的缺失是"教育贫困"（教育水平低下）这一概念的突出表现，充分保障受教育权也是打破"经济欠发达—教育贫困—人力资本匮乏—经济发展滞后加剧……"这一恶性循环最有效的手段。因此，改善"教育贫困"现象，才能从根本上消除贫困。

普及基础教育、开展技术技能培训，能够帮助社会成员获得知识和提升技能、提高他们的生产效率，有助于使他们拥有应对贫困、饥饿、社会排斥等风险的能力，从而帮助贫困家庭摆脱贫困。教育为农村家庭提供从事非农工作的选择，能够促使他们增强自身创收能力，拓宽他们的收入渠道。除了提高知识和技能水平，教育还为人们提供对有效参与社会转型进程至关重要的价值观、信念和态度。从人力资本的角度来看，人力资本的积累能帮助人们摆脱贫困、加快经济增长。通过促进针对最弱势群体的终身学习，有助于打破贫困的代际传递。[1] 有证据表明，受教育程度越高，贫困程度越低。如果低收入国家的所有学生都掌握了基本的阅读技能，这些国家的贫困人口将减少 1.71 亿。[2] 同样地，25~34 岁人口群体的平均受教育年限与其贫困状况（以每天不到 2 美元为衡量标准）之间存在很强的相关性。联合国儿童基金会 2015 年发布的《教育和公平投资案例》（The Investment Case for Education and Equity）显示，受教育年限每增加一年，贫困率就会降低 9 个百分点。[3]

受教育程度也与人们把握摆脱贫困机会的意识与能力高度关联。联合国教科文组织统计研究所曾分析 1965~2010 年教育对发展中国家经济增长和减贫的影响。报告指出，如果所有成年人能够多接受 2 年的教育，全球近 6000 万人就可以摆脱贫困。同样，如果所有成年人能完成中等教育，全球 4.2 亿人就可以摆脱贫困，全球贫困人口将减少一半

---

[1]　World Bank, *Global Monitoring Report 2014/2015: Ending Poverty and Sharing Prosperity*, 2015, pubdocs. worldbank.org.

[2]　United Nations Educational, Scientific and Cultural organization (UNESCO), *Education for All 2000-2015: Achievements and Challenges, EFA Global Monitoring Report 2015*, 2015, unesdoc.unesco.org.

[3]　United Nations International Children's Emergency Fund (UNICEF), *The Investment Case for Education and Equity*, 2015, www.unicef.org.

以上。① 此外，在教育降低收入不平等方面，根据114个国家在1985~2005年的数据，平均受教育时间延长1年能够让基尼系数降低1.4个百分点。②

提升妇女受教育水平能够有效改善儿童福祉，对实现两性平等、女性赋权至关重要。2011年，时任联合国常务副秘书长阿莎－罗丝·米吉罗（Asha-Rose Migiro）在联合国妇女地位委员会第五十五届会议上强调，为妇女和女童投资是社会发展的强力推进器。教育则是最好也是最正确的一种投资，因为教育不仅是经济增长的主要推动力，更是赋予女性权利的催化剂。通过教育，妇女有更多机会从事有报酬的工作，保持健康状态并参与社会生活的各个领域，在提高经济收入水平的同时，增进其子女和家庭的福祉。2015年，联合国儿童基金会指出，如果低收入和中等收入国家的所有妇女都完成了中学教育，儿童接受免疫疫苗接种的机会将增加43%。联合国教科文组织称，在低收入国家，如果所有妇女都完成初等教育，发育不良儿童的数量将减少170万。此外，女童的受教育程度与晚婚、晚育也有关联。联合国教科文组织在2014年进行的一项预测显示，如果南亚、西亚和撒哈拉以南非洲的所有女孩都达到中等教育水平，童婚女童数量将从290万下降到100万（下降66%），早孕人口也会相应从340万下降到140万（下降59%）。

事实表明，教育普及和技术技能培训对想要摆脱贫困的人口尤为重要。消除贫困的关键是使人们拥有基本素养与技能，让他们拥有生产力并获得从事有尊严的工作所需要的能力，由此有效地帮助他们减少挫折和风险，打破社会歧视枷锁。

研究表明，教育与技能获取、教育与就业机会之间存在联系。教育

---

① United Nations Educational, Scientific and Cultural organization (UNESCO), *Reducing Global Poverty through Universal Primary and Secondary Education, Policy Paper 32, Fact Sheet 44*, 2017, uis.unesco.org.

② United Nations International Children's Emergency Fund (UNICEF), *The Investment Case for Education and Equity*, 2015, www.unicef.org.

打开了通向更好和高薪工作的大门。受过中等教育的人与没有受过中等教育的人、受过中等教育的人与受过高等教育的人之间的差异是明显的。受过高等教育的人比没有大学文凭的人更有可能找到工作。在经济困难时期，教育通常是防止失业的良好保障。

三　可持续发展议程中的教育与消除贫困

（一）《2030 年可持续发展议程》与全球减贫

2015 年 9 月，联合国大会第七十届会议在纽约召开，各会员国的国家元首、政府首脑和高级别代表制定了新的全球可持续发展目标，即《2030 年可持续发展议程》。该议程强调消除一切形式和表象的贫困，其中消除极端贫困是世界的最大挑战，是实现可持续发展目标必须完成的任务。在全世界消除一切形式的贫困也成为所有可持续发展目标中的首要任务，其中，"到 2030 年，在全球所有人口中消除极端贫困""到 2030 年，按各国标准界定的陷入各种形式贫困的各年龄段妇女和儿童至少减半"等 7 个具体目标共同构成了全球可持续发展的宏大愿景。

可持续发展目标致力于寻求应对全球挑战的方略，包括减轻贫困（可持续发展目标 1）、零饥饿（可持续发展目标 2）、良好健康与福祉（可持续发展目标 3）、优质教育（可持续发展目标 4）、性别平等（可持续发展目标 5）、清洁饮用水和卫生（可持续发展目标 6）、体面工作和经济增长（可持续发展目标 8）、减少不平等（可持续发展目标 10）以及负责任消费和生产（可持续发展目标 12），上述所有目标是减贫的关键。虽然每个目标都有其自身的重要性，并代表着特定的全球挑战，但 17 个可持续发展目标作为一个整体是紧密相连的，这意味着在一个目标上的停滞不前将阻碍在其他目标上取得进展。因此，向可持续、和平、繁荣的社会发展需要一种全面和综合的方法，明确认识可持续发展目标之间错综复杂的相互关系。例如，减轻贫困（可持续发展目标 1）、良好健康与福祉（可持续发展目标 3）以及优质教育（可持续发展目标 4）与大多数其他目标具有协同关系。同样，在其他可持续发展目标方面取得的进展也将对减轻贫困、良好健康与福祉以及优质教育产生积极影响。可持续发展目标的相互联系和综合性质对实现包括减贫目标在内的可持续发展目标至关重要。特别是教育，它是所有可持续发展目标实现的基础，教育作为实现人类发展挑战的支柱，其重要性是众所周知的。在通过《2030 年可持续发展议程》后不久，联合国驻华系统与中国政府联合发布了《2016–2020 年联合国对华发展援助框架》（下文简称《框架》），为联合国和中国未来 5 年的伙伴关系奠定了基础。该框架是联合国系统与中国政府以及一系列利益攸关方，经过严格协商后达成一致的结果。《框架》是一份战略性文件，旨在为中国实现国家发展重点的努力提供综合支持。该框架确定了 3 个工作重点：第一，减贫和公平发展；第二，环境改善和可持续发展；第三，加强全球参与。《框架》的意义不仅在于帮助中国应对自身面临的发展挑战，还在于帮助中国更多地参与包括减贫在内的全球发展挑战。

经过各国的共同努力，特别是中国等新兴国家的重要贡献，过去几十年，全球减贫事业取得显著进展。2018 年，联合国秘书长安东尼奥·古特雷斯（António Guterres）向联合国可持续发展高级别政治论坛提交的实现可持续发展目标进展情况报告指出，在过去 20 年中，每人每天生活费不到 1.90 美元的工人的比例大幅下降，从 2000 年的 26.9% 降至 2017 年的 9.2%，世界许多地区在扩大社会保障方面也取得了重大进展。但近年来，由于减贫驱动力不足，全球减贫速率呈现下降趋势。有数据显示，2017 年平均每秒钟就有 1 个人脱离贫困，但由于全球经济增速放缓，这一数据在 2018 年下降为 0.8 人 / 秒，2019 年已减缓为 0.6 人 / 秒。[1] 从地

---

① Kharas, H., Hamel, K., Hofer, M., & Tong, B., "Global Poverty Reduction Has Slowed Down Again," 2019, www.brookings.edu.

区来看，在《2030 年可持续发展议程》开始实施的 2016 年，非洲贫困人口占全球贫困人口的 60%，2019 年这一数字达到 70%，且非洲贫困人口仍在不断增长中。[①] 因此，全球减贫事业面临的挑战十分严峻，非洲很可能是 2030 年终结全球极端贫困的最后阵地。据预测，到 2030 年全球仍将有约 6 亿人生活在极端贫困中。

突如其来的新冠肺炎疫情重创全球经济，给全球人民带来了直接和长期的消极影响。全球极端贫困人口数量自 1998 年以来首次增加，有 1.19 亿 ~1.24 亿人陷入极端贫困，不平等现象加剧。2020 年，全球减少了 2.55 亿个全职工作岗位，1.01 亿儿童和青少年没有达到最低阅读水平，未来 10 年面临童婚风险的女童将增加 1000 万。新冠肺炎疫情对发达经济体和发展中经济体都有较大影响，对发展中国家贫困人口和弱势群体的冲击更为巨大。新冠肺炎疫情使可持续发展目标自 2015 年启动以来在减贫领域取得的所有成果都被抵消了。

新冠肺炎疫情导致的极端贫困人口预测数据的变化如表 1-1 所示，其展示了 2019 年年底（新冠肺炎疫情发生前）极端贫困预测数据与 2020 年 10 月（新冠肺炎疫情发生后）极端贫困预测数据的对比。其中，第一列是 2019 年的基线，估计 2019 年有 6.5 亿人处于极端贫困[②]。值得注意的是，根据 2019 年的估计，极端贫困率在 2019~2030 年总体上呈稳步下降的趋势：从 2019 年的 8.4% 下降到 2020 年的 8%、2021 年的 7.6%、2030 年的 6.3%。然而，根据 2020 年的预测，受新冠肺炎疫情的影响，2020 年极端贫困人口比例上升到 9.9%，2021 年略有下降（9.3%），到 2030 年将下降到 7%。

---

① Kharas, H., Hamel, K., & Hofer, M., "Rethinking Global Poverty Reduction in 2019," 2018, www.brookings.edu.

② 极端贫困的定义：按 2011 年购买力平价（Purchasing Power Parity, PPP）计算，每日人均花销低于 1.90 美元的家庭。

表 1-1　新冠肺炎疫情导致的极端贫困人口预测数量和占比的变化

单位：人，%

		2019 年	2020 年	2021 年	2030 年
2019 年年底（新冠肺炎疫情发生前）	极端贫困人口	650433712	621931609	598347067	536923904
	极端贫困人口占世界总人口的比例	8.4	8.0	7.6	6.3
2020 年 10 月（新冠肺炎疫情发生后）	极端贫困人口	646806659	766032180	726524822	597902578
	极端贫困人口占世界总人口的比例	8.4	9.9	9.3	7.0

资料来源：Kharas, H., The Impact of Covid-19 on Global Extreme Poverty, 2020。

世界陷入经济、健康和教育方面的危机，暴露了各国内部以及国家之间的脆弱和不平等。其中，受新冠肺炎疫情严重影响的群体之一就是发展中国家的"低技能人群"。新冠肺炎疫情引发经济发展迟缓甚至倒退，大量低技能人口找不到工作或者失业，无法获得固定收入而引发的贫困现象比比皆是。这体现了掌握技能和能力的紧迫性，更反映了教育增权赋能以及运用教育手段减贫的重要性。

（二）《教育 2030 议程》的开启

保障受教育权、减少文盲数量、促进全社会教育发展等手段能够改变欠发达地区贫困人口的生活困境，逐渐成为国际社会的共识。21 世纪以来，全球各个国家在普及全民教育、扫盲、提升教育水平等方面做出了积极的努力。2000 年 4 月，国际社会在塞内加尔达喀尔通过了聚焦全民教育的《达喀尔行动纲领》。其重申了 1990 年在泰国宗滴恩通过的《世界全民教育宣言》的全球愿景，承诺到 2015 年满足所有儿童、青少年和成年人的学习需求，而其体现在六个目标中。这些目标包括改善幼儿保育和教育、普及初级教育、提供生活技能学习机会、减少成人文盲、确保教育中的性别平等和提高教育质量。2000 年 9 月，联合国在纽约通过了《联合国千年宣言》，提出了八项千年发展目标（Millennium Development Goals, MDGs），其中有两项目标均与教育有关。

2015 年是全球实现全民教育目标以及实现同教育相关的千年发展目标的终结年，为此，需要全面评估各个国家自 2000 年以来取得的成果和经验，以反映在不同国家、地区和国际方面采用的为实现该教育目标的策略。2015 年 4 月，联合国教科文组织发布《2015 年全民教育全球监测报告》（后改名《全球教育监测报告》），对国际社会在过去 15 年中所取得的成果进行了总结和分析，时任联合国秘书长潘基文在为报告发布而发表的致辞中指出："过去 15 年来，国际社会在促进全民教育方面取得了诸多进展。例如，进入小学接受教育的儿童比以往增加了 5000 万，而失学儿童和青少年的数量减少了近一半，许多国家在增加包括女童在内的小学注册率方面取得了长足的进展。"报告指出，2015 年有 47% 的国家实现了全民教育六个目标中的第一个目标，改善幼儿保育和教育；52% 的国家实现了第二个目标，确保所有儿童尤其是女童，完成优质免费的初级教育。同时，报告的评估结果显示，全民教育目标仍是一个尚未完成的议程。虽然在增加男孩和女孩就学人数方面取得了重大进展，但总体而言，全民教育的六个目标和千年发展目标未能在 2015 年最后期限之前实现。[①] 世界各地的教育系统继续受低学习质量的困扰。基于性别、种族、语言和残疾的教育差距仍在扩大。文盲率居高不下，群众技能水平低，且获得职业技术教育和高等教育的机会有限。儿童和青年未具备在全球化世界中发挥作用的知识、价值观、能力和态度，也未能为建立一个包容、和平、文明、可持续的社会做出贡献。显然，世界需要一个新的教育议程，其不仅要关注全民教育目标未完成的工作和千年发展目标中与教育相关的内容，而且要有效应对当前和未来在全球范围内的教育挑战。

---

① United Nations Educational, Scientific and Cultural organization (UNESCO), *Education for All 2000-2015: Achievements and Challenges. EFA Global Monitoring Report 2015*, 2015, unesdoc.unesco.org.

在此背景下，2015 年 5 月，国际社会在韩国仁川举办了世界教育论坛，各国际组织代表、国家元首与政府首脑积极参会。论坛上通过了《仁川宣言》（Incheon Declaration），在 2015 年 9 月，联合国大会第七十届会议也正式通过《2030 年可持续发展议程》，《仁川宣言》明确的 2030 年全球教育发展目标成为 2030 年可持续发展目标的重要内容之一。同年 11 月，联合国教科文组织第三十八届大会通过了旨在落实 2030 年可持续发展目标 4 的"教育 2030 行动框架"。该行动框架包括四项原则，即提供免费和高质量的义务教育、重申教育是一项社会必须承担的公共责任、有必要为成年人提供终身学习的机会、优先致力于实现性别平等，从而为各国政府与合作伙伴提供了行动指南。

（三）《教育 2030 议程》面临的挑战

《教育 2030 议程》发布以来，世界各国纷纷采取措施，将提高学习质量、促进社会包容和性别平等、增强技能和能力、推动终身学习、教师发展等作为谋求可持续发展目标高度相关的行动领域。然而，实现《教育 2030 议程》目标仍然面临很多挑战。

1. 失学儿童数量仍然庞大，且主要集中在发展中国家特别是欠发达国家，保障儿童受教育权面临巨大挑战

依靠发展教育消除贫困任重道远。联合国教科文组织统计研究所的一份分析报告指出，自 2008 年以来，教育事业停滞不前。据报道，2015 年约有 2.64 亿儿童、青少年和青年未能接受学校教育。2000~2015 年按受教育程度和性别划分的全球失学率如图 1-2 所示，自 2008 年以来，失学儿童的比例几乎一直居高不下。2015 年，由于各种原因，小学儿童失学比例为 9%，初中失学青少年比例为 16%，高中失学青少年比例则达到 37%。

联合国教科文组织《2020 年全球教育监测报告》显示，受到社会身份、家庭背景和个人能力等因素影响，全球有 2.58 亿儿童和青少年无法

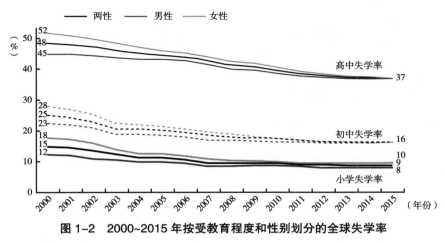

图 1-2　2000~2015 年按受教育程度和性别划分的全球失学率

资料来源：联合国教科文组织《2017 年全球教育监测报告》。

接受教育，新冠肺炎疫情则进一步加剧了教育排斥现象。据估计，全球约有 40% 的低收入和中低收入国家在学校因疫情停课期间未能向贫困学生提供任何帮助。此外，在出勤率方面，贫富家庭学生的差距较大。在65 个中低收入国家中的小学学龄儿童里，最贫穷家庭和最富有家庭的学生的入学率平均差距为 9 个百分点，初中学龄青少年的平均差距为 13 个百分点，高中为 27 个百分点。由于贫穷家庭的学生更有可能中途辍学，贫穷和富有家庭的学生在教育完成率上的差距更大，小学完成率相差为30 个百分点，初中为 45 个百分点，高中为 40 个百分点。

2015 年不同收入水平国家的小学、初中、高中辍学率和辍学人数分别如表 1-2、表 1-3、表 1-4 所示，低收入国家的辍学率明显高于中低收入、中等收入和高收入国家。例如，低收入国家的小学辍学率为 19.1%，而中低收入国家、中高收入国家和高收入国家的小学辍学率分别为 9.7%、4.3% 和 2.8%。低收入和高收入国家的初中辍学率分别为 38.5% 和 1.5%，高中辍学率分别为 62.3% 和 7.1%。

性别、种族、语言、地理位置、人口迁移和许多其他因素进一步加剧了教育发展的差距，使得社会处境不利的群体在接受教育时面临更多困难。鉴于这些趋势，2019 年联合国可持续发展高级别政治论坛得出结论，世界还没有真正走上实现可持续发展的道路。如果该状况在未来十年得不到改变，到 2030 年将仍有 2.2 亿儿童和青少年不能接受学校教育。如果青少年不能完成中学学业、不能取得相关学习成果，那将会对实现其他可持续发展目标造成不利影响。

表 1-2　2015 年不同收入水平国家的小学辍学率和辍学人数

单位：%，百万人

	辍学率				辍学人数		
	两性	男性	女性	女／男比例	两性	男性	女性
低收入国家	19.1	16.7	21.4	1.28	19.9	8.8	11.1
中低收入国家	9.7	9.0	10.6	1.18	31.0	14.8	16.2
中高收入国家	4.3	4.1	4.5	1.10	8.4	4.2	4.2
高收入国家	2.8	3.0	2.6	0.87	2.2	1.2	1.0
世界（平均水平）	8.8	8.1	9.7	1.20	61.4	29.0	32.4

资料来源：UNESCO, Education 2030: Incheon Declaration and Framework for Action for the Implementation of Sustainable Development Goal 4, 2015。

表 1-3　2015 年不同收入水平国家的初中辍学率和辍学人数

单位：%，百万人

	辍学率				辍学人数		
	两性	男性	女性	女／男比例	两性	男性	女性
低收入国家	38.5	35.7	41.3	1.16	19.4	9.1	10.3
中低收入国家	19.2	20.4	17.9	0.87	33.7	18.6	15.1
中高收入国家	7.1	7.3	7.7	1.05	8.2	4.1	4.1
高收入国家	1.5	–	–	–	0.6	–	–
世界（平均水平）	16.4	16.4	16.3	0.99	61.9	32.1	29.8

资料来源：UNESCO, Education 2030: Incheon Declaration and Framework for Action for the Implementation of Sustainable Development Goal 4, 2015。

表 1-4　2015 年不同收入水平国家的高中辍学率和辍学人数

单位：%，百万人

	辍学率				辍学人数		
	两性	男性	女性	女／男比例	两性	男性	女性
低收入国家	62.3	58.2	66.4	1.14	24.6	11.6	13.0
中低收入国家	46.8	45.6	48.0	1.05	91.0	46.1	44.9
中高收入国家	21.6	23.9	19.2	0.80	22.4	12.9	9.5
高收入国家	7.1	7.7	6.4	0.83	3.0	1.7	1.3
世界（平均水平）	37.1	36.7	37.5	1.02	141.0	72.3	68.7

资料来源：UNESCO, Education 2030: Incheon Declaration and Framework for Action for the Implementation of Sustainable Development Goal 4, 2015。

2. 低质量教育仍然广泛存在，全球特别是欠发达国家和地区面临学习危机

优质教育是社会发展、进步和减贫的基础，低质量教育几乎等于没有教育。正如国际红十字会指出的，获得受教育机会未必等同于获得高质量的教育服务和学习效果，让学生进入没有质量保障的学校对学生帮助甚少，甚至还会提高其辍学的可能性。在很多发展中国家，很多儿童和青少年因各种原因进不了学校；很多学生即使接受了学校教育却未获得有质量的学习。这是发展中国家普遍存在的"教育贫困"问题。低质量教育体现在教师素质低、教学水平低、学校教学设备简陋或不足、没有合理的教育教学安排和评估手段、区域教育发展不均衡等方面。这导致数以亿计的儿童和青少年在离开学校时连最基本的技能都未掌握，更不用说应对生活和就业所需的学习技能。

低质量教育和学习危机也会对社会繁荣造成危害。联合国教科文组织统计研究所报告称，2015 年，超过 6.17 亿小学和初中适龄儿童和青少年未达到阅读和数学的最低合格水平，这占全球该群体总数的 55% 以上。小学和初中适龄儿童和青少年的不合格率仍然主要出现在撒哈拉以南非洲，其次是中亚和南亚（见图 1-3）。

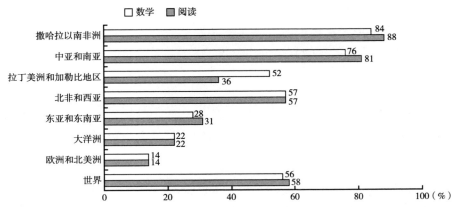

图 1-3 2015 年阅读和数学能力未达到最低合格水平的儿童和青少年的占比

资料来源：联合国《2019 年可持续发展报告》。

其他一些国际评估也显示了类似的情况。发展中国家学生评估项目
（Programme for International Student Assessment for Development, PISA-D）[①]
是一项考察中低收入国家学生表现的国际项目。该项目报告称，2018 年
学生的整体学习水平较低。该测试的对象是 15 岁的在校学生，尽管只有
7 个国家参加了 PISA-D 测试，但结果显示只有 12% 的学生在数学方面达
到最低水平，仅 23% 的学生达到阅读最低水平。相比之下，经济合作与
发展组织（OECD）的成员国在这两方面的比例分别为 77% 和 80%。

儿童不能达到最低教育水平的要求是一种全球性的学习危机。世界
银行还引入了"学习贫困"的概念，对儿童不学习的现象提出了警示。[②]
这一术语指的是儿童特别是 10 岁之后的儿童还不能阅读和理解简单文章
的现象。世界银行认为，正如收入贫困使人们无法获得经济、社会和政
治机会一样，缺乏基本阅读和理解技能或者说"学习贫困"也使人们无
法在现代社会过上富有成效、充实的生活。教育质量和学习效率不仅关
乎一个人摆脱贫困的能力，也关乎各国经济繁荣的前景。因此，要实现
减贫脱贫的目标，必须应对"学习贫困"和学习危机的挑战。

3. 欠发达地区，尤其是极端贫困地区严重缺乏合格教师

教师是影响贫困地区教育发展的关键因素，是教学质量的关键，是
各级各类学校在开展教学项目、提升教育效能方面的关键。然而，在世
界范围内的很多欠发达地区尤其是极端贫困地区，许多学生毕业时仍然
不具备基本的阅读、书写与计算技能，其中一个主要原因就是缺乏训练
有素的教师。

合格教师严重缺乏是一个全球性问题，撒哈拉以南非洲的问题最为
严重。联合国教科文组织统计研究所的数据显示，70% 的撒哈拉以南

---

① 2013 年，经济合作与发展组织和一些合作伙伴发起了发展中国家学生评估项目
（PISA-D），旨在促进中低收入国家参与国际学生评估项目。它采用与国际学生评估项目
（PISA）相同的量表，但评估工具是特别设计的，以符合中低收入国家的情况。

② World Bank, *Ending Learning Poverty: What Will It Take?* 2019, openknowledge.worldbank.org.

非洲国家面临教师严重缺乏的问题，在中等教育层面，这一比例上升至90%；而初等教育层面的学生—教师平均比例为 42：1，一些国家的这一比例甚至超过 60：1。2020 年，撒哈拉以南非洲中等教育和初等教育的合格教师数量缺口为 900 万，全球范围缺口达 3200 万。根据预测，这一数字在 2030 年将达到 1700 万和 6900 万。

解决合格教师缺乏的问题，需要实施全面的教师政策，内容涉及与教师职业相关的所有领域，例如培训、招聘、地位、工作条件和薪资。在教师普遍缺乏的许多国家，教师培训机构没有能力培养出数量充足的合格教师，加之受新冠肺炎疫情的影响，诸多教师培训机构临时关闭，合格教师的培训需求更加难以满足，这使得欠发达地区教育发展面临更为严峻的挑战。

4. 对贫困地区和贫困人口的教育投入不足

《教育 2030 议程》指出，为了实现可持续发展目标 4，全球教育支出必须从每年的 1.2 万亿美元增加到 2030 年的 3 万亿美元。2016 年，主题为"为了人类与地球的教育：为全人类创造可持续的未来"的《2016年全球教育监测报告》指出，很多教育投入远未实现公共教育支出占GDP 比例达 4% 或占全部公共支出 15% 以上的目标，特别是很多欠发达国家教育支出捉襟见肘。需要明确的是，没有足够的财力资源，就无法实施教育发展计划或战略。严重的资金缺口也是 2000~2015 年全民教育（Education For All, EFA）未取得足够进展的一个重要原因。

5. 弱势群体的受教育权需要特别关注

由于身体障碍，残疾人往往因为劳动能力弱、受教育程度低而导致相关生存技能缺失，这使得他们更容易陷入经济困境。贫困残疾人是贫困人口中贫困程度最深、脱贫难度最大、返贫率最高的特殊困难群体。因此，残疾人群体的受教育权是否受到保障直接关系到其是否能较为迅速地获得符合其自身需求的生存、生产、生活技能。如何有针对性地为残疾人提供帮助，使其更好地融入社会、有尊严地生活，是国际减贫工作普遍面临的挑战。

6. 新冠肺炎疫情加重了中低收入国家教育面临的挑战，其破坏性影响波及 190 多个国家的 19 亿学习者，教育发展遭受重创

据估计，由于新冠肺炎疫情期间学校和教育机构的关闭，全球约 94% 的学生受到影响，而在低收入国家，这一比例高达 99%。经济衰退最严重的国家将大幅削减包括教育在内的公共开支。短期和长期的学习缺失将严重影响来自贫困家庭的学生，特别是生活在贫困农村地区的学生，他们的受教育机会受到严重威胁。据联合国估计，新冠肺炎疫情期间，大约有 2400 万名包括从学前到高等教育阶段的儿童和青少年永久辍学。如果不采取适当措施减轻这一冲击带来影响，世界将经历由于全球未能实现可持续发展目标 4 而带来的世代灾难。[1]

在世界范围内消除贫困，全面实现《教育 2030 议程》目标，对各国政府来说都是一个挑战。许多事实和研究表明，贫困是全球实现《教育 2030 议程》目标的主要障碍，发展教育则成为消除贫困的关键举措，可持续发展目标 1 和目标 4 紧密相关，需要统筹推进。提升脱贫致富的能力被视为贫困人口改变生活困境的最主要手段，教育是加速能力提升最直接的方式。因此，将教育与减贫紧密结合起来、增加政府投入、调动更多公共资源、统筹推进落实《教育 2030 议程》和全球减贫目标是全面落实 2030 年全球可持续发展目标的重要战略内容。在这一过程中，还需要系统推进各级各类教育发展。学前教育、基础教育、高等教育、职业教育、继续教育、特殊教育、可持续发展教育、终身教育等都与促进减贫紧密相关。例如，大力发展职业教育，让更多家庭都有具备一技之长的成员，进而通过高质量就业实现贫困人口脱贫；发展继续教育，使得贫困人口树立终身学习理念、不断提高生产和生活技能，补齐农村地区贫困人口的技能学习短板；特殊教育旨在为残疾儿童提供适宜的教育，

---

[1]　United Nations, *The Sustainable Development Goals Report 2020*, 2020, unstats.un.org.

让残疾人学习掌握技能，帮助他们更好地融入社会，成为有用之才，活出自主人生。相关各方的协同推动，是保障教育扶贫成效的基础。贫困有着复杂的成因，教育又涉及政府、社会的方方面面，要发展教育、有效推进减贫必须汇聚各方面力量，统筹推动，特别是要形成政府、社会、家庭的强大合力，这是从落实千年发展目标、实现全民教育中得到的重要经验，因此，需要在国家与地方各级政府之间、政府的不同部门之间，以及政府与来自社会的各类合作伙伴之间建立协调、合作机制，形成统筹推动教育发展和减贫的行动，有效推进可持续发展目标的实现。

第二章
中国教育精准扶贫的行动与成效

一 中国的脱贫攻坚战

1949 年中华人民共和国成立后，中国开展了大规模社会主义建设，建立了独立的、比较完整的工业体系和国民经济体系，积极发展社会事业特别是教育事业，广泛开展扫除文盲运动，为摆脱贫困、改善人民生活打下了坚实基础。

1978 年改革开放以来，中国在致力于经济和社会发展的进程中，实施了大规模、有计划、有组织的扶贫开发，减贫进程加快推进，贫困人口大幅度减少，1978~2020 年中国生活在国家贫困标准以下的人口如图 2-1 所示。按照中国现行贫困标准计算，1978 年中国农村贫困人口数量超过 7.7 亿，农村贫困发生率高达 97.5%；2012 年，农村贫困人口下降为 9899 万，贫困发生率降为 10.2%。2005 年 10 月，时任世界银行行长的保罗·沃尔福威茨来中国考察扶贫开发情况时说："近 30 年来，东亚见证了人类历史上涉及人口最多、速度最快的财富增长，如果没有中国的增长尤其是其数亿贫困人口的减少，这是不可能实现的。"

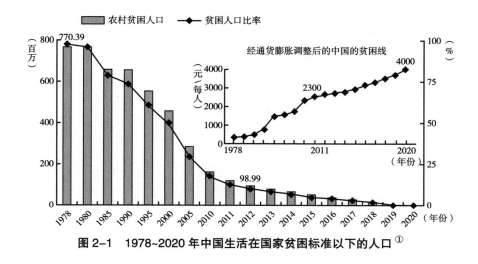

图 2-1　1978~2020 年中国生活在国家贫困标准以下的人口①

　　2012 年，中国剩余的 9899 万贫困人口主要分布在 832 个贫困县，其中有 5067 万贫困人口生活在六盘山区、秦巴山区、武陵山区、乌蒙山区等 14 个集中连片特困地区。14 个集中连片特困地区基础设施和社会事业发展滞后、生态环境脆弱、自然灾害频发、交通不便，具有贫困程度深、致贫原因复杂、自我发展能力弱、返贫现象突出等特点。一般的经济增长无法有效带动这些地区的发展，常规的扶贫思路和办法难以奏效，扶贫开发工作任务异常艰巨，且越往后脱贫成本越高、难度越大。

　　面对贫中之贫、坚中之坚，中国政府把脱贫攻坚摆在治国理政的突出位置，把消除绝对贫困作为全面建成小康社会的底线任务，从 2012 年起，在习近平的亲自倡导和领导下，中国政府先后开展精准扶贫，实施脱贫攻坚，出台了一系列政策举措，构建了一整套行之有效的政策体系、工作体系、制度体系，走出了一条中国特色减贫道路，形成了中国特色

---

① "Targeted Poverty Relief: China's Way to Achieve Prosperity," CGTN, 2021, news.cgtn.com.

反贫困理论。其中，很重要的一点就是将教育与减贫结合起来，把教育作为扶贫的重要内容和重要手段，既扶教育事业发展之贫，也通过提供教育服务扶持贫困人口，这被实践证明是有效发展贫困地区教育的方式和扶贫的方式。

（一）精准扶贫、精准脱贫战略的提出

2012 年年底，中国共产党第十八次全国代表大会召开后不久，习近平强调，"小康不小康，关键看老乡，关键在贫困的老乡能不能脱贫"，承诺决不能落下一个贫困地区、一个贫困群众。2013 年，习近平在贫困地区湖南湘西考察时，首次提出"实事求是、因地制宜、分类指导、精准扶贫"的理念，标志着中国开始从扶贫开发向精准扶贫、精准脱贫的战略转变。2015 年 6 月，习近平在贵州考察期间进一步提出了"六个精准"，对精准脱贫的战略构想进行了补充，即做到扶贫对象、项目安排、资金使用、措施到户、因村派人（第一书记）、脱贫成效"六个精准"。"六个精准"是对扶贫精准性的界定，通过精准识别、建档立卡，对所有贫困人口建立档案，建设全国扶贫信息网络系统，解决"扶持谁"的问题；通过加强领导、建强队伍解决"谁来扶"的问题；通过区分类别、靶向施策解决"怎么扶"的问题；通过严格标准、有序退出解决"如何退"的问题；通过跟踪监测、防止返贫解决"如何稳"的问题。精准扶贫、精准脱贫战略，涵盖了从扶贫到脱贫再到巩固的全过程，体现了精准扶贫思想的深刻内涵，是中国打赢脱贫攻坚战的制胜法宝，是中国减贫理论和实践的重大创新。

（二）脱贫攻坚战的提出与实施

2015 年年底，习近平在出席中央扶贫开发工作会议时指出，"要立下愚公移山志，咬定目标、苦干实干"，吹响了脱贫攻坚战的冲锋号。为确保 2020 年所有贫困地区和贫困人口实现脱贫、全面建成小康社会，

中共中央、国务院发布的《关于打赢脱贫攻坚战的决定》明确提出，到2020年稳定实现农村贫困人口不愁吃、不愁穿，义务教育、基本医疗和住房安全有保障。实现贫困地区农民人均可支配收入增长幅度高于全国平均水平，基本公共服务主要领域指标水平接近全国平均水平。确保中国现行标准下农村贫困人口实现脱贫，贫困县全部摘帽，实现区域性整体贫困的总目标，要求在"六个精准"指导下，实施发展生产、易地搬迁、生态补偿、发展教育、社会保障兜底"五个一批"脱贫工程（见图2-2），发出打赢脱贫攻坚战的总攻令。2017年，中国共产党第十九次全国代表大会全面部署精准脱贫攻坚战，锚定全面建成小康社会目标，聚力攻克深度贫困堡垒，决战决胜脱贫攻坚。2018年，中共中央、国务院印发《关于打赢脱贫攻坚战三年行动的指导意见》，进一步为脱贫攻坚工作做了全面部署，推动脱贫攻坚工作更加有效开展。2020年，为克服新冠肺炎疫情的不利影响，中央政府对决战决胜脱贫攻坚进行再部署、再动员，要求以更大的决心、更强的力度，做好"加试题"、打好"收官战"。

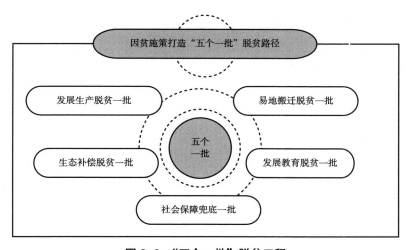

图2-2 "五个一批"脱贫工程

2012~2020 年，习近平先后主持召开 7 次中央扶贫工作座谈会，开展 50 多次调研扶贫工作，走遍全国 14 个集中连片特困地区，连续 5 年审定脱贫攻坚成效考核结果，连续 7 年在全国扶贫日期间出席重要活动或做出重要指示，连续 7 年在新年贺词中强调脱贫攻坚，每年在全国两会期间同代表委员共商脱贫攻坚大计，多次回信勉励基层干部和群众投身减贫事业。全国累计选派 25.5 万个驻村工作队、300 多万名扶贫干部（包括派驻贫困村的第一书记和驻村干部），近 200 万名当地乡镇干部和数百万名村干部奋战在扶贫一线，其中 1800 多名干部在扶贫工作中殉职。

中国坚持中央政府对脱贫攻坚的集中统一领导，把脱贫攻坚纳入经济建设、政治建设、文化建设、社会建设和生态文明建设"五位一体"总体布局和全面建成小康社会、全面深化改革、全面依法治国、全面从严治党"四个全面"战略布局，建立中央统筹、省负总责、市县抓落实的脱贫攻坚管理体制和片为重点、工作到村、扶贫到户的工作机制，构建省、市、县、乡、村五级一把手负责制。

中国广泛动员全国各族人民和社会各方力量共同向贫困宣战，构建专项扶贫、行业扶贫、社会扶贫互为补充的大扶贫格局，形成跨地区、跨部门、跨单位，全社会共同参与的社会扶贫体系，加强东西部扶贫协作，推动省市县各层面结对帮扶。组织开展定点扶贫，各级党政机关、人民团体、国有企事业单位和人民军队积极帮扶贫困县或贫困村。推动各行各业发挥专业优势，开展产业扶贫、科技扶贫、教育扶贫、文化扶贫、健康扶贫、消费扶贫。动员民营企业、社会组织、公民个人积极参与脱贫攻坚，开展扶贫公益活动。调动广大贫困群众的积极性、主动性、创造性，激发脱贫内生动力，引导贫困群众依靠勤劳双手和顽强意志摆脱贫困、改变命运。

中国发挥政府投入在扶贫开发中的主体和主导作用，优先保障脱贫攻坚资金的投入，2012~2020 年中央、省、市、县财政累计投入专项扶贫资金近 1.6 万亿元,其中中央财政累计投入 6601 亿元。打响脱贫攻坚战以来,土地增减挂钩①指标跨省域调剂和省域内流转资金 4400 多亿元,扶贫小额信贷累计发放 7100 多亿元,扶贫再贷款累计发放约 6688 亿元,金融精准扶贫贷款发放 9.2 万亿元,东部 9 省市共向扶贫协作地区投入财政援助和社会帮扶资金 1005 多亿元,东部地区企业赴扶贫协作地区累计投资约 1 万亿元。

中国坚持对扶贫对象实行精细化管理、对扶贫资源实行精确化配置、对扶贫对象实行精准化扶持,建立了全国建档立卡信息系统,确保扶贫资源真正用在扶贫对象上、真正用在贫困地区。坚持把发展作为消除贫困的根本途径,改善发展条件,增强发展能力,实现由"输血式"扶贫向"造血式"扶贫转变,让发展成为消除贫困最有效的办法、创造幸福生活最稳定的途径。实行严格的考核评估制度,开展扶贫领域腐败和作风问题专项治理,建立全方位监督体系,坚决反对形式主义、官僚主义,把一切工作都落实到为贫困群众解决实际问题上,做到"真扶贫、扶真贫、脱真贫"。

2020 年年底,中国在有力应对新冠肺炎疫情影响的同时,取得了脱贫攻坚战全面胜利,现行标准下 9899 万农村贫困人口全部脱贫,2012~2020 年,平均每年 1000 多万人脱贫,相当于一个中等国家的人口。贫困人口收入水平显著提高,全部实现"两不愁三保障",即脱贫群众不愁吃、不愁穿,义务教育、基本医疗、住房安全有保障,饮水安全也都有了保障。千百万贫困家庭的孩子享受到更公平的教育机会,他们告别了天天跋山涉水上学的生活,实现了住学校、吃食堂。832 个贫困县全部摘帽,12.8 万个贫困村全部出列,区域性整体贫困得到解决,困扰中华民族几千年的绝对贫困问题得到历史性解决,创造了彪炳史册的人间奇

---

① 土地增减挂钩即城镇建设用地增加与农村建设用地减少相挂钩,是指依据土地利用总体规划,将若干拟整理复垦为耕地的农村建设用地地块(即拆旧地块)和拟用于城镇建设的地块(即建新地块)等面积共同组成建新拆旧项目区,通过建新拆旧和土地整理复垦等措施,在保证项目区内各类土地面积平衡的基础上,最终实现增加耕地有效面积、提高耕地质量、节约集约利用建设用地、城乡用地布局更合理的目标。

迹。中国也为全球减贫事业做出了重大贡献，1978 年以来，按照现行贫困标准计算，中国 7.7 亿农村贫困人口全部脱贫；按照世界银行国际贫困标准，中国减贫人口占同期全球减贫人口的 70% 以上。特别是在全球贫困状况依然严峻，一些国家贫富分化加剧的背景下，中国提前 10 年实现《2030 年可持续发展议程》的减贫目标。同时中国还积极参与国际减贫合作，做世界减贫事业的推动者和贡献者，与各国携手合作，共建没有贫困、共同发展的人类命运共同体。

联合国开发计划署 2019 年发布的《中国人类发展报告特别版》记录了新中国成立以来中国的非凡发展，特别是 1978 年改革开放后，中国的人类发展指数从 1978 年的 0.410 上升到 2017 年的 0.752。凭借这一成就，中国被公认为世界上唯一一个从低人类发展群体发展到高人类发展群体的国家。报告指出，中国 1978 年的人类发展指数还很低，但现在已经成为全球经济大国，是对外投资、发展融资和援助的主要来源国。2000~2018 年，中国收入最底层 40% 人口的收入以 263% 的惊人速度增长，这为快速减少极端贫困做出了贡献。联合国官员指出精准扶贫是中国减贫的重要经验，中国能将扶贫工作细化到每个社区、每户居民，通过因地制宜的方案逐步完成总体目标，这种中国经验是全球减贫工作的重要参考。

二 中国在教育精准脱贫和教育脱贫攻坚中的行动

2012 年以来，中国中央政府在教育系统内外，建立起了涵盖各级各类机构，多层级、多渠道的细分管理体制①，构建起了一套完善的教育脱贫攻坚制度与政策体系，其主要在八个方面明确目标、落实责任、确保落实。

---

① 中国的政府体制由中央政府、省级政府、地市级政府、县级政府以及乡镇政府五个级次组成。义务教育实行国务院领导，省、自治区、直辖市人民政府统筹规划实施，县级人民政府为主管理的体制。教育工作涉及的中央部门包括教育部、国家发改委、财政部、人社部、科技部等。

（一）构建职责与分工明确的责任体系

教育部成立脱贫攻坚领导小组，统筹推进教育行业扶贫等工作，全国教育系统建立健全各负其责、协同配合、狠抓落实的责任体系。与13个扶贫任务较重的省级人民政府签订《打赢教育脱贫攻坚战合作备忘录》，明确责任，合力攻坚克难。为充分发挥高等教育机构的科技、人才优势，2012年以来，先后牵头组织中央政府直属高校履行定点扶贫职责，与高校签订定点扶贫责任书、立下"军令状"，定时督促进展、考核成效。切实履行教育部牵头负责的滇西扶贫职责，与26个部委建立滇西部际联系机制、与云南省建立部省协商工作机制，集中会商与及时沟通相结合，帮助滇西协调解决脱贫攻坚重点、难点问题，协调多种资源合力推进滇西教育脱贫攻坚。统筹做好教育脱贫攻坚工作，利用视频会议、信息技术等方式推进定点联系滇西、直属高校定点扶贫等工作，同时积极参与其他部委牵头负责的集中连片特困地区扶贫工作，配合开展教育扶贫工作。

（二）构建精准扶贫、问题导向的工作体系

针对贫困地区比较突出的辍学问题，集中开展控辍保学工作。建立健全全国中小学生学籍系统库、国家人口信息库、建档立卡贫困人口库"三库"对比核查机制。同时，建设控辍保学工作台账管理平台，精准识别每一名因贫辍学学生，并实行疑似辍学问题复核销号制度（即建立清单，确认每名辍学学生，确保其复学才销号）。在此基础上，地方政府建立多部门、多机构的联防联控机制，确保贫困地区辍学儿童和青少年能够返回学校上学。针对适龄未上学的、学习困难的、厌学的、受家庭思想观念影响以及身体残疾等原因而失学、辍学的儿童和青少年，按照"一人一案"原则，通过重返课堂、就读中等职业学校、送教上门等手段，使失学、辍学的儿童和青少年得到妥善安置。

针对贫困地区义务教育基础薄弱、发展不均衡的问题，中央政府从基础设施建设入手，有序推进全面改善贫困地区义务教育薄弱学校基本办学条件工作和义务教育薄弱环节改善与能力提升工作，结合国家教育资源公共服务平台，将优质教育资源输送到贫困地区，全面提升乡村贫困地区教育教学质量。

针对贫困地区优质教育资源匮乏、师资投入不足、教师队伍结构不完善、人才质量不高问题，持续实施乡村教师"特岗计划"[1]和"三区"[2]人才支持计划教师专项等，选派优秀教师及教育管理人员到边远贫困地区、边疆民族地区等学校任教，支持各地实施地方师范生公费教育，为农村学校定向培养师资，在有效缓解贫困地区师资总量不足的同时，带动当地学校教学水平和育人管理能力的整体提升。实施"国培计划"（中小学幼儿园教师国家级培训计划），面向中西部乡村教师开展大规模在职培训，累计投入约200余亿元，培训教师约1700余万人次，覆盖了全部贫困地区乡村教师，大幅度提升了乡村教师的专业素养。

针对经济困难学生上学难问题，中央政府建立了全学段覆盖、公办民办学校全覆盖、家庭经济困难学生全覆盖的学生资助体系。在扩大资助对象、提高资助标准的基础上，将"全国学生资助信息系统"与国务院扶贫办、民政部等部门的信息系统全面对接、定期对比，建立中央政府、省、市、县、学校五级学生资助管理机构和队伍，有力推进困难学生认定和精准资助工作，确保学生不因家庭经济困难而辍学。

需要说明的是，中国一直主张男女平等，中国有着从宪法到专门法如《妇女权益保障法》《母婴保健法》等较为完善的法律体系保障男女平等。中国妇女劳动参与率居于世界前列，中国在各级教育入学率方面也

---

① 特岗教师是中国中央政府实施的一项对中西部地区贫困地区农村义务教育的特殊政策。通过公开招聘高校毕业生到中西部地区县以下农村学校任教，引导和鼓励高校毕业生从事农村义务教育工作，逐步解决农村学校师资总量不足和结构不合理等问题，提高农村师资队伍的整体素质，促进城乡教育均衡发展。2020年全国招聘特岗教师达到10.14万名。

② "三区"是指边远贫困地区、边疆民族地区和革命老区。

已经实现了男女平等。在教育脱贫攻坚中，也始终坚持男女平等，不论男女都要享受同等的教育扶贫政策，特别是把女童和妇女教育作为工作重点，确保平等的受教育权利。

（三）构建多层面统一协调的政策体系

中央政府进行顶层规划，出台了一系列指导性政策文件，为各级各类部门指明了教育扶贫的发展方向与实施路径。2013 年，《关于实施教育扶贫工程意见的通知》发布，成为中国首个教育行业扶贫的指导性意见。2016 年，《教育脱贫攻坚"十三五"规划》发布，部署推动了 2016~2020 年中国脱贫攻坚关键期的教育脱贫工作。2017 年，中央政府印发《深度贫困地区教育脱贫攻坚实施方案（2018—2020 年）》，将中国的教育脱贫工作重点进一步向深度贫困地区聚焦。2020 年，《打赢教育脱贫攻坚收官战总攻方案》印发，进一步为教育系统完成各项减贫任务明确了工作目标。

针对教育脱贫攻坚的重点任务、重点领域、重点区域等，中央政府制定了一系列政策文件，提升政策供给的精准性、有效性。在义务教育控辍保学方面，印发《关于进一步加强控辍保学提高义务教育巩固水平的通知》《关于进一步加强控辍保学工作 健全义务教育有保障长效机制的若干意见》，进一步落实控辍保学工作责任制、细化工作举措，形成多部门合力控辍、聚力保学的有效机制。在改善办学条件方面，印发《关于全面改善贫困地区义务教育薄弱学校基本办学条件的意见》《关于切实做好义务教育薄弱环节改善与能力提升工作的意见》，加快补齐义务教育基本办学条件短板，同时印发《构建利用信息化手段扩大优质教育资源覆盖面有效机制的实施方案》《教育信息化 2.0 行动计划》，加快贫困地区教育信息化建设。在教师队伍建设方面，印发《乡村教师支持计划（2015—2020 年）》《教育部等六部门关于加强新时代乡村教师队伍建设的意见》，指导各级地方政府、教育行政部门、高等院校、职业院校等，为中国的贫困地区打造了一支热爱乡村、素质优良、充满活力的乡村教师队伍。在教育投入保障方面，印发《关于进一步调整优化结构提高教育经费使用效益的意见》，着力加大贫困地区义务教育财力投入力度。在加大深度贫困地区支持力度方面，印发《关于进一步加强财政投入管理深入推进"三区三州"教育脱贫攻坚的指导意见》《关于进一步加大支持力度持续做好义务教育有保障工作的通知》，深入推进了贫困人口多、贫困发生率高、脱贫难度较大的深度贫困地区的教育脱贫攻坚工作。

同时，在学生资助、学前教育、高中教育、职业教育、招生倾斜、就业帮扶等方面，中央政府出台了系列政策性文件，各地教育部门也全面制定和实施了本地区的教育脱贫攻坚规划、计划、方案、意见等政策制度文件，共同形成了与国家部署相衔接、部门协作、地方协同的政策体系。

为保障各级各类政策的落实，中央政府建立了年初部署、年中推进、年底总结与日常跟踪进展相结合的常态化工作机制，同时依托各类教育脱贫培训班，着力提升扶贫干部的政策水平和工作能力。教育部自2018年以来委托相关机构开展第三方评估，深入检验了农村义务教育营养改善计划、全面改善贫困地区义务教育薄弱学校基本办学条件等重点项目的政策实施效果，进一步提升了检视问题、优化政策、确保落实的整体工作水平。

（四）构建多渠道的资金、人才与智力投入体系

2012年以来，中央政府结合财税体制改革和脱贫攻坚"义务教育保障"任务，在财政资金投入方面调整多项中央财政教育转移支付政策，支持教育脱贫攻坚的财政投入政策体系不断完善。如完善城乡义务教育经费保障机制方面，建立城乡统一、重在农村的义务教育经费保障机制，实现城乡统一的生均公用经费基准定额标准。脱贫攻坚干部队伍建设方面，教育部建立优秀年轻干部队伍和直属高校领导人员援派挂职干部储

备库。2012年以来选派了300多万名扶贫干部到中国贫困地区一线工作。

贫困地区人才建设方面，教育部不断加大对贫困地区人才支持力度，依托高等院校组织实施一系列教育系统培训和项目，通过教育行政干部班、专业技术人才培训班等，为贫困地区的脱贫攻坚工作培养了一大批优秀干部人才。

智力投入方面，中国各高等院校持续实施《高等学校乡村振兴科技创新行动计划（2018—2022年）》，依托高等学校国家和教育部重点实验室，围绕遗传育种、土壤改造等涉农专业领域，不断开展创新和关键技术突破工作，为贫困地区产业发展提供科技源头支撑。一大批具有典型示范作用的科技服务新模式以及多种农业科技推广的新做法，源源不断地将高校创新成果和人才优势转化为推动扶贫产业发展的新动能。

（五）构建因地制宜、因人施策的院校帮扶体系

在高等教育方面，中国各高等教育机构自承担定点扶贫、专项扶贫任务以来，与贫困县密切配合，结合实际坚持定点帮扶、重点突破与全面提升相结合，逐步形成了应贫困县所需、尽高校所能的特色扶贫路径。在教育扶贫方面，中国高等院校坚持硬件建设和软件提升同步，援建捐赠、师生支教、师资培训、资源共享、学生资助、结对关爱等成为所有高校的共同行动，进而帮助贫困地区有效缓解基础薄弱、师资短缺、资源不足等突出矛盾，使贫困县的教育教学质量有了较大提升。在产业扶贫方面，各高校发挥学科、科技、智力和人力优势，通过制定产业规划、引入专业力量、促进成果转化、拓展农业多种功能、发展农业新形态、开展招商引资等一系列举措，有效实现了贫困地区农业的品种改良、品质提升、品牌升值，农村第一、第二、第三产业融合发展的新格局加快形成，很多贫困县、贫困村集体产业从无到有、从弱到强，产业扶贫的减贫效果持续提升。

针对贫困地区特别是深度贫困地区在减贫过程中面临的突出问题，

中国各高等教育机构也有针对性地提出了解决办法。面对贫困地区技术技能人才短缺问题，国家开放大学持续实施"一村一名大学生"计划，在中国中西部贫困地区的近千个县设县级教学点，有力促进农村实用技术人才、致富带头人和乡村管理人才的培养。

在推进高校毕业生就业方面，中国各高等院校始终把贫困地区和贫困家庭毕业生就业作为重点。特别是2020年，面对新冠肺炎疫情影响和总体就业形势严峻的状况，把帮扶建档立卡贫困毕业生就业作为重中之重，专门出台了升学培训、政策岗位、专场招聘等专项政策。持续举办贫困毕业生就业专场招聘活动，提供数十万个就业岗位与针对贫困地区学生的岗位信息。各高校实行一人一档、一人一策，实施有针对性的专人帮扶。近年来，在各项就业支持政策的合力扶持下，中国家庭经济困难毕业生就业率均高于全国平均水平1~4个百分点，有效缓解了贫困地区家庭因就业困难而导致的经济困境。

在中等职业教育方面，面对贫困地区职业教育基础薄弱的问题，对未设中等职业学校的贫困县，通过支持新建学校、推动就近异地就读、在普通教育序列中开设职业教育班等措施，有效填补贫困地区职业院校的空白。对已设中等职业学校的贫困县，通过倾斜支持改善办学条件、促进校企合作、增强就业指导等措施，帮助贫困地区提升职业教育质量。

（六）形成广泛参与的社会动员体系

中国中央政府实施《职业教育东西协作行动计划（2016—2020年）》，落实东部与西部职业院校在资金援助、技能培训、劳务协作等方面的协同发展，全面提升了中国贫困地区职业院校教育质量，改善了贫困地区的就业状况。2020年，相继组织27所职业本科学校对口支援民族地区职业学校发展，提升民族地区职业教育水平。

中国各高等院校持续推动高校对口支援工作，实施东部高校对口支援西部地区高等学校计划，119所部属和东部高水平大学支援中西部103

所高校，形成了全方位、多层次、立体式的帮扶格局。2018 年启动实施的慕课西部行动计划，组织 10 余个在线课程联盟和课程平台开放优质课程资源，将其输送至新疆、西藏、青海、陕西、贵州等地区，促进了东西部高校教学资源共享，提升了教育教学质量。2020 年，相继组织 27 所职业本科学校对口支援民族地区职业学校。在教师发展层面，中国各高校集合教育系统帮扶团队的优质资源持续加大对贫困地区的教育帮扶力度，依托"国培计划"名师名校长领航工程，建立"校长＋教研组长＋骨干教师"支教团队，组团式"一对一"帮扶凉山州、怒江州等深度贫困地区。创新的支教模式同步带动了贫困地区学校管理队伍、骨干教师和教研团队能力和素质的整体提升。在动员社会力量方面，中央政府协调公益组织、爱心企业、民办教育机构等社会力量助力教育脱贫攻坚。各类基金会、中央企业、民办教育机构等在资助家庭经济困难学生、教师以及贫困地区基础办学条件改善等方面投入大量资金，为贫困地区学生健康发展、教育信息化建设、数字教育资源完善等提供了有力支持。

（七）构建全方位的监督体系

中国中央政府把教育脱贫攻坚作为巡视巡察监督重点，按照巡视反馈意见，逐项研究落实举措，制定实施整改方案，建立问题清单、任务清单和责任清单，将整改任务细化为具体整改举措，明确完成时间节点，加强对教育脱贫攻坚业务的监督。在国家层面成立督导委员会，会同相关机构主要业务部门，建立跟踪调度制度，对地方"义务教育有保障"工作中出现执行政策进度缓慢等问题及时反馈，督促认真落实整改，确保进度不落后、方向不走偏。以基本办学条件 20 条"底线要求"为重点，开展"全面改薄"专项督导，采用调研检查、绩效管理等多种方式，加强对重要教育扶贫专项资金的监管。中央政府落实教育脱贫攻坚外部监督机制，每年组织开展脱贫攻坚督查巡查，加强日常涉及脱贫攻坚问题的反馈处理工作，确保各级各类教育扶脱贫政策得到充分落实，取得积极成效。

（八）构建全面覆盖的考核评估体系

2016 年以来，中国中央政府在国家层面逐步形成了全面的考核体系，内容主要包括各级政府的脱贫攻坚成效、东西部扶贫协作、中央单位定点扶贫工作成效，形式包括专项工作成效组省际交叉考核、第三方评估、扶贫资金绩效评价等。对中国各级教育精准扶贫、精准脱贫工作进行详细、全面、深入的评估，提高了发现问题、解决问题和总结经验的效率，为推动教育脱贫攻坚成果同乡村振兴有效衔接奠定了坚实基础。

三　中国教育精准脱贫的成效

2012~2020 年，中国积极实施教育精准扶贫、开展教育脱贫攻坚战，取得了决定性成就。主要实现了以下成效。

（一）"义务教育有保障"目标全面实现

2020 年，中国九年义务教育巩固率 95.2%，其中贫困县九年义务教育巩固率达到 94.8%，较 2015 年提高了近 5 个百分点，接近全国平均水平。截至 2020 年年底，全国义务教育阶段 1.45 亿名学生中，辍学学生数量由台账建立之初的 60 多万降至 682，其中 20 多万名建档立卡贫困辍学学生实现动态清零，长期存在的建档立卡贫困学生的辍学问题得到历史性解决。

（二）贫困地区学校面貌发生整体变化

中国贫困地区办学条件得到根本性改善。2013 年以来，760 个贫困县通过了县域义务教育基本均衡国家实地督导检查，全国 99.8% 的义务教育学校（含教学点）办学条件达到基本要求。全国中小学（含教学点）互联网接入率从 2012 年的 25% 上升到 100%，拥有多媒体教室的学校比例从 48% 上升到 95.3%。

乡村教师队伍建设水平整体提升。依托教育脱贫中各项教师专项工作，中国贫困地区拥有了一支"留得住、教得好"的教师队伍。"特岗计划"累计招聘教师 95 万名，地方师范生公费教育每年为农村地区输送教师 4 万名，"国培计划"培训中西部乡村学校教师、校长 1700 万余人次。原连片特困地区乡村教师生活补助惠及 8 万所乡村学校近 130 万名教师，选派 19 万名教师到贫困地区、边疆地区等学校支教，有力提升了当地的教育教学质量。乡村教师队伍的整体素质大幅提升，本科以上学历教师占 51.6%。

（三）教育脱贫成效显著

职业教育助力脱贫攻坚成效快速显现。2012 年以来，累计有 800 多万贫困家庭学生接受中等、高等职业教育，其中仅通过实施职业教育东西协作计划一项举措，就招收西部贫困家庭学生 100 多万人，目前职业院校的学生大多来自农村，切实发挥了职业教育"职教一人、就业一人、脱贫一家"的作用。西部地区职业院校的教育质量和整体办学水平明显提升，实训装备水平等基础办学条件大幅改善，教师实践教学水平和技术服务能力显著增强，学生实践操作能力进一步适应地方经济特点和产业发展需求。

高等教育助力贫困学生纵向流动的通道更加宽广。2012 年以来，累计有 514.05 万名建档立卡的贫困学生接受高等教育，数以百万的贫困家庭有了第一代大学生。特殊的支持政策为贫困地区学生创造了更为公平的受教育环境和就业机会，其中面向贫困地区定向招生计划累计招收农村和贫困地区学生 70 万人，为中部、西部农村定向培养 7 万余名本科医学生，平均为每个乡镇卫生医院培养 2 名本科医学生，"一村一名大学生"

计划累计为贫困地区培养了 60 万余名乡村干部、乡村致富带头人。

完善的资助体系构建牢固的保障网络。政府主导、学校和社会积极参与，使覆盖学前至研究生各个教育阶段的学生资助政策体系更加完善，从制度上保障了不让任何一个学生因家庭经济困难而失学。义务教育营养改善计划覆盖 1643 个县的 13.63 万所学校，每年惠及学生 4000 万余人。监测表明，2019 年，营养改善计划试点地区男、女生各年龄段平均身高比 2012 年分别提高 1.54 厘米和 1.69 厘米，平均体重分别增加 1.06 千克和 1.18 千克，高于全国农村学生平均增长速度。

开展国家通用语言文字教育培训助力脱贫攻坚并取得明显成效。针对贫困地区少数民族青年由于不懂国家通用语言文字，难以与其他地区人们沟通，导致脱贫能力较弱的现象，国家在保护其使用少数民族语言权利的同时，开展国家通用语言文字普及攻坚工程，帮助他们学会国家通用语言文字，拓展信息渠道，拓宽致富之路。据不完全统计，累计有350 万余的乡村教师、青壮年农牧民接受了国家通用语言文字教育培训。与社会力量联合开发的"语言扶贫"App 累计用户 88.4 万人。"扶贫先扶智、扶智先通语"的理念深入人心，中国政府在推广国家通用语言文字助力脱贫的同时，也非常重视保护少数民族传统语言文化，加强当地非物质文化遗产的保护传承，并通过教育传承传播优秀传统文化，支持当地群众将传统文化转化为产品与服务，从而成为脱贫致富的手段。贫困地区群众用普通话对外交流交往、脱贫致富的意愿和能力得到明显增强。

（四）教育综合扶贫格局基本形成

教育脱贫攻坚得到了各级行政机构、教育机构、企业、社会组织的大力支持，中国脱贫攻坚工程的各专项计划都将教育作为脱贫攻坚的重要任务，加大人力、物力、财力的投入，从捐款捐物、援建学校、资助学生逐步向支持教师队伍建设、扩大优质教育资源等拓展，专项扶贫、行业扶贫、社会扶贫"三位一体"的扶贫格局基本形成。在教育系统内部，协同发展机制不断完善。2016~2020 年，据不完全统计，职业教育东西协作的援助资金达 18.2 亿元，其共在受援点建设专业点 683 个、实训基地 338 个，各类培训人员达 40 万人。对国家重点扶贫开发地区西藏、新疆、青海的教育援助投入资金达 1300 亿元。119 所教育部直属和中国东部地区高水平大学加大支援力度，支持中西部 103 所高校提升办学水平，发挥脱贫攻坚辐射带动作用，实现西部 12 个省（区）全覆盖。"三区"人才支持计划教师专项计划累计派出 17 万名教师到 1272 个县支教帮扶，实现贫困县全覆盖。这一扶贫格局的形成不仅为彻底解决绝对贫困问题提供了支撑，也为解决相对贫困、推进乡村振兴奠定了良好基础。

第三章

中国教育减贫的实践案例

中国教育减贫的过程，也是在贫困地区推进《教育 2030 议程》的过程，其涉及各级各类教育。为了从不同角度展现中国教育减贫的实践，本书针对国际社会在落实《教育 2030 议程》过程中面临的 5 个方面的共性问题，选取了一批中国教育扶贫的典型案例，力图以此呈现中国推进教育精准扶贫的实践与经验，为国际社会落实可持续发展目标 1 和目标 4 提供参考。

一 教育的普及性和公平性，确保贫困学生有平等的受教育机会

（一）如何确保所有孩子不因家庭贫困失学而失去改变命运的机会

让贫困家庭的孩子都能接受公平、有质量的基础教育，并让他们有更多的机会走进职业学校、高等院校，不因贫困失去改变命运的机会，是中国教育减贫工作的重点。《中共中央国务院关于打赢脱贫攻坚战三年行动的指导意见》强调，要切实解决义务教育学生因贫失学、辍学问题，保障贫困家庭的孩子接受九年义务教育，确保有学上、上得起学。中国政府建立了从学前教育、义务教育、高中阶段教育到高等教育各学段全

覆盖，公办民办学校全覆盖，家庭经济困难学生全覆盖的家庭经济困难学生资助体系。

学前教育：按照"地方先行、中央补助"原则，地方政府对经县级以上教育行政部门审批设立的普惠性幼儿园中的家庭经济困难儿童、孤儿和残疾儿童予以资助。

义务教育：统一城乡"两免一补"政策，对城乡义务教育学生免除学杂费，免费提供教科书，对家庭经济困难学生补助生活费。对集中连片特困地区县、其他国家扶贫开发工作重点县、省级扶贫开发工作重点县、民族县、边境县、革命老区县等地区农村义务教育阶段学生提供营养膳食补助。

中等职业教育：建立了以国家奖学金、国家助学金和免学费为主，以地方政府资助、学校和社会资助等为补充的资助政策体系。

普通高中教育：建立了以国家助学金、建档立卡等家庭经济困难学生免学杂费为主，以地方政府资助、学校和社会资助为补充的资助政策体系。

本专科教育：建立了国家奖学金、国家励志奖学金、国家助学金、国家助学贷款、基层就业学费补偿国家助学贷款代偿、服兵役高等学校学生国家教育资助、师范生公费教育、新生入学资助、勤工助学、校内奖助学金、困难补助、伙食补贴、学费减免及新生入学"绿色通道"等相结合的资助政策体系。

研究生教育：建立了研究生国家奖学金、学业奖学金、国家助学金、国家助学贷款、"三助"岗位津贴、基层就业学费补偿国家助学贷款代偿、服兵役高等学校学生国家教育资助、校内奖助学金及新生入学"绿色通道"等相结合的资助政策体系。

《2020年中国学生资助发展报告》显示，中国全年资助资金2408.20亿元，资助学生14617.50万人次，确保"不让一个学生因家庭经济困难而失学"。

1. 案例：福建省宁化县建立"三全三扶一档"教育精准扶贫机制

近年来，福建省宁化县创新性地建立了"三全三扶一档"教育精准扶贫机制，其主要通过全员参与、全面覆盖、全程管理和"扶志"工程、"扶智"工程、"扶助"工程，为每个贫困家庭学生建立专门档案，做到档随人走，实现动态跟踪、信息共享。全县教育精准扶贫实现了学前教育、义务教育、高中教育和大学教育全学段覆盖，相关学校通过档案全面了解学生成长脉络，有利于其在每个阶段采取不同措施，因人"扶助"，因材施教，最大限度实现育人目标。真正让每一个贫困家庭的孩子有书读、读好书，有学上、上好学，走出了一条教育精准扶贫的新路子。

张媛媛是宁化一中高二年级的建档立卡贫困学生。在刚考入高中时，她还很担心自己的学习和生活会遇到困难。进入校园后，她的担心被打消了，学校安排了3名帮扶教师与她"结对子"。宁化一中王盛镰是张媛媛的"扶智"教师，他说张媛媛在理科方面，特别是数学和物理的基础相对较弱，后面跟她讲了一些理科方面的学习方法，并带她请教相关的老师，经过一段时间辅导，她的数学和物理成绩有了明显提高。除了功课学习上的帮扶，学校"扶志"教师张斌非常关心张媛媛的思想和心理情况，鼓励她珍惜时间、刻苦学习、树立信心、不断进步。同时，宁化一中的"扶助"教师张炜斌帮助张媛媛通过减免学费、享受资助等方式解决了学费和生活上的问题，让她没有后顾之忧，全身心投入学习。经过"扶智""扶志""扶助"的全方位帮助，张媛媛同学成了一名开朗进取的好学生。她说："老师无微不至的关怀，让我增强了信心，掌握了许多学习方法，成绩也稳步提高。"2019~2020学年度，宁化一中共有97位建档立卡家庭经济困难学生，他们都和张媛媛一样，得到了学校的精心帮扶。①

从2016年开始，宁化全县实现全学段精准扶贫，在全面落实国家助学政策的基础上，向学前教育和大学教育延伸，实现了学前教育、义务

---

① 高建进：《福建宁化县：创新"三全三扶一档"教育精准扶贫机制》，《光明日报》2020年11月14日。

教育、高中教育和大学教育全覆盖。据当地介绍，宁化县实施大学教育"45810 资助"政策，县财政对全县建档立卡贫困家庭在校就读的省内大专生、省外大专生、省内本科生、省外本科生，分别给予每学年 4000 元、5000 元、8000 元和 10000 元资助金帮扶。截至 2020 年，共发放资助金 699.60 万元，惠及 972 人次。对学前教育实施"保教费补差"政策，在落实国家资助标准的基础上，县财政向建档立卡贫困幼儿补助发放"保教费补差"资金，2018~2019 学年共发放 14.08 万元，惠及 332 人次，保障贫困幼儿顺利入园。

2. 案例：河南省落实"两免一补"，推进城乡教育均衡发展

"两免一补"指中国政府向城乡义务教育阶段（小学和初中）的学生免费提供教科书、免除学杂费，并对家庭经济困难学生（含寄宿生和非寄宿生）补助生活费。从 2006 年起，国家逐步建立分项目、按比例分担的城乡义务教育经费保障机制，对中国全面普及九年义务教育发挥了重要作用。随着中国城镇化持续推进，大量农村剩余劳动力转移到城市，进城务工人员随迁子女的受教育权保障，尤其是义务教育保障，成为中国政府在利用教育阻断贫困代际传递过程中的工作重点。2015 年，国务院印发了《国务院关于进一步完善城乡义务教育经费保障机制的通知》，统一了城乡义务教育"两免一补"政策，依托有关统计信息系统，做到义务教育生均公用经费基准定额资金可携带，即"钱随人走"，对保障 1400 万进城务工人员随迁子女的受教育权起到积极作用。2020 年，中央财政下拨城乡义务教育补助经费 1695.9 亿元，金额比 2019 年增加 130.6 亿元，增长 8.3%。

河南省郑州市郑东新区小学四年级的学生李诚，四年前随进城务工的父母从驻马店农村来郑州。"户口马上迁城里了，家里经济条件也慢慢好起来，没想到孩子在郑州还能享受到'两免一补'，算一算，几年下来，给我们减轻了不小经济压力。"李诚家长说。与李诚一样处于义务教育阶段的 1344 万名河南学生，从 2016 起，无论是在农村还是在城市，都将享受同样的"两免一补"政策。2016 年，河南补助资金达 133 亿元，约 103 万名家庭经济困难的学生受益。从 2017 年春季学期开始，河南省统一城乡义务教育学生"两免一补"政策，在整合农村义务教育经费保障机制和城市义务教育奖补政策的基础上，建立城乡统一、重在农村的义务教育经费保障机制。实现教育经费"随学生流动可携带"，包括"两免一补"资金和生均公用经费基准定额资金，"人到哪里钱同样就到哪里"，进而推进城乡教育均衡，减轻群众经济负担。①

3. 案例：学生资助让寒门学子完成大学学业

随着《关于进一步落实高等教育学生资助政策的通知》《关于进一步加强和规范高校家庭经济困难学生认定工作的通知》等政策的印发和实施，中国高等教育学生资助范围不断扩大，资助更加精准有效，资助育人成果显著。中国高等教育学生资助体系以"奖、贷、助"为主，"勤、补、免"为辅，形成了以政府为主导、学校和社会互为补充的三位一体资助格局，形成了普惠性资助、助困性资助、奖励性资助和补偿性资助有机结合的多元混合资助模式，具体资助方式包括国家奖学金、国家励志奖学金、国家助学金、国家助学贷款、师范生免费教育、勤工助学、校内资助、绿色通道等。各级各类资助政策的大门，向每一位家庭经济困难学生敞开。据统计，2020 年，政府、高校及社会设立的各项普通高等教育学生资助政策共资助全国普通高等教育学生 3678.22 万人次，资助资金共计 1243.79 亿元。其中，财政资金 653.04 亿元，占 2020 年普通高等教育资助资金总额的 52.50%。银行发放国家助学贷款 378.12 亿元，占普通高等教育资助资金总额的 30.40%。高校从事业收入中提取并支出的资助资金 183.62 亿元，占普通高等教育资助资金总额的 14.76%。社会团体、企事业单位及个人捐助资助资金（简称社会资金）29.01 亿元，占普通高等教育资助资金总额的 2.33%。这些综合资助有力保障了家庭贫困学

---

① 《河南：133 亿用于"两免一补"推进城乡教育均衡发展》，央广网，2016，hn.cnr.cn。

生的受教育权。

中国农业大学经济管理学院 2014 届的马玉，在入学报到时是通过"绿色通道"直接入学的。在国家助学贷款项目中他选择了校园地贷款，"我一共借了 2 万多元，十年内还清，在校四年是免息的，办理过程非常便捷。"马玉说。助学贷款是目前中国在高等教育阶段对贫困家庭学生资助的主要方式之一，国家通过财政贴息，保障了大学生的受教育权利，并让他们能够安心完成学业。

"感谢国家的好政策，让我摆脱困境，进入大学安心读书。我要加倍珍惜来之不易的学习机会，学成本领回报社会。"2018 年年初，在收到中国银行帮扶国家连片贫困县在校大学生资助项目的 2000 元资助金后，西安医学院 2017 级学生刘小花热泪盈眶。刘小花来自陕西省咸阳市淳化县，其家庭贫困，父亲也罹患恶性肿瘤。2017 年 8 月，在她收到大学录取通知书后，一家人一时陷入了"看病"还是"上学"的纠结。在县教育局学生资助中心工作人员的帮助下，刘小花陆续获得生源地信用助学贷款 5500 元、社会爱心捐助 7000 元。进入大学后，学校又给她发放了 6000 元资助金。这些帮扶让刘小花摆脱了贫困的桎梏，心中重燃对美好未来的信心。

魏祥是甘肃省定西市的一名考生，患有先天性脊柱裂、椎管内囊肿，出生后双下肢运动功能丧失。更不幸的是，魏祥的父亲早逝，只有母亲陪着他一路求学。考上清华大学后，为了方便求学，他希望学校能给他们母子提供一间宿舍。6 月 28 日，清华大学给魏祥回信，清华大学表示将为魏祥母子提供两室一厅的宿舍，并承诺在确认录取后会立刻开始提供资助。清华大学多位校友也在看到消息的第一时间，主动表达了资助和协助他治疗的意愿。清华大学在信中回复："请你相信，校内外有足够多的支持，清华不会错过任何一位优秀学子。""很激动，这封回信处处都很打动我，处处都体现着对我的关心。我当时只是设想过，有可能给我一个肯定的答复说可以帮我，但没想到这么隆重地写一封回信。"魏祥说。确实有学子像魏祥一样是因病致贫，也有学子是因为其他原因致贫，面对教育改变命运的希望，资助不仅仅是钱的事，更是重大的民心、民生工程。[①]

近年来，在学生资助体系的基础上，中国高等院校将"扶贫"与"扶志"相结合，设立了"勤工俭学"机制，让贫困地区学子在高校学习期间，可以利用课余时间在图书馆、食堂等兼职进而增加收入，促进他们树立通过自身努力改变贫困境遇的意识，为他们在毕业后带动自己的家庭、社区摆脱贫困奠定思想基础。同时，依托大数据技术支持，中国广大高等院校可以更加及时准确地了解在校学生的日常生活情况，因而更加精准地采取针对贫困地区学生的资助手段、帮扶方式。

4. 案例：北京大学多渠道帮扶助力贫困学子成长成才

为增加特殊贫困地区学生接受优质高等教育的机会，2012 年 3 月，教育部等部门发布《关于实施面向贫困地区定向招生专项计划的通知》，组织国内优质高等院校在普通高校招生计划中专门安排适量招生计划，面向集中连片特困地区生源实行定向招生，并引导和鼓励学生毕业后回到贫困地区进行就业、创业。截至 2019 年，该计划的实施区域覆盖了中国所有集中连片特困县、国家级扶贫开发工作重点县等边远、贫困、民族等地区，招生人数由 2012 年的 1 万增至 2020 年的 11.7 万，计划开展以来，超过 70 万名特殊贫困地区学生得以接受优质高等教育。

彭玉恒是北京大学地球与空间科学学院地质专业的一名学生，2014 年她以贵州省瓮安县理科第一名、全省理科第九十九名的成绩进入北京大学。事实上，如果按照当年北京大学在贵州的最低录取分数线，彭玉恒不会有机会进入北京大学。"我十分幸运，赶上了好政策，北京大学降分录取了我。"彭玉恒说的"好政策"就是贫困地区定向招生专项计划。从改革开放到 21 世纪初，有 48 万人口的瓮安县仅有 22 人考入北京大学、

---

① 董鲁皖龙：《学生资助 更加精准有效——全国学生资助工作不断取得进展述评》，《中国教育报》2018 年 3 月 12 日。

清华大学。但是，自 2012 年贫困地区定向招生专项计划在贵州省实施以来，瓮安县平均每年都能有 1 人考入北京大学、清华大学。[①]

经济帮扶不是帮助贫困学生摆脱困难境遇的唯一手段，经济帮扶与其他帮扶手段相结合往往能帮助家庭经济困难的学生进入大学，更好地适应大学生活，更好地处理学习、生活中遇到的困难和问题。2010 年，北京大学针对家庭经济困难学生设立"燕园领航"项目，邀请校内知名学者、社会企业家和曾受资助的优秀毕业生等作为领航导师，安排他们与在校家庭经济困难学生"结对子"，密切关注并悉心指导学生的学习、生活。"燕园领航"项目启动以来，已覆盖两万名家庭经济困难学生，取得了良好的效果。用北京大学学生罗双双的话说："一只来自农村的燕子飞进了燕园，一切是那么陌生与新奇。好在有国家和学校的资助政策，特别是在领航老师的指导下，让我从一个什么都不懂的农村小姑娘变成了一个阳光、自信的学姐。在燕园的这些日子，我学到了很多的专业知识，我也学到了很多的为人处世的方法。'领航人'的关怀让我树立了信心在学校去发挥自己的能力，我也就更不惧怕什么，努力地做好自己的每一件事，无论是学习上的、工作上的，还是同学之间的。在这个过程中，我学会了担当，学会了合作，学会了付出。"罗双双说的"领航人"就源自北京大学"燕园领航"项目。[②]

（二）如何让失学、辍学的儿童返回学校并完成学业

中国在全面普及义务教育后，一直着力解决在少数贫困地区仍存在的辍学问题。中国政府结合精准扶贫方略，持续常态化开展控辍保学工作，建立"一生一表"工作档案，组织各地特别是农村贫困地区定期开

---

①　董鲁皖龙:《贵州大力推进贫困地区专项计划和精准扶贫——让更多寒门学子上重点大学》,《中国教育报》2015 年 12 月 5 日。

②　赵婀娜、朱佩娴、侯琳良:《虽然清贫些，但内心很温暖》,《人民日报》2015 年 8 月 13 日。

展数据比对核查，对失学、辍学现象采取针对性措施，让学生返回学校课堂，完成义务教育。2017年7月，国务院办公厅印发《关于进一步加强控辍保学提高义务教育巩固水平的通知》，要求进一步防控义务教育学生失学、辍学，确保实现2020年全国九年义务教育巩固率达到95%的目标，切实保障适龄儿童、青少年依法接受义务教育。文件要求针对学生辍学原因，加强分类指导，因地因人施策，做到"三避免"，即提高质量控辍，避免学生因学习困难或厌学而辍学；落实扶贫控辍，避免学生因贫失学、辍学；强化保障控辍，避免学生因上学远、上学难而辍学。

1. 案例：云南省为控辍保学开"药方"

云南是集边疆、民族、山区、贫困"四位一体"的西部省份。受地理环境、经济社会发展和民族文化习俗等因素影响，在一些深度贫困地区、少数民族聚居地区仍然存在不同程度的失学、辍学现象。围绕控辍保学目标要求，云南省设计规划了一整套措施。一是建立领导机构和协调机制，省教育厅成立由主要负责同志抓总负责、由相关部门负责人参与的控辍保学工作专班，加强对全省控辍保学工作的领导、指导和督查落实。各地政府成立由主要负责人任组长的控辍保学工作领导小组，全力推进云南少数民族地区义务教育控辍保学工作。二是开展全范围的调查，制定"四查三比对"数据核查方法（查户籍、学籍、学生、建档立卡贫困户适龄儿童少年，比对户籍、学籍与失学儿童，比对学籍、实际在校生与辍学学生，比对辍学学生、扶贫数据库与建档立卡户辍学学生），在全省组织大排查，准确摸清辍学、失学底数。三是制定精准方案和问责机制，督促县级政府依法履行控辍保学主体责任，全面落实"一县一方案"，精细做实"一校一方案、一人一方案"，强力推进依法劝返工作，针对控辍保学突出问题开展专项整治。四是运用法律手段保障儿童的受教育权利。五是通过普职融合的教育形式，帮助辍学学生继续返校学习。指导各地按照"集中管理、提供食宿、因材施教"的原则，统筹经费、师资、学习和生活条件等资源举办普职融合班，使学生在增长文化知识的同时也能学到技能。截至 2020 年 5 月，云南省控辍保学专项行动劝返辍学学生 16058 名，劝返率达 97.10%，其中家庭经济困难学生 4512 名。

云南省红河哈尼族彝族自治州金平县学生晓妹，12 岁才进入当地一所民办学校读一年级，由于年龄偏大、家中姊妹多、父母经常更换工地，上了一个学期后她便辍学在家。按照省州部署，金平县在深入开展控辍保学专项行动过程中，经过细致排查，发现了晓妹的辍学情况。随后，由政府工作人员、教师、村组干部组成的专班工作组迅速开展工作，与其父母进行深入沟通交流，说服其父母同意送她返回学校。同时，鉴于晓妹辍学时间长、几乎零基础的实际情况，当地专班工作组在晓妹返校后将其安置到普职融合班，让她在掌握基础知识的同时也掌握一项专业技能。此外，还在其就读的学校指定了一对一辅导教师，开展心理疏导工作，让她走出由辍学带来的负面影响，进而继续学道理、学知识、逐梦想。截至 2020 年，金平县普职融合班共有在校学生 106 人，这为当地培养了一批在结束义务教育后可以无缝对接选择升入职业高中或技校学习，进而能够尽快改变自己贫困境遇的年轻学子。[①]

2017 年 11 月 24 日，云南省怒江傈僳族自治州兰坪县啦井镇新建村的一场巡回法庭的公开审理引来数百名村民旁听。为依法维护适龄儿童少年享受义务教育的权利，啦井镇人民政府将 5 名学生的家长告上法庭，要求依法判令学生家长立即送其子女入学并完成义务教育。兰坪县啦井镇人民政府为原告，依据《中华人民共和国义务教育法》相关规定，这 5 名儿童、青少年应依法在校接受义务教育，但原告方多次对被告进行敦促、动员、批评、教育，被告方始终拒绝履行将其子女送入学校接受义务教育的义务。为此，啦井镇人民政府向兰坪县人民法院依法提起诉讼。法院在立案后，对被起诉的学生家长进行了走访调查，认为 5 名被告家

---

① 《云南：为控辍保学难题开出"药方"》，腾讯网，2020，new.qq.com。

长作为法定监护人，没有履行法定义务，以各种理由放任本应接受义务教育的子女辍学，违反了法律规定。庭审现场，法庭针对每名被告家长及其子女的实际情况，对原告、被告双方进行调解，既严肃申明违反国家法律、不履行法定义务将受到的惩处，又组织、劝导双方共同协商、探讨依法解决纠纷的具体方法。双方当场就学生返校时限、劝导事宜等达成共识，法庭当场下达调解书。经过庭审，家长认识到不让子女上学是违法的，纷纷表示今后要好好教育子女，尽力为子女创造良好的学习环境。村民纷纷表示，以前不懂法，目光短浅，不重视子女的学习，进而造成子女辍学，通过法院的这次判决，不但普及了法律常识，也使村民认识到了自身的错误，其表示今后一定充分尊重未成年人受教育的权利，使自己的子女依法入学，接受并完成义务教育。①

2. 案例：临夏回族自治州东乡族自治县，适龄儿童接受义务教育"一个都不能少"

受自然环境等因素的影响，甘肃省临夏回族自治州东乡族自治县巴苏池村是一个群众思想相对保守、适龄儿童入学特别是女童按时上学面临很多挑战的贫困村。教育精准扶贫工作开展以来，为落实控辍保学政策要求，派驻该村的扶贫干部通过细致负责的工作，使当地很多贫困家庭的适龄儿童走进学校、走上了改变人生的道路，并保障阻断了贫困代际传递。

张学红是临夏回族自治州教育局派驻巴苏池村的扶贫干部，从事教育工作多年。他对适龄儿童上学问题格外关注，让适龄儿童特别是女童按时上学是他的重点工作。经过走访，张学红发现当地建档立卡贫困户马哈入的 10 岁女儿马白给也曾在巴苏池小学报名入学，但之后一直辍学在家。经过家访，他了解到孩子不上学的原因除了上学路途较远，还有家长对女童上学的不重视。为此，张学红与其他扶贫干部多次到马白给

---

① 《不送娃娃上学 家长吃官司——全省首例控辍保学公益诉讼案在兰坪开庭》，怒江州人民政府网，2017，www.nujiang.gov.cn。

也的家中走访，耐心的政策讲解使马白给也的父母对适龄儿童入学有了新的认识，打消了让孩子上学的顾虑，马白给也终于重返学校，开始了新的学习生活。

东乡族自治县除了依托基层扶贫干部的细致工作，还落实所有就读女生从小学到大学的学费、食宿费等费用全免工作，同时在村民中树榜样，推动控辍保学政策有效落实。从县政府的主要工作人员到各级各类学校的校长，不少职务由女性担任，东乡族自治县常常组织这些榜样与当地村民分享自己的成长故事，引导当地贫困户村民形成接受教育可以改变命运、摆脱贫困的认识。通过多方努力，当地众多贫困村落的适龄儿童上学远、上学难的问题得到了有效解决。2017 年，临夏回族自治州义务教育巩固率达到了 95.11%，而张学红所在的东乡族自治县也在 2019 年实现了县辖 24 个乡镇所有辍学学生动态清零。①

3. 案例：张桂梅，照亮大山女孩的梦想

云南省丽江市华坪女子高级中学有一位女校长——张桂梅。她扎根云南贫困山区 40 多年，创办了中国第一所免费女子高中，是华坪儿童之家 130 多个孤儿的"妈妈"。她把全部身心投入边疆少数民族地区的教育事业和儿童福利事业，像一束希望之光，照亮学生的追梦人生。

1997 年，时年 40 岁的张桂梅被调动到华坪县民族中学执教。时间一长，她发现总有女生在课堂上"消失"，那些如花般的孩子，连世界的面貌都没有认全，就稀里糊涂地回家嫁人生子，一代又一代地重复着贫困的生活。张桂梅校长在一次次的家访中，看到一个个山区女孩因贫困辍学而深感心痛，因为她相信，培养一个女孩，最少可以影响三代人。如果能培养有文化、有责任的母亲，大山里的孩子就不会辍学，更不会成为孤儿。她在这座贫瘠的大山里建立了一所费用全免的女子高中，让华坪县的女孩公平地接受教育。初建女校，没有资金，她就挨家挨户地去

---

① 林焕新、苏令、尹晓军、郑芃生：《希望在沟沟坎坎中闪耀——甘肃省东乡族自治县教育脱贫攻坚纪实》，《中国教育报》2020 年 7 月 14 日。

"乞讨"来募集资金；没有学生，她就翻山越岭找辍学的女生来上学；没有教师，她就用理想和信念感动6名教师留了下来。她对教学和管理的要求非常严格，努力帮助大山里的女孩寻求改变命运的每一丝希望。尽管物质条件十分艰难，但张桂梅从来没有利用女孩的贫穷去博取同情，她小心翼翼地呵护着女孩的自尊，亲切地称呼她们是"大山里的姑娘"。

办学十几年来，华坪女子高级中学顺利送出了十一届毕业生，先后帮助1800多名贫困山区女孩圆梦大学。这所大山里的全免费女子高中，是当地的教育奇迹，它的历史很短，招收的大多是贫困、辍学或落榜的女学生，全校高考上线率、升学率却连年高达百分之百，本科上线率稳居丽江市前列，张桂梅校长"阻断贫困的代际传递"的目标正在逐渐实现。①

4. 案例：农村义务教育学生营养改善计划帮助贫困地区在校学生健康成长

为下一代提供充足营养，既是帮助贫困地区孩子摆脱营养贫困、让他们健康成长的关键措施，也是吸引这些地区的贫困家庭愿意送子女上学、让孩子愿意上学的有效措施。这有助于提高贫困地区义务教育质量，缩小城乡教育差距，对减贫具有重要现实意义。

21世纪初，中国仍有数以亿计的贫困人口，其主要集中在中西部农村地区，而儿童营养不良的问题也主要发生在这些地区。除因经济困难孩子营养不达标外，还存在很多农村学生饿着肚子上学的情况。2002年，中国学龄儿童少年生长迟滞检出率最高的是西南地区的国家扶贫工作重点县，5~12岁阶段，男生和女生的生长迟滞检出率分别达38.0%和38.2%，13~17岁阶段分别达40.0%和36.5%。西北地区的国家扶贫工作重点县的学龄儿童少年生长迟滞检出率也很高，5~12岁阶段，男生和女生的生长迟滞检出率分别为15.4%和20.9%，13~17岁阶段分别为27.4%

---

① 徐元锋：《照亮大山女孩的梦想》，《人民日报》2021年7月17日。

和 11.4%。

2011 年 11 月，为进一步改善农村学生营养状况，提高农村学生健康水平，国务院办公厅发布《关于实施农村义务教育学生营养改善计划的意见》（以下简称《意见》），率先在集中连片特困地区启动农村义务教育学生营养改善计划试点工作。2012 年 5 月，教育部等部门印发《农村义务教育学生营养改善计划实施细则》等 5 个配套文件，进一步规范农村义务教育学生营养改善计划的实施和管理工作。《意见》规定，集中连片特困地区的营养餐补助标准为每生每天 3 元（全年按学生在校时间 200天计算），所需资金全部由中央财政承担。2015 年，国家进一步将营养餐补助标准提高至每生每天 4 元。以贵州省长顺县第四中学为例，学校食堂的菜品十分丰富，每餐的标准都是三菜一汤，菜谱一周一换。除每生每天的营养餐补助 4 元外，家庭经济困难寄宿学生还有额外的 7 元补助，大部分学生都可以在食堂吃到免费的一日三餐。从 2021 年秋季学期起，学生营养餐补助标准从每生每天 4 元提高至每生每天 5 元，让学生不仅能吃饱，更能吃好。营养餐在贫困农村地区学校的推广有力巩固了这些地区义务教育普及的成果。

在实施营养改善计划的过程中，中国很多地方政府结合当地实际，采取创新性实施策略，确保营养餐被快速推广，以此造福农村学生。如在提供学生营养餐的工作中，确保营养餐的卫生安全是最重要也是最底线的要求。贵州省铜仁市由政府主导建立了学生营养餐智慧云综合服务管理平台，进而对学校食堂进行信息化监管。该平台不仅可用于对学校食材的采购与管理，还可以对出库食材的营养品质进行分析和提醒，对保质期只有 1 天的食材进行预警提醒。此外，市、县、校管理人员随时可以通过相关 App 对学校食堂进行网上巡察，提高了学校食堂管理的实效性和精准度。为了确保营养餐计划的资金安全，安徽省舒城县不仅建立了严格的财务审计制度，还直接与银行对接，并由学校申请委托付款、审核把关，食堂食材款直达供应商，从而实现了无现金结算。

中国的农村义务教育学生营养改善计划覆盖了中国大部分经济较不发达的农村地区，并在促进学生的健康成长和巩固义务教育方面发挥了显著作用。2020年6月，教育部发布的报告显示，全国有28个省份（含兵团）1647个县实施了营养改善计划，覆盖农村义务教育阶段学校13.72万所，占农村义务教育阶段学校总数的81.7%，受益学生达3728.3万人，占农村义务教育阶段学生总数的39.6%。2019年，中国疾病预防控制中心的跟踪监测数据显示，在营养改善计划试点地区，男生、女生各年龄段平均身高比2012年分别提高1.54厘米和1.69厘米，平均体重分别增加1.06公斤和1.18公斤，高于全国农村学生平均增长速度。同时中国义务教育巩固率不断提升，从2009年的90.8%提高到2020年的95.2%，营养改善计划的实施，不仅提高了贫困地区义务教育阶段学生的身体健康水平，让更多家庭经济困难的学生留在学校，也明显减轻了这些学生家庭的经济支出负担，推进了当地减贫工作的开展。

（三）如何在贫困地区发展学前教育来帮助孩子为上学做好准备

中国政府高度重视儿童早期发展，在全国范围内普及了九年义务教育后，将普及教育的工作重心向学前教育和高中阶段教育延伸。一是国家制定规划，强力推进学前教育的普及。2010年中央政府颁布《国家中长期教育改革和发展规划纲要（2010—2020年）》，确立了用10年基本普及学前教育，并提出要坚持学前教育公益普惠的发展方向，按照扩资源、调结构、建机制、提质量的发展思路，以县为单位连续实施三期"学前行动计划"。二是明确政府责任，部门分工协作。中国确立了国务院领导、省市统筹、以县为主的管理体制。地方各级政府积极落实建设和监管责任，大力发展公办幼儿园，积极支持和规范民办幼儿园。教育部、财政部等部门根据职责分工，密切合作、共同推进。三是加大财政投入，实施重大项目。地方各级政府制定生均财政拨款标准和生均公用经费标准。中央财政设立专项资金，2011~2020年，支持学前教育发展资金达 1519.8 亿元。建立学前教育资助制度，2011~2020 年各级政府总计投入 643 亿元，资助家庭经济困难幼儿 5500 万人次。各地出台并落实公办幼儿园生均财政拨款标准、生均公用经费标准普惠性民办幼儿园财政补助标准。

1. 案例：四川省乐山市彝区开展"一村一幼"建设

受历史、地理、社会、经济等因素的影响，四川省乐山市彝族聚居区的学前教育发展严重滞后，普及学前教育面临很大困难。2013 年，乐山市彝区村级幼儿园只有 9 所（其中公办幼儿园 1 所），适龄幼儿 417 人、教师 20 人，彝区学前三年毛入园率只有 62.6%，低于全市平均水平 23.54 个百分点。为补齐乐山教育的短板，加快彝区教育事业发展，有效阻断贫困代际传递，2014 年 4 月，乐山市政府把彝区"一村一幼"建设写入《关于进一步加快推进小凉山综合扶贫开发的通知》，在四川省彝区率先实施"一村一幼"建设。目的是以"一村一幼"建设为突破口，加快彝区学前教育发展，乐山市政府决定用三年的时间，通过"一村一幼"建设基本实现彝区适龄幼儿入园全覆盖。到 2017 年年底，在乐山市彝区286 个行政村中建设了 295 所村幼儿园，在园幼儿达 9947 人，基本实现了彝区适龄幼儿入园全覆盖的目标。

在"一村一幼"建设实施过程中，乐山市政府分别从基础设施、资金保障、师资队伍建设及帮扶网络建设四个方面推动当地彝区学前教育发展。在基础设施方面，以现有场地为主解决园舍难题。按照"保基本，广覆盖"的原则，利用闲置的村小学教室和村级活动室，建设最基本的、安全有保障的幼儿园。2014~2017 年，在 295 所"一村一幼"幼儿园中，修缮闲置村小学教室的有 157 所，利用村级活动室作园舍的有 63 所，附设中心校的有 56 所，新建园舍的有 19 所。在资金保障方面，以财政投入为主解决经费难题。中央财政设立支持学前教育发展资金，重点补足普惠性学前教育资源短板，健全普惠性学前教育经费投入机制，巩固幼儿资助制度，提高保教质量，并引导激励地方加大资金投入，增加支持学前教育发展资金，其中省财政主要解决"一村一幼"保教人员的工资问题，每年投入资金 1372.8 万元。市财政按每所幼儿园 5 万元的标准，投入资金 1475 万元，将其作为"一村一幼"的启动建设资金，投入资金 235.2 万元，将其作为"一村一幼"购置教具、学具和安全监控设备安装经费补助，同时每年投入 686.4 万元，给予保教人员工资补助。县级财政共投入 3000 多万元来建设"一村一幼"并对其进行升级改造，按每人每年 1000~4000 元的标准给予保教人员工资补助；按每生每年 800 元的标准给予学生营养补助，解决幼儿生活难题；按每生每年 100~200 元的标准给予生均公用经费补助。在师资队伍建设方面，乐山市政府以拓宽用人渠道解决师资缺乏难题。乐山市通过转岗、公招等办法切实落实"一村一幼"保教人员。同时强化教师培训，市、县教育行政部门每年都对"一村一幼"保教人员进行全员培训，提高保教人员的素质和能力。在帮扶网络建设方面，依托市、县优质学前教育资源的引领和带动，乐山市于 2016 年大力实施彝区"一村一幼"提升工程，举全市之力实现彝区"一村一幼"整体升级。不断完善全覆盖式帮扶模式，实现市与县的定点帮扶、县与县的对口帮扶、县域内片区结对帮扶等，进而提高帮扶实效。乐山市已成立市实验幼儿园幼教集团、市机关幼儿园幼教集团。金口河、马边、峨边三个民族地区同时被纳入集团，在集团中学习优质高效的管理模式、先进科学的保教理念，不断提高办园质量。[①]

2. 案例：安徽省通过结对帮扶助农村学前教育提高质量

2010~2020 年，中国学前教育普及程度快速提高，但仍存在发展不平衡的问题，特别是农村学前教育存在不同程度的教育资源短缺、资金投入不足、师资队伍不健全等难题。中国采取城市支持农村的措施来帮助农村学前教育发展。很多地方开展了结对帮扶活动，即由城市办学水平较高的示范幼儿园与农村幼儿园结成帮扶对子，充分发挥城市示范幼儿

---

① 《干在实处 走在前列 夯实阻断贫困代际传递基石——乐山市彝区"一村一幼"建设案例》，中华人民共和国教育部，2016，www.moe.gov.cn。

园的示范引领作用，把优质学前教育资源向农村幼儿园辐射与拓展，帮助农村幼儿园提高教师专业能力，提高保教质量。结对帮扶活动在促进农村学前教育发展方面取得显著成效。

2017年10月，安徽省合肥市庐阳区教育行政部门启动了对临泉县的教育扶贫工作。截至2020年7月，共有156名庐阳区幼教专家、名园长赴临泉县开展讲座，共有3300多名幼儿园教师参加培训。合肥市庐阳区先进的幼教理念已在临泉县377所幼儿园的教学中得到运用，临泉县700余名幼儿园教师的保教能力得到全面提升，先后有10万余名在园幼儿从中受益，其有效提升了临泉县幼儿园规范办园水平并提高了保教质量，为促进城乡幼儿教育的均衡发展做出了积极贡献。

李峥是安徽省合肥市庐阳区安庆路幼儿园教育集团总园长，也是安徽省级名园长。2018~2020年，合肥市庐阳区与阜阳市临泉县开展学前教育结对帮扶，李峥多次往返两地，帮助指导临泉县乡镇幼儿园办园。2018年10月，李峥第一次走进临泉县城东街道中心幼儿园时，发现幼儿家长在育儿观念上存在误区——很多家长希望幼儿园可以多教孩子文化课知识。李峥立即号召组织了一次全员幼儿家长会，幼儿家长、幼儿园教师全员参与。她用富有亲和力的话语向家长讲述了幼儿园"小学化"的危害。接下来的几场家长会，每一场都座无虚席。通过一个个案例的讲述、一张张日周计划表的讲解，"适合孩子身心发展才是最好的"这一观念逐渐渗入家长心中。随后，李峥对幼儿园的环境建设也给出了具体、可操作的建议。在李峥的指导和帮助下，临泉县城东街道中心幼儿园成功评上阜阳市一类幼儿园。

像李峥一样的省级名园长深入贫困地区乡镇幼儿园帮其制定发展方案并创先争优的案例在当地并非个案。2018年11月，临泉县杨桥镇中心幼儿园在争创"阜阳市级一类园"的过程中就得到了合肥市委机关幼儿园教育集团的精准指导。园长崔利红动员集团内精英幼教力量，将一类园要求细化为区域游戏创设指导、园务管理、教学提升、卫生保健安全、材料管理等具体工作，并有针对性地建立指导小组，派集团专业人士带着做，短短三个月内，让杨桥镇中心幼儿园从内到外都有了质的变化。在崔利红看来，幼教帮扶具有特殊性，因此必须把工作做细，细到幼儿水杯怎么选择、饮用水温度如何控制等。就这样，手把手带、一点点教，成功帮助杨桥镇中心幼儿园实现办学水平的巨大跨越。

在临泉县很多园长心中，庐阳区这一批名园长的到来，改变的不仅是临泉县幼儿园的面貌，更把幼儿园教师的志气给扶了起来。让当地教师明白，自己不是保姆、不是看孩子的，而是有专业精神和专业自信的幼儿园教师。乡镇幼儿园教师刘玲玲觉得，这两年自己最大的收获就是学会了站在幼儿的角度思考问题。"以前总觉得做环创、搞区角、做活动，展现的是老师的艺术水平，是做给大人看的。现在才发现这个想法错了。"刘玲玲说。在安庆路幼儿园专业团队手把手带着干的过程中，她慢慢体会到幼儿园教师"蹲下来"的重要性，"蹲下来，和孩子处于一样的高度，用他们的眼睛去看这个世界，才会看到自己这份职业的闪光点"。[①]

（四）如何确保特殊群体的受教育权

确保残疾人等特殊群体的平等受教育权是《教育2030议程》的重要内容。由于治病康复的花费较大，有残疾儿童少年的家庭更容易陷入贫困甚至是绝对贫困，而这些残疾儿童少年如果没有接受必要的教育，长大后同样会陷入贫困境地。要解决绝对贫困问题，必须重视解决残疾儿童少年的受教育问题。中国政府高度重视保障残疾人受教育权利，《中华人民共和国教育法》以及专门修订颁布的《残疾人教育条例》等法律法规都对残疾人教育事业提出了明确要求。同时，中国政府颁布实施的教育规划，如五年规划以及《中国教育现代化2035》也都对发展面向残

---

① 方梦宇：《合肥庐阳区2017年启动对临泉县教育扶贫以来，已形成幼儿园教师学习共同体——结对帮扶助学前教育爬坡过坎》，《中国教育报》2020年7月5日。

疾人的教育做出专门部署。各级政府密集发布实施细则和相关落实文件，政策推进力度之大前所未有，特殊教育实现了快速发展，其主要表现在以下几方面。

一是特殊教育的普及水平显著提升。2020年，全国有特殊教育学校2244所，比2015年增加191所，增长约9.3%；在校生88.08万人，比2015年增加43.9万人。残疾儿童少年接受义务教育从"基本普及"发展到"全面普及"。同时，残疾人接受学前教育、以职业教育为主的高中阶段教育和高等教育的机会也不断增加。二是特殊教育保障力度明显加大。2016~2020年的5年间，中央财政特殊教育专项补助经费年均投入约4.1亿元，累计投入20.5亿元，重点支持中西部地区加强特殊教育资源建设，改善特殊教育办学条件。特殊教育学校和随班就读残疾学生的生均公用经费标准提高到6000元，为普通学生的6~8倍，保障了特殊教育的正常运转。三是特殊教育师资队伍建设得到显著加强。2020年，全国特殊教育学校共有专任教师6.6万人，比2015年增加约1.3万人，教师专业化水平不断提高。已有20多个省（区、市）出台特殊教育学校教职工编制标准，各地普遍落实了特殊教育教师享受基本工资15%的特殊教育津贴政策，已有超过18个省（区、市）提高了津贴标准或增加了岗位补贴。四是特殊教育质量稳步提高。中国推进融合教育，随班就读工作机制进一步健全，随班就读工作水平不断提高。开展残疾人高等融合教育，探索为残疾学生学习、生活、就职指导等方面提供支持服务。发布实施盲、聋、培智三类特殊教育学校义务教育课程标准，组织专门力量开展统编教材的编审工作，截至2020年年底，已编写审定并投入使用统编教材239册，这为特殊教育学校师生提供了基本的教学标准和依据。布局合理、学段衔接、普职融通、医教结合的特殊教育体系初步建立，财政为主、社会支持、全面覆盖、通畅便利的特殊教育服务保障机制逐步完善，政府主导、部门协同、各方参与的特殊教育工作格局基本形成。

1. 案例：江西省融合教育和送教上门给特殊儿童温暖的爱

江西省信丰县作为国家特殊教育改革实验区，在 2016 年建立了特殊教育资源中心，对特殊儿童进行专业评估，确定特校就读、随班就读、送教上门等不同教育形式，让这一特殊困难群体都能接受教育。

李晓强就读于信丰县某小学普通班，他有一定程度的识字障碍，为此学校老师专门成立了帮助小组。在老师和同学的陪伴下，他的学习有了很大的进步，识字障碍的问题得到很大缓解，并且在融合教育过程中李晓强也有了正常的社交能力。

李晓强的变化源于信丰县大力推进的融合教育。信丰县在对特殊儿童一对一评估后，对 565 名轻度特殊儿童采取随班就读方式，同时建立专门档案，按照每人每年 6000 元的标准下拨经费到特殊儿童所在学校。此外，对于有特殊儿童的班级，学校加大师资配比，定期由资源中心专业教师巡回指导，研究实施符合随班就读学生特点的教学方法，根据学生需求配备助理教师，完善融合教育保障机制，让特殊儿童得到高质量的教育和关爱。

为了让重度残疾学生公平接受义务教育，信丰县组建了 171 支"送教小分队"，走遍全县 300 多个村组社区，把"小课堂"搬进学生的家中。家住信丰县正平镇九渡村的刘嘉怡，4 岁时因意外导致颅内损伤而被鉴定为极重度残疾。从刘嘉怡 6 岁开始，由 1 名特殊教育老师和 2 名普教老师组成的"送教小分队"就敲开了她的家门。除了每周一次上门送教，"送教小分队"还通过视频、微信等远程方式对刘嘉怡的家人进行培训，指导其开展日常的肢体康复和文化教学，从而形成了线上线下互动，学校、家庭共同参与的送教模式。刘嘉怡的健康状况和认知能力都得到了明显提高。

在信丰县，像刘嘉怡一样重度和极重度残疾的学生有 171 人，他们都享受了送教上门服务。而这得益于 2014 年教育部等 7 部门启动的《特殊教育提升计划（2014—2016 年）》，其针对重度残疾学生居住分散且许多住在偏远乡村的问题，发挥普通学校属地就近的特点，建立了以特殊教育为支撑、普教共同参与的多元化送教模式。截至 2021 年，信丰县已累计为 386 名重度和极重度残疾学生制定了个性化教学方案，送教上门课时 4.5 万多节。送教上门让重度和极重度残疾学生接受了适合自己的教育。[①]

2. 案例：福建省泉州市推进职业教育发展，让残疾学生拥有出彩人生

长期以来，支持残疾人就业创业是特殊教育的重要目标。福建省泉州市以实施特殊教育提升计划为抓手，积极发展残疾学生职业教育，帮助残疾学生掌握一技之长、顺利融入社会。

萍萍是泉州市特殊教育学校职专毕业生，有听力障碍，同时她也是泉州市静土文创院的员工，每天安心绘画就是她的工作。萍萍表示："我喜欢在这里工作，这里就像我的家一样。别人喜欢我的作品，我特别开心，这是一种自我价值的实现。"在这里，还有 4 名来自泉州市特殊教育学校的实习生，他们专心投入创作，内心的充盈让他们由内而外洋溢着快乐。

萍萍是残疾学生通过接受职业教育成功就业的一个缩影。泉州市以市场需求为导向，紧紧围绕"特殊教育职业化，职业教育社会化"的办学思路，整合闽南文化资源、工匠大师和电商平台，在特殊教育学校设置听障部工艺美术、文化创意、生活服务及视障部推拿按摩、艺术表演五个专业，开设陶艺、油画、书画装裱、版画、影雕、推拿按摩等 15 门职教课程。学生在确定一个规划专业的基础上，可选择学习多门职教课程，实现"1+N"职业培养模式。学校为每一名学生提供个性化的职业教育，搭建展示平台，让学生能迅速地融入就业岗位。萍萍在校学习期间，参加过市级残疾人艺术作品展，其绘画作品多次获奖。

---

① 《江西信丰：171 支"送教小分队"》，央视网，2021，tv.cctv.com。

借助泉州市教育基金会设立的特殊教育专项基金，泉州市特殊教育学校创办了残疾学生就业创业孵化基地——静土文创院，为学校职业教育提供实习场所，解决部分学生的就业问题，打通职业培训、职业鉴定、岗前培训等教育渠道，铺就残疾学生从学校到社会顺利就业创业的道路。残疾学生的职业技术素养和就业创业能力不断提高，其融入社会、自立于社会、奉献社会的信心得到极大增强。泉州市越来越多的"萍萍"正通过接受多样化的职业教育，走上适合的工作岗位，发挥自身所学技能，创造幸福而出彩的人生。①

二 提高教育质量，确保贫困地区孩子学得好

（一）如何解决贫困地区城乡之间和学校之间办学水平差距过大的问题

在 2011 年中国全面普及九年义务教育后，中国教育的发展仍存在不平衡的情况，特别是东部经济发达地区与中西部地区之间的差距较大，城乡之间、学校之间的发展差距也十分明显。为了缩小义务教育阶段过大的差距，推动义务教育均衡发展，让孩子享受更公平、更有质量的义务教育，中国政府采取了综合措施，集中力量推动县域内义务教育均衡发展。2012 年 9 月，《国务院关于深入推进义务教育均衡发展的意见》对推进县域内义务教育均衡发展进行全面部署，其中一条重要举措就是实施"农村义务教育薄弱学校改造计划"和"中西部农村初中校舍改造工程"，着力支持农村学校和薄弱学校改善办学条件，提升办学水平，努力让所有适龄儿童少年"上好学"。2013 年 1 月，中国教育部启动义务教育均衡发展督导评估工作，明确师生比、专任教师学历合格率、生均校地面积、生均校舍面积等十项国家义务教育均衡发展指标，中国贫困地

---

① 《泉州推进特教职业化 打通残疾人就业创业渠道》，《泉州晚报》2019 年 5 月 16 日。

区义务教育均衡发展有了更明确的方向。近年来中国在各个教育阶段的总投入一直在不断增加，2020 年全国教育经费投入为 53033.87 亿元，其中义务教育投入最多。2020 年 12 月底，全国累计 26 个省份 2809 个县实现县域义务教育基本均衡发展，县数占比 96.8%，其中，中西部地区县数占比达到 95.3%。

1. 案例："全面改薄"工作保障农村贫困地区办学条件，助力义务教育均衡发展

2013 年 12 月，为了改善贫困地区义务教育办学条件，促进基本公共教育服务均等化，国家启动实施全面改善贫困地区义务教育薄弱学校基本办学条件工作（简称"全面改薄"工作）。"全面改薄"工作以中西部贫困地区为主，兼顾东部部分困难地区；以集中连片特困地区为主，兼顾其他国家扶贫开发工作重点地区、民族地区、边境地区等贫困地区。其包括保障基本教学条件、改善学校生活设施、办好必要教学点、解决县镇学校大班额问题、推进农村学校教育信息化、提高教师队伍素质等 6 项重点任务，直指贫困地区义务教育的薄弱环节和存在的主要问题。

湖南省武冈市湾头桥镇铜湾小学曾因教学质量太差而被撤并。2016 年，在"全面改薄"工作的驱动下，铜湾小学恢复修建。70 年代的老旧平房变成了两层教学楼，泥巴地上修建了风雨连廊，每间教室都装上了网络校校通、优质资源班班通、网络学习空间人人通等设备，学校办学条件有了根本性改善，教学水平也有了明显提升。武冈市稠树塘镇凉山小学是一所覆盖 3 个村的乡村小学。先前，这所学校还只有 5 个学生，濒临撤并。2017 年，武冈市依托"全面改薄"工作，在 3 个村中心选址重建学校。2018 年 9 月，凉山小学新校开学，当年就招了 76 名学生。一年之后，村民对学校非常满意，又强烈要求增加五、六年级。截至 2020 年，凉山小学已经有了 6 个年级，在校学生 132 名。在武冈市，像凉山小学这样，通过新建改建"长大"的农村学校还有不少。武冈市通过统一规划设计，按照"实用、够用、安全、节俭"和"缺什么补什么"原

则，全面建设农村标准校园。截至 2021 年，武冈市累计投入教学点建设资金约 1.1 亿元，新建和改扩建教学楼和学生食堂等 169 栋、篮球场 61 个，将全市小规模学校各班级全部配齐配足教学设备。新建农村教师公租房、周转房 800 余套，改善教师生活条件。2019~2021 年，全市共补充 400 余名优秀教师到农村教学点。同时，武冈市创新管理模式，按照"大校托小校"原则，将全市 73 所农村小规模学校就近纳入完全小学以上学校，按照教育教学统一管理、教师统一配置、教育设施统一调配、教育经费统一使用的原则，推动完全小学与所辖教学点一体化办学、协同发展。截至 2020 年年底，武冈全市 73 所农村小规模学校全部完成标准化学校建设，教育教学质量大幅提高，吸引 700 余名在外地学校就读的农村学生回流，有效提升了当地农村教育教学水平。[①]

2. **案例：安徽省农村小规模学校运用信息技术提升教学质量**

针对农村教育基础薄弱、提升质量难度大的问题，安徽省将信息技术的广泛应用作为提升农村学校教育质量的关键措施，并取得了良好成效。安徽省将农村中小学，特别是贫困地区小规模学校的智慧学校建设纳入省政府重点工作和民生工程。六安市下辖的金寨县地处大别山区，是安徽面积最大、山库区人口最多的县，有小规模学校 127 所，其大部分地处山区。金寨县天堂寨中心小学下辖的 6 个教学点地处偏远且师资力量严重不足，多年来一直无法开设英语、美术、音乐等课程。2015 年，金寨县开始在全县推广在线教育，借助在线课堂平台，学校的 6 个教学点实现了与中心小学课堂同步、教研同步，偏远教学点的学生也有了英语、美术、音乐等课程。同时，安徽省实施了乡村教师信息素养专项提升计划，对农村中小学教师教育技术能力进行全面培训，重点加强乡村教师信息化应用能力。截至 2021 年年初，安徽省已组织智慧学校应用培训近 1800 次，并将信息技术应用作为新任教师上岗和教师资格注册的考

---

① 《昔日"痛点"，今成"亮点"：武冈累计投入 1.1 亿元建设小规模学校》，搜狐网，2021，www.sohu.com。

核内容。在金寨县天堂寨中心小学，传统的在线课堂已升级为"在线课堂＋智慧课堂"的智慧空中课堂 2.0 模式，教学点学生也可以和中心小学师生同步课堂互动、同步作业测评。学生可以在课后利用智慧空中课堂进行自主学习，教师还可以给学生推送名校名师录制的精品课程。农村学校第一次通过线上教学，弥补了学生在获取教育资源上的不均衡。①

（二）如何解决偏远农村学校教师数量不足、教师质量不高的问题

贫困地区特别是一些偏远山区，受交通、地理、语言等多种因素的影响，加之财政困难，无法聘请足够数量的合格教师，制约了当地教学质量的提升，造成乡村学校学生外流甚至辍学、失学。因此，解决偏远乡村学校教师的数量不足、质量不高等问题，成了提高乡村学校教育教学质量的关键。针对这个问题，中国中央政府主导实施了若干有针对性的教师专项计划，有效推动了农村贫困地区教师整体水平的提升。

1. 案例："特岗计划"为乡村学校补充合格师资

2006 年 5 月，中国教育部、财政部、人事部、中央编办四部门联合印发《关于实施农村义务教育阶段学校教师特设岗位计划的通知》，启动实施了农村义务教育学校教师特设岗位计划（简称"特岗计划"），即通过公开招募高校毕业生到西部地区"两基"②攻坚县，中部地区的少数民族自治州，西部地区一些有特殊困难的边境县、少数民族自治县和少数民族县的农村义务教育阶段学校任教，引导和鼓励高校毕业生从事农村教育工作，逐步解决农村师资总量不足和结构不合理等问题，提高乡村教师队伍的整体素质。特岗教师聘期为 3 年，中央财政对特岗教师给予工资性补助。鼓励高校毕业生投身农村教育事业，促进农村教育发展，助力脱贫攻坚。2015 年 6 月，国务院办公厅印发《乡村教师支持计划（2015—2020 年）》，分别从补充渠道、生活待遇、编制标准、职称评定、

---

① 方梦宇：《安徽：智慧校园为乡村小规模学校赋能》，中国教育新闻网，2020，www.jyb.cn。
② "两基"是基本实现九年义务教育和基本扫除青壮年文盲的简称。

交流制度、能力素质和荣誉制度等方面对乡村教师给予优惠支持政策和保障。

"特岗计划"实施以来，招聘规模逐步扩大，从2006年的1.6万人，逐步增加到2019年的10万人，累计招聘近85万名特岗教师，覆盖中西部地区的1000多个县、3万多所农村学校，服务期满后的特岗教师留任率在90%以上。2006年专科及以上学历的乡村小学专任教师仅占53.61%，2015年达到了86.49%，2019年高达94.79%，"特岗计划"对此起到了重要作用。特岗教师平均年龄24岁左右，极大地改善了乡村教师尤其是偏远地区教师老龄化的现象。"特岗计划"集中补充了大量的英语、信息技术、音乐、体育、美术等短缺课程教师，信息技术、音乐、体育、美术等薄弱课程专任教师的比例从2006年的6.38%、2015年的11.54%，提高到2019年的16.72%。

广西壮族自治区田阳县采用多种方式帮助特岗教师"下得去、留得住、教得好"。一是创便利条件，让特岗教师"下得去"。田阳县将新招聘特岗教师优先安排在交通条件相对便利、生源相对集中的乡镇学校，让远离父母、初涉社会的特岗教师能够顺利度过乡村工作适应期。教师周转房优先建设在有特岗教师服务的乡镇学校，学校优先为特岗教师提供单人单间的教工宿舍，避免因环境落差而导致教师"打退堂鼓"。特岗教师服务学校开设教师食堂，刷卡就能吃到现成的饭菜，让每一名特岗教师不因柴米油盐问题而产生工作和生活上的不便。二是给优厚待遇，让特岗教师"留得住"。县财政每年预算600多万元用于实施乡村教师生活补助政策、发放乡镇工作补贴。工作在乡镇的特岗教师最高补助达每月700元，最低也有每月500元，切实提高特岗教师的获得感。将特岗教师纳入县政府发放年终绩效考评奖金范围，个人最高可领到绩效奖励金达2.3万元，这大大增强特岗教师安心留任田阳县的决心。破格提拔重用特岗教师，将适应能力强、入行快、工作成绩突出的特岗教师提拔进入学校中层。在每年教师节表彰中，专门划出名额指标向特岗教师倾斜，截至 2017 年已有 52 名服务期内的特岗教师接受了县级以上的表彰。三是搭事业平台，让特岗教师"教得好"。切实解决特岗教师的后顾之忧，服务期满后的特岗教师，经考核合格后个人自愿留任，县政府将其全部按时安排入编聘用，让特岗教师在乡村安心从教。同时，师徒"结对子"，做好"传帮带"，通过城乡学校"结对子"送教下乡，校内师徒"结对子""传帮带"等途径让特岗教师从老教师、优秀教师的言传身教中得到启发，通过切身的感悟解决他们的入门入行问题。落实经费保障，抓好继续教育培训，新招聘的特岗教师必须完成不少于 120 学时的岗前集中培训。特岗教师上岗后，县教育局统筹安排其参加"国培计划"和"区培计划"培训。搭建展现个人才华的平台，让教坛新秀能够脱颖而出，充分发掘特岗教师的优势，开展各级各类教学技能比赛，鼓励特岗教师参赛。①

2. 案例：定向为贫困地区培养优秀教师——北京师范大学的"志远计划"

为帮助农村地区特别是贫困地区培养高素质教师，中国教育部依托国内一流师范院校，从贫困地区师资队伍建设入手，实施了专项人才培养计划，北京师范大学设立的"志远计划"就是其中之一。该计划从 2020 年本科招生开始，其基本原则是"定向招生、定向培养、定向就业"，招生面向当时尚未摘帽的 52 个国家级贫困县所在省份的优秀高中毕业生，择优招收本科毕业后到国家级贫困县定向就业的师范生，为这些地方培养志存高远、乐教适教的高素质教师。

2020 年，"志远计划"面向广西、四川、贵州、云南、甘肃、宁夏和新疆等 7 个当时尚未摘帽国家级贫困县所在的省（区）招收本科定向就业师范生 156 人，开设汉语言文学、数学与应用数学和英语三个专业。"志远计划"学生毕业后，将经双向选择，由省级教育行政主管部

---

① 《教师队伍建设典型工作案例一：农村义务教育阶段学校教师特设岗位计划实施工作优秀案例》，中华人民共和国教育部，2017，www.moe.gov.cn。

门安排至生源省份国家级贫困县域中小学任教，入编入岗，任教服务不少于 6 年。对履行协议到国家级贫困县域中小学任教的定向就业师范毕业生，北京师范大学将返还其本科四年的学费和住宿费，并将其纳入学校"四有"好老师启航计划的奖励范围，服务满一学期且符合条件者，可申请免试攻读北京师范大学教育硕士专业学位。定向就业师范生在服务期内，可申请参加北京师范大学举办的基础教育教师在职培训项目，共享北京师范大学精品课程、在线教育资源等优质教育教学资源，获得学科教育专家团队的业务指导，并有机会参与学校面向一线基础教育的教育教学改革研究、基础教育集团组织的教学改革实践等职后培养与培训活动。

3. 案例：通过招募退休教师支持贫困地区教育——高校和中小学银龄讲学计划

提高贫困地区的教育质量，高水平教师是其关键。中国政府采取了招募退休高水平教师对贫困地区扶教的举措。2018 年 7 月，中国教育部、财政部联合印发《银龄讲学计划实施方案》，从 2018 年起，面向社会公开招募一批优秀退休校长、教研员、特级教师、高级教师等到农村义务教育学校讲学，目的是发挥优秀退休教师引领示范作用，为农村学校提供智力支持，帮助提升农村学校教学水平和育人管理能力，缓解农村学校优秀师资总量不足和结构不合理等矛盾，促进城乡义务教育均衡发展。该项目以县为单位，主要是国家确定的集中连片特困地区县、国家扶贫开发工作重点县、省级扶贫开发工作重点县等，重点向深度贫困地区倾斜。受援学校为县镇和农村学校。招募的讲学教师可以根据自己的专业特长开展以课堂教学为主的讲学活动，同时也可以根据受援学校的教育教学需求进行听课评课、开设公开课、研讨课或专题讲座，协助学校做好教学管理工作并开展丰富多彩的讲学活动，发挥示范和辐射作用，提升受援学校教育教学和管理水平。招募工作由省级教育部门负责，遵循"公开、公平、自愿、择优"和"定县、定校、定岗"的原则，从受援县学校的实际需要出发招募讲学教师，结合讲学教师专业特长，选准学科专业。招募工作按以下 6 个程序进行：公布需求、自愿报名、资格审核或遴选、公示公布、签订协议、上岗任教。讲学教师服务时间原则上不少于 1 学年，鼓励考核合格的教师连续讲学。各受援县教育局与拟招募讲学教师签订银龄讲学服务协议，协议一年一签，明确双方的权利和义务，正式签约前，讲学教师需提供近 6 个月体检报告。讲学教师服务期间，由受援县对其进行跟踪评估，对不按协议要求履行义务的，或因身体原因不适合继续讲学的，予以解除协议。讲学教师服务期间的人事关系、现享受的退休待遇不变，按月发放工作经费，工作经费主要用于向讲学教师发放工作补助、交通差旅费用及购买意外保险费等。该计划于2018 年启动，首先在河北、江西、湖南、广西、四川、云南、甘肃、青海这 8 个中西部省（区）开展试点。2018~2020 年，该计划实施范围扩大至 16 个省（区）及新疆生产建设兵团，招募近 1 万名退休讲学教师参与支教，同时招募名额向最困难的贫困地区倾斜。

为了支持欠发达地区高等学校发展，2020 年，中国教育部又启动实施了高校银龄教师支援西部计划，从教育部直属的高水平高校遴选 140 余名一线教学和科研经验丰富、师德高尚、爱岗敬业、业务精良的退休教授、副教授到西部高校支教，这些教师的工作以课程教学、教学指导、课题研究、团队建设指导为主，以短期授课、远程教育、同步课堂、学术讲座（报告）为辅，采取"传帮带"的方式，指导受援高校教师做好教学和科研工作，把先进教学方法和科研理念传授给受援高校教师。长期援派教师，其支援服务时间原则上不少于 1 学年，每学年承担不少于64 课时的教学工作，参与指导 1 项课题研究，组织开展若干学术讲座、教研等活动。短期授课和远程教育支援教师，按照"突出实效、形式多样、时间灵活"的原则，根据受援高校需求，认真做好支教、支研工作。教育部直接划拨资金，用于发放援派教师补助。同时，积极协调受援高校提供岗前培训费、派出地往返交通差旅费、意外保险费、必要的商业医疗保险费、采暖费等保障性经费，援派具体工作由援受双方高校共同负责。

（三）如何通过现代信息技术帮助乡村薄弱学校提高教学质量

现代信息通信技术的快速普及与发展，为贫困地区共享优质教育资源提供了新可能、新渠道。中国政府极其重视利用现代教育技术推动教育发展，实施教育信息化工程，推动教育信息化设施建设、学校信息化设备配备及应用，重视通过信息化手段将经济发达地区优质教育资源与农村特别是贫困地区学校共享，从而提高贫困地区教育质量，为当地减贫提供支撑。

1. 案例：广东省佛山市禅城—凉山远程支教项目助力精准脱贫

广东省佛山市禅城区对口支援贫困的四川省凉山彝族自治州昭觉县、普格县、布拖县，禅城区教育局充分利用互联网技术，开展禅城—凉山远程支教项目，实现了与对口帮扶地域的教育无缝对接。2018 年 8 月，禅城区分别与三个县相互交流教育工作情况，就远程教育硬件建设、远程教育具体应用等问题进行了研讨，同时派遣教育部门相关人员对受援地的远程教育软硬件情况、人力资源情况进行了深入调研。基于调研结果，2018 年 9 月，禅城区教育局拨付专项经费 96 万元，启动建立了禅城—凉山远程支教平台。通过该平台，禅城区教育局教育技术装备室为禅城—凉山 6 所高中、初中、小学支教点学校的师生建立账号，组织两地完成支教点学校主页上线，增强两地的认识与交流。组织两地近百名优秀教师在线建立个人主页以便增强两地教师进行点面结合、互帮互助的交流活动。组织禅城区优秀教师上传 150 余个教学视频与优质课件至平台，实现了优质教学资源的共享。2018 年 10 月以来，平台共推送优质课程 41 门，包括管理和技术、中小学学科、幼儿园课程、特殊教育、职业教育等，课程总时长 2460 分钟。截至 2018 年年底，两地教师共计 4351 人进行线上学习。为配合开展远程培训，帮助受援地教师掌握微课技术、教学课件制作与运用等现代教学技术，支教教师在凉山共开展线下培训 5 场次，培训教师 725 人次，真正实现远程培训质量提升。

禅城—凉山远程支教项目的启动，有效降低了支教的时间成本和人力成本，加强了两地之间和学校之间的教研交流，让相隔千里的两地学生可以共同享有更多优质的教学资源。通过远程支教项目和派遣教师支教，禅城区帮助受援地教师掌握了先进的教育理念和现代教学技术，受援地师生的视野得到有效拓展，从而帮助当地建立起完善的集体教研制度和教师专业学习制度，培养了一支属于凉山的优质教育人才队伍。

2. 案例：宁夏回族自治区建设"互联网＋教育"示范区，推进公平而有质量的教育

近年来，宁夏回族自治区教育信息化管理中心建设了"互联网＋教育"示范区、开展了"人工智能助推教师队伍建设行动"等，以"互联网＋教育"促进优质教育资源共享和教育质量提升，推进公平而有质量的教育，让农村学校、薄弱学校的学生也能通过信息通信技术接受优质教育、实现全面发展。主要有以下做法。

一是完善基础设施建设，为贫困地区学校配齐教育信息化设施设备。宁夏以项目机制为重点，为偏远农村学校配齐计算机、互动教学大屏等教学设备，通过在全区开展学校联网攻坚行动，所有学校（含教学点）全部以不同方式接入网络，形成"云—网—端"的架构，只要学校和师生需要，其可以随时从宁夏教育云平台调用需要的专业资源。二是建设资源服务平台，促进优质资源共享。宁夏建设了从省级层面为各级各类教育、社会公众服务的宁夏教育云平台，通过积极对接国家和发达省份精品课程，汇集本地名师优课，实现了优质教育资源快速普惠应用。面对突如其来的新冠肺炎疫情对教育的冲击，宁夏教育系统依托教育云平台架起空中课堂，打通电视、网络同步播出渠道，实现了空中课堂全覆盖、无死角送达全区城乡每一个学生家中，让所有学生停课不停学、离

校不离教。三是搭建在线互动课堂，形成城乡帮扶机制。宁夏通过教育云平台搭建自治区统一在线互动课堂，推动城市教学名师与乡村教师牵手结对，形成了外省优质学校帮扶区内城市学校、区内优质学校帮扶山区薄弱学校、县城学校帮扶农村薄弱学校、乡（镇）中心小学帮扶教学点的四帮扶工作机制，被帮扶学校按需"点菜"、帮扶学校照单"配菜"，在云平台上开展跨区域、跨学校的互动教学与教研活动，实现名校、名师优质资源共享。

2020年，宁夏3456所各级各类学校全部接入网络，63%的学校网络带宽达到100M以上，山区学校互联互通，网络教学畅通无阻，为城乡教育均衡发展提供了基础和条件。过去，西吉县震湖乡堡玉村的学生为了接受更优质教育，经常选择乡镇学校，自从设施和网络覆盖了教学点后，学生可以通过网络在最近的教学点享受名校名师资源。教育云平台共登记注册全区90%的教师，记录全区80%的学生学习档案，接入了学科网、教学助手等100多个应用，提供1800多万件教学资源、10万多节辅导微课、5000多节名师课堂，全区80%的家长实现家校互联。通过一块屏幕、一台电脑、一部平板实现全区不同区域、不同经济水平的师生都能享受来自全区乃至全国的名校、名师优质教育资源，有效解决了偏远、薄弱学校获取优质教育资源难、课堂教学质量不高的问题。教师在宁夏教育云平台注册使用"人人通"学习空间，开展线上线下混合式研修。28%的中小学校覆盖在线课堂，114万余名学生和9万余名教师在宁夏教育云平台上开通了网络学习空间，100%的中小学校开通了学习空间，基本形成了课堂用、经常用、普遍用的良好局面。

（四）如何提高少数民族地区教育质量并为学生的后续学习打下基础

中国政府着眼于改善教学机构基础设施、增强教师专业能力、提升教育教学质量等少数民族地区教育发展的关键环节与问题，持续实施发达地区与欠发达地区间的教育协同发展专项计划，全方位提升中国少数民族地区的教育质量，有力推动教育减贫工作。少数民族多数都有本民族的语言文字，学习和掌握本民族语言是文化传承的需要。如果少数民族地区儿童仅掌握本民族语言文字，就难以与本民族地区之外的人群进行语言交流，由于很多少数民族语言文字难以准确表达现代科技相关内容，学生在学习现代科技与专业技能时也会面临很大困难。因此，在学习掌握本民族语言文字的同时掌握国家通用语言文字，是少数民族地区学生接受更加公平和更有质量教育，实现可持续发展的重要基础。采取少数民族语言文字与国家通用语言文字教学相结合的方式，结合开展英语教学，正在成为中国提高少数民族地区教育质量、增强少数民族学生可持续学习发展能力的普遍做法。

1. 案例：贵州省榕江县宰荡侗寨国家通用语言文字教育试验项目

20 世纪 50 年代，贵州省榕江县宰荡侗寨能认识较多国家通用文字的人很少，多数人只会讲一些汉语，并不认识国家通用文字。当地适龄儿童在接受学校教育时，学习积极性低、辍学率较高。为摆脱这一困境，贵州大学与世界少数民族语文研究院合作，在该村寨开展国家通用语言文字教育试验项目，旨在帮助当地贫困家庭学生更好地学习科学知识，融入现代社会，为未来就业与发展奠定基础。

项目组成员由中国学者和外国学者组成，中外学者共同策划设计该项目。项目注重借鉴地方经验，在教学中结合少数民族生活、语言和文化实际，组织编写了少数民族题材的辅助性读本教材，采取国家通用语言和本民族语言并用的双语教学模式。在课程教学内容上，教师首先以侗语授课，其次在识字环节和其他课程（数学、音乐、美术、体育等）的安排上尽可能反映当地侗族文化中的地方性知识内容，让学生感受到课堂学习的内容同自己的生活是切近的、有用的，从而有效提升学生的学习兴趣和热情。在教师层面，参与该项目的都是当地人，项目实施过程中，当地教师在双语教学上的经验以及他们提供的意见建议，成为项目组推进相关工作的重要支撑。国家通用语言文字教育试验项目开展后，宰荡侗寨学生辍学现象逐渐减少，因语言问题造成学习困难进而辍学的现象再没有出现。①

2. 案例：成都市构建"三位一体"对口帮扶模式，帮助四川省民族地区教育发展

四川省涉藏重点工作区和凉山彝族自治州是中国脱贫攻坚工作重点关注的地区，尤其是藏区，其地域辽阔、人们居住分散、信息闭塞，导致教育发展基础薄弱、教学手段和方法较为单一、教育整体质量和水平较低。四川省成都市把对口帮扶民族地区教育纳入教育事业发展规划与年度工作计划，举全市之力开展民族地区教育减贫工作。成都市教育系统先后投入资金 5 亿元，实施对口援助项目 80 个，采取了"学校 + 教师 + 学生""散插班 + 民族班 + 计划班""政府 + 学校 + 企业"三位一体的模式，推进成都市和受援地区教师学生人才共育、学校企业资源共享，惠及师生达 10 万人次。

一是结对帮扶，形成教育互动。成都市组织全市 22 个区（市）县 458 所小学（幼儿园）与甘孜、阿坝、凉山三州 20 个县（市）477 所小学（幼儿园）建立"县对县""校对校"的结对帮扶关系。采取双向沟通、双向制定方案的手段，建立共同发展、协同进步的工作机制。为推进教师互派，实施民族地区人才支持计划教师专项计划，高标准落实支教教师待遇，先后选派 2000 余名优秀干部和教师到甘孜、凉山、阿坝三州支教，同时成都接收三地 2000 余名教师跟岗学习，快速推进贫困地区教师专业成长。成都市先后接收贫困地区 1 万余名学生在成都市优质普通高中和中等职业学校就读。

二是普通教育与职业教育并行。成都市组织双流中学、温江中学、

---

① 罗宏炜：《少数民族地区开展双语教育对文化交往的现实意义——以贵州榕江县宰荡侗寨"侗汉双语教育"为例》，《民族教育研究》2015 年第 3 期。

成都三中等优质高级中等学校，设立专项招生计划，每年招收贫困少数民族地区学生，并根据民族地区学生学习的实际情况，开设专门职业教育课程，让民族贫困地区学生在接受优质普通高中教育的同时，能根据兴趣掌握职业技能。学生的学习兴趣明显提升，辍学率下降，升学率、就业率均得到明显提升。

三是远程共享优质教育资源。成都市统筹实施《成都市教育信息化发展规划（2014—2020年）》《成都市"互联网＋教育"工作方案》，建立和完善多方协同发展的远程教学帮扶机制，建成覆盖从幼儿园到高中的全日制远程教育体系，结合成都七中网校等远程教育平台，将成都优质教育资源覆盖到全部贫困地区。

成都市实施的"三位一体"帮扶模式，数年来使逾万名民族地区贫困学生受益，使他们得以走出大山，接受优质高等教育，改变自己的命运。

三　技术赋能帮助贫困家庭直接脱贫

（一）如何让每一个家庭至少有一个人学到技术并找到工作

贫困家庭大多收入来源单一，多数农村贫困家庭仅以农作物种植为生，缺少具有多元创收技能的成员。因此，让贫困家庭的劳动力能够掌握一技之长，获得更多收入，是帮助贫困家庭直接脱贫的一个重要渠道。

1. 案例："职教＋"驱动致富车——海南省经济技术学校扶贫巾帼励志中专班

2009年，一项对海南省贫困家庭子女就读职业教育的意愿进行的调研发现，60%左右的农村贫困家庭没有能力也没有意愿让女儿初中毕业后继续上学。她们中的一部分选择外出打工补贴家用，从事繁重、技术含量低的工作；另一部分则留在农村，选择早婚、早育。

为改变当地贫困女性群体的困境，2009 年，海南省经济技术学校联合海南省妇联，于当年 7 月面向全省贫困家庭子女招生，创办扶贫巾帼励志中专班。"培养一个好女孩，造就一位好母亲，带出一个好家庭"是海南省经济技术学校对扶贫巾帼励志中专班提出的发展愿景。学校制定了扶贫巾帼励志中专班发展计划，准备用 10 年（2009~2018年）时间培养 1 万名学生。学校紧紧抓住海南省建设国际旅游岛、迫切需要大量高素质技能人才的契机，为扶贫巾帼励志中专班开设了酒店服务与管理、农产品加工与检验技术、烹饪与糕点制作、企业财务与超市收银、服装设计与制作、高尔夫服务与管理等 13 个专业。针对来自贫困家庭的学生，学校除免除学费、住宿费外，还提供每月每生350 元的生活费，减轻学生家庭的经济负担。在职业技能培训层面，以该校开设的美发专业为例，该校同海南品牌美发企业建立校企合作，每周都会有企业的专门技术人员来校开展创业就业体验训练，使学生在校期间就可以熟练掌握护理、染发、造型等扎实过硬的实操技术和经营管理经验。经过扶贫巾帼励志中专班的职业技能培训，每年都有30 余名学生从学校进入美发行业，从而成为店长、技术骨干，实现自己的职业和创业梦想。

2009~2016 年，扶贫巾帼励志中专班共招收培养贫困学生 7914 人，已毕业五届学生，总计 5070 人，在校学生 2844 人。不少贫困学生经过三年的扶贫励志教育，树立了脱贫致富的志向，毕业后凭借技术技能实现优质就业。扶贫巾帼励志中专班改变了许多当地女孩的命运，使她们成长为生产经营骨干，在生活中也逐步成长为家庭脱贫致富的顶梁柱。

2. 案例：扶"智"更扶"志"——贵州装备制造职业学院精准扶贫班对口帮扶荔波县

荔波县隶属于贵州省黔南布依族苗族自治州，地处贵州最南端，是全省的深度贫困地区，也是贵州装备制造职业学院帮扶县。2015 年秋季，贵州装备制造职业学院成立了精准扶贫班，该班学生可以选择学校办学能力强、就业质量高的传统优势专业——机械制造技术、电梯安装与维修、汽车维修技术等专业，学校安排最优秀的教学团队授课。学院依托学校驻村干部，广泛走访荔波县当地贫困学生家庭，了解不同贫困学生的困难，结合学校专业课程制订符合每名贫困学生实际的教学计划与帮扶计划。精准扶贫班采用双导师制度，做到既扶"智"又扶"志"，配备生活导师和职业导师，在关心学生生活、学习的同时，注重学生心理健康辅导。该校免除贫困学生学杂费，在政策允许的范围内给予助学金资助，并帮助安排勤工俭学岗位，助力贫困学生改善生活。该校依托优势专业，使贫困学生掌握适合市场需求的职业技能，从而在较短时间内获得稳定的经济收入，家庭生活质量得到改善，实现了"一人就业，一家脱贫"的目标。截至2017年，该校精准扶贫班已招收学生460余人，其中对口服务的荔波县已招收学生56人，截至2020年已有三批毕业生走上就业岗位，精准扶贫班为学生家庭走出贫困提供了有力支撑。

3. 案例：职业教育东西协作行动计划促进就业脱贫

2016年，教育部、国务院扶贫办联合印发《职业教育东西协作行动计划（2016—2020年）》，这一行动计划是中国政府在东西部扶贫协作框架下，以职业教育为重点，以就业脱贫为导向，为服务西部贫困地区群众而实施的职业教育专项计划。其主要包括三大行动：一是实施东西职业院校协作全覆盖行动，实现东部地区职业教育集团、高职院校、中职学校对西部地区的结对帮扶全覆盖。二是实施东西中等职业学校招生协作兜底行动，东部地区大幅增加对西部地区贫困家庭子女的招生数量，让他们接受优质中等职业教育，毕业后根据学生意愿，优先推荐他们在东部地区就业，实现就业脱贫。三是支持职业院校全面参与东西劳务协作，让每个有劳动能力且有参加职业培训意愿的贫困人口，都能接受满足就业创业需求的公益性职业培训。

2017年7月和9月，中国分省份签署职业教育东西协作落实协议。以支持职业院校全面参与东西劳务协作为例，各省（区、市）利用财政扶贫基金、东西扶贫协作财政援助资金等经费，开展公益性职业培训项目，支持职业院校开展劳动预备制培训、就业技能培训、岗位技能提升培训、创业培训等。

2017年4月，国务院扶贫办在处于中国东部地区且产业发达的福建省泉州市的泉州海洋职业学院设立全国扶贫就业创业培训基地，重点面向宁夏、甘肃、四川、安徽和河南等五省（区）开展贫困家庭新成长劳动力职业技能培训和稳岗就业工作。该校在国务院扶贫办指导下先后成立闽宁劳务协作输转基地、闽黔劳务输转培训基地、闽黔东西部人才数据中心等机构，招收宁夏、贵州等省（区）的贫困学生，免除他们的学杂费，为他们提供特色岗位的高质量技能培训、创业致富带头人培训等一系列适应劳动力市场需求的培训项目。泉州海洋职业学院还联合有关物流和电商企业，发挥自身地域优势，牵头搭建中经海农扶贫电商平台，通过冷链物流连接分布在中国东、西部地区各特色生鲜产区的移动冷库，形成具有特色的冷链集市。同时成立校企联合体的海农扶贫电商平台，购买移动冷库并配备部分流动资金，邀请贫困村脱贫致富带头人等以合伙人的身份参与经营"冷链集市"，在共同发展的基础上，带动所在村寨发展连片种植、养殖业，实现居家创业、脱贫致富。

截至2020年，泉州海洋职业学院下属各个职业、劳动培训基地共培训致富带头人310人，培训各类船员2200余人，培训企业新员工2000余人，为4200多个贫困家庭新增劳动力解决了高质量就业问题，为300多个贫困村的农民送去了脱贫致富新技能。同时，该校积极开展船员、远洋渔民、创业致富带头人、企业新员工等培训项目，惠及2万余人次，减免培训费用216.26万元。接受培训的学员全部在泉州及周边企业就业，开创了贫困地区、贫困家庭、发达地区企业和学校"多方共赢"的扶贫新模式。

（二）如何通过成人教育与培训帮助农村脱贫

在农村贫困地区，受历史、文化、地理等因素的影响，有相当一部分成年人未能在学龄期接受系统的学校教育，缺少就业的专业知识和生产技能，其成为农村贫困地区家庭经济困难的主要原因。中国政府认为成人教育与培训，尤其是涉农成人教育具有贴近农村群众生活实际、有利于贫困农村社区群众发展生产与务工择业的特点，将做好面向农村的成人教育与培训作为帮助贫困地区群众补上技能短板、实现精准扶贫的有效手段。2013 年 1 月，中国教育部印发《关于开展国家级农村职业教育和成人教育示范县创建工作的通知》，启动了农村职业教育和成人教育示范县创建活动，旨在通过示范县创建活动，树立一批农村职业教育和成人教育典型，让贫困农村社区群众学习身边的榜样、感悟学会技能才能长久脱贫的道理，激励更多人参与成人教育与培训，通过学习改变人生。截至 2019 年年底，国家级农村职业教育和成人教育示范县（市、区）共创建 261 个，成为农村职业教育和成人教育服务"三农"工作、助力脱贫攻坚和乡村振兴的重要抓手。2016 年教育部、中华全国总工会决定联合实施农民工学历与能力提升行动计划——"求学圆梦行动"，该行动计划将学历与非学历教育并重，打造产教融合、校企合作、工学结合的农民工继续教育新模式。截至 2020 年，在有学历提升需求且符合入学条件的农民工中，共有 150 万人接受资助并进行学历继续教育，使每一名农民工都能得到相应的技术技能培训、通过学习免费开放课程提升自身素质与从业能力，从而帮助农民工实现体面劳动和幸福生活，同时有效服务经济社会发展和产业结构转型升级。据不完全统计，截至 2020 年年底，全国共有 710 所高校、1796 家教育培训机构参与该行动计划，共 130 多万人次接受学历继续教育，950 多万人次接受非学历培训，有效促进了农民工学历的提升、技能的增长和就业质量的改善，在扶贫方面发挥了重要作用。

1. 案例：河南省南阳市新型农民专项技能培训促进精准扶贫

镇平县是河南省南阳市下辖县，位于河南省西南部，总面积1560平方公里，辖3个街道、19个乡镇，截至2019年，总人口104万人。当地贫困群众长期面临技能培训缺失、新型农业技术掌握不足、就业水平与收入水平低下等困境。2014年，中国成人教育协会在全国开展第二批"农村社区学习中心（CLC）能力建设项目"，建立16个实验点，镇平县杨营镇成人学校被选为项目实验点，同时被河南省成人教研室命名为"河南省农村成人教育教学改革实验学校"。

该成人学校的学员主要来自当地贫困户，学校采用集中讲授与分散自主学习相结合的方式进行教育培训。为了紧密结合杨营镇实际情况，培训内容将教师授课与视频讲座相结合，采用互动课堂模式，由学员提出问题，由专业教师进行专题解答。该校还聘请专家开展家庭教育讲座，进行家庭教育重要性、家庭教育方法等内容的培训。以2018年该校暑期课程为例，学校和县工艺职专联合举行了为期25天的精准扶贫玉雕专题培训，共计培训54人次。2018年年底，学校联合镇政府举办精准扶贫新型农民专班技术培训，共计培训60人次。当地一批贫困群众掌握了实用性强、易上手的技能，并对获取谋生手段、实现脱贫致富充满信心。

2. 案例：浙江省丽水市遂昌县旅游资源开发技能培训助力村民脱贫致富

一些欠发达地区的贫困村落风景优美、民风淳朴，有优质的有机农副产品资源，具有较高的旅游资源开发价值。然而，当地群众缺乏旅游资源开发技能，无法将身边优质自然资源转化为经济收入从而实现脱贫致富。浙江省丽水市遂昌县大柘镇大田村就是这样一个地方。该村风景优美，民风淳朴，是远近闻名的茶叶生产基地。先前，村里家家户户都种茶叶，但那时村民所获收入不过维持温饱而已。村里农民的住宅基本为泥瓦房，房前屋后堆积了各类杂物，村容村貌较差。该村地理位置优越，是通往遂昌西部 10 个乡镇的枢纽，也是通往国家 4A 级景区千佛山、南尖岩、九龙山国家级自然保护区的必经之地，但这一优势并未得到充分利用，相关产业一直未能得到发展。2010 年大柘镇政府制定了以茶产业为基础、大力发展乡村休闲旅游业、走绿色和谐之路的发展策略。经过多年努力，当地形成了大田村、车前村等农旅融合发展的专业村和新农村建设示范村，相继获得了省级农家乐特色村、省级旅游特色村等称号，当地农民的生活变得富足。遂昌县大柘镇的大柘中心成技校在此过程中发挥了重要作用。

该校在当地贫困村落围绕农家乐的开发组织开展了面向当地贫困村民的农业休闲旅游技能培训，主要是结合当地自然资源和农副产品资源优势，开展茶文化、餐饮住宿服务等技能培训。同时，为当地村民送信息、送项目。在大柘中心成技校的帮助下，大田村依托优越的地理位置和良好的生态资源优势，逐步走上茶文化和农家乐旅游发展之路，建成集餐饮、住宿、停车、接待于一体的茶香苑农家乐接待中心，在全省乃至全国都小有名气。现如今，遂昌县大柘镇大田村的经济收入以茶叶种植与加工、乡村休闲旅游为主，农民的生活条件越来越好。2018 年，全村农家乐共有 50 多家，村民人均收入 22135 元，居全县村级人均收入之首。这个只有 600 多户的小山村，共接待游客 11.8 万人次，实现收入 1210 多万元，农民彻底摆脱了贫困，过上了富裕的生活。

（三）如何把当地的传统技能与教育脱贫相结合并发挥脱贫致富的作用

很多农村社区有自己独特的文化资源甚至非物质文化遗产，挖掘传统文化资源，特别是当地非物质文化遗产中的传统技能，例如，流传于不同地区的刺绣、剪纸、皮影、花灯制作、刻葫芦等。开发传统技能中蕴含的商业价值和文化价值，不仅能让农村社区传统技能代代传承，还能给农村贫困家庭带来一定收益。

1. 案例：西安石油大学结对帮扶永寿县，发掘非物质文化遗产，打造永寿县旅游特色文化

陕西省永寿县人杰地灵，历史文化源远流长，其中监军战鼓、民间剪纸、土梁油制作等均被列入省级非物质文化遗产保护名录。但因为缺乏系统规划与开发利用，当地的非物质文化遗产资源在较长时间内并没有成为带动当地贫困人口增收、助力贫困群众脱贫的优质资源。

西安石油大学自结对帮扶永寿县以来，经过充分调研论证，将学校科研、人才优势与永寿县独特的文化资源结合，设立了"发掘非物质文化遗产，打造永寿县旅游特色文化品牌"课题，旨在帮助永寿县推出具有核心竞争力的文化产品，打造具有鲜明特色的文化品牌，助推当地特色产业与经济发展。

课题分为非物质文化产业品牌全面提升方案、非物质文化市场化开发包装设计及展览以及非物质文化遗产项目申报援助计划三部分，通过非遗发掘、包装设计、产品推广等开发非遗、民间工艺项目，结合市场需求，推出适销对路的产品，打造优势手工艺项目链条，同时发展永寿县文化产品电子商务，形成开发设计、生产、推广、销售链条。在开发设计及展示方面，西安石油大学结合人文学院设计系包装设计课程，利用课程实践环节安排针对性课题，对非物质文化遗产资源进行市场化开发策划与包装设计，同时联合永寿县委、县政府举办了2场永寿县非物质文化市场化开发包装设计展览。参与展览的设计作品，展示了永寿县非物质文化遗产的整体面貌，为永寿县非物质文化遗产挖掘、开展品牌提升项目打下了坚实基础。在非遗项目申报援助方面，西安石油大学设立永寿县非物质文化遗产项目申报援助计划，组织相关人员深入永寿县，对非遗现状进行调研，并与当地相关人员建立紧密联系，为非遗项目申报援助的开展做了充分准备，帮助非遗调研和申报部门梳理现有11个县级非遗项目，撰写并修改完成11个非遗项目申报书。同时，依托调研论证与后期设计打造的非物质文化遗产保护项目，衍生许多具有当地特色

的文创品牌，促进了当地文化旅游资源开发，使贫困群众获得了一条脱贫致富的新道路。①

2. **案例：广西壮族自治区乐业县磨里村依托非遗手艺技能培训脱贫**

磨里村位于广西壮族自治区乐业县城东部、新化镇东北部，全村耕地稀少贫瘠，人均耕地面积 0.65 亩。农民收入主要依靠种养殖和劳务输出。近年来，乐业县不断挖掘和打造该村的卜隆文化，发展文化产业和旅游产业，推动文化与经济共同繁荣，众多贫困群众发家致富，罗美烈就是其中一员。

罗美烈于 1955 年出生，是个土生土长的卜隆后代，12 岁就跟随母亲学习壮族土布纺织技艺。她勤奋好学、刻苦钻研，织出来的布非常精美，颜色也搭配得当。虽然纺织文化在磨里村已有 400 多年的历史，但是村里年轻一辈都嫌纺织技艺复杂、烦琐，生产产品效率低、成本高。因此，年轻人不愿学习壮族纺织技艺，乐业壮族土布纺织面临即将失传的窘境。

当地政府高度重视通过非遗特色产业助推贫困群众脱贫工作。为保护和传承流传 400 多年乐业壮族纺织技艺，2008 年起，乐业县每年举办一届旅游手工艺品比赛，并评出创意奖和巧手奖，对保护传统乐业壮族纺织技艺起到良好促进作用。同时，该县每年都选派壮族纺织技艺县级代表性传承人到市里和自治区民族大学进修，使她们的技艺得到更大的提高。在地方政府的带动下，罗美烈也逐渐将日常工作的重点转向纺织生产，不仅继续努力学习各种壮族纺织技术，还带领其他群众一起学习，定期或不定期地在家中或壮族纺织技艺传习基地举办壮族纺织技艺培训班，向本村的中青年妇女等免费传授壮族纺织技艺，把祖辈流传下来的这一壮族文化遗产传承下去。因此，她成了当地有名气的壮族纺织能手，2017 年 11 月她荣获了自治区级非物质文化

---

① 　中国人民大学课题组编《党的十八大以来教育脱贫攻坚总结（典型案例汇编）》，2020。

遗产"乐业壮族纺织技艺"项目代表性传承人称号，并通过纺织壮族土布、销售土布制作服装过上了富裕的生活。在罗美烈的带领下，当地做传统纺织业的妇女越来越多，以壮族纺织技艺制作的产品有壮族服装和壮族被心、背带、布鞋、鞋垫、门帘、窗帘、蚊帐帘、挎袋、枕套等，深受农村壮族群众的喜爱，在市场上很畅销。磨里村全村464户2270人，从事壮族纺织制作的有427户2045人，靠纺织每人每天平均可收入50元，纺织户每年靠纺织可以带来10000多元的收入。2014年全村建档立卡贫困户为165户742人，从2014年到2019年就有155户706人成功实现脱贫。[①]

四　高等学校与职业学校帮助贫困地区发展产业及经济

（一）如何培养农村地区致富带头人

一些农村地区群众生活贫困，不是因为当地缺少资源、缺少发展机会，而是缺少发现优势资源并将其转化为优势产业的致富带头人，而通过各类涉农、涉产业发展的技术技能培训，培养农村贫困地区致富带头人就是帮助一些贫困农村社区发展的关键。

1. 案例："一村一名大学生计划"项目实现农民大学生本地化培养

2004年，国家开放大学实施了"一村一名大学生计划"（简称"一村一"）项目，致力于通过远程教育为农村培育一批优秀的村干部、农村致富带头人及农村专业技术人员。2017年以来，该项目将人工智能技术融入教育教学，将高等教育输送到农村，面向基层干部或种养殖户提供专属学习方案，精准推送优质教育资源。截至2021年，该项目为贫困地区累计培养60多万名乡村干部、乡村致富带头人，实现"输血式"扶贫，

①　韦美兰、冉涛：《乐业县"非遗＋扶贫"带头人罗美烈：妇女撑起半边天 非遗手艺引领致富路》，广西县域经济网，2020，www.gxcounty.com。

2021 年该项目获评联合国教科文组织教育信息化大奖。

国家开放大学湖南分部——湖南开放大学实行"订单式"培养，聘请了一批省内外名师线上授课，当地"土专家"线下实训，开设了农村行政管理、农业经济管理、畜牧兽医等农村实用专业，增开了农村政策法规、村级财务管理、信息技术运用等必修课。其中，养猪技术这门课程就是由中国工程院院士、中国科学院亚热带农业生态研究所畜禽健康养殖中心主任印遇龙院士讲授。在教学方法上，学校充分利用现代化技术手段，以网络空间为载体开展线上教学。学校给每位学生建立个人学习空间，学生借助电脑、智能手机或 iPad 等终端，登录"农民大学生学习网"，进入个人学习空间自主学习、考试，同时还可进入公共学习平台参与集体学习活动。学校给每位教师建立教师空间，教师可充分利用空间平台建设特色化教学资源，适时调整教学方式，并通过教师空间实行个性化指导。学校根据课程性质特点并针对学生需要，围绕线上教学开展线下辅助教学，各市州分校及县级教学点组织开展入学教育、面授辅导和实践教学等线下教学活动。各教学点还将课堂直接设在田间地头，聘请技术专家、行家能手进行手把手实践指导，让学生掌握一项以上的实用技能。

湖南省怀化市芷江侗族自治县古冲村的妇女龙四清就是湖南开放大学的毕业生。过去的古冲村是远近闻名的贫困村，以致没有女青年愿意嫁到该村。龙四清不仅在湖南开放大学拿到了成人高等教育专科文凭，而且利用学到的柑橘种植知识和电商营销知识脱了贫，在她的带动下，2018 年村里 200 多户村民立足本村优势产业，种植了 6000 余亩柑橘，年总产值近 8000 万元；圈地 300 多亩养殖绿壳蛋土鸡；建设了一个年产万头生猪的标准化养猪场。同时在她带动下，多名村民参加此成人教育项目，成为大学生和致富能手。她本人也成为古冲村党总支书记，当选中国共产党十七大、十八大代表，获得"全国劳动模范"荣誉称号。据不完全统计，截至 2014 年，湖南开放大学培养的农民大学生中，85% 已担任村干部，60%以上成为当地致富带头人，7%考入公务员队伍。他们有的成长为村镇干部，成为带领村民致富的领路人；有的创办产业卓有成就，成为科技致富的带头人和新农村建设的骨干力量。[①]

2. 案例：大学教授李保国言传身教扶贫助农

岗底村是河北省内丘县侯家庄乡有名的贫困村，曾经山秃、人穷、观念旧。岗底村有160户690人，早年间全部家当是8000亩荒山、250多亩山间农田，人均年收入较低。2017年的岗底村，山绿、水清、人富、观念新，植被覆盖率达82%；总资产达10553万元，年总产值6800万元；人均年收入大幅提高。这一切都离不开中国知名经济林专家、山区治理专家、河北农业大学教授李保国呕心沥血的奉献。

1996年，一场山洪来袭，河北省内丘县岗底村仅有的250多亩耕地被冲毁。村里仅存的几十亩果园成为当时全村的希望，然而当时结出的苹果是"一咬一层皮"的"小黑蛋子"，无法卖上好价钱。面对这样的情景，李保国教授带着同在河北农业大学任教的妻子郭素萍搬到了岗底村。为了摸清当地山区的"脾气秉性"，解决果树种植难题，李保国起早贪黑，跑遍了山上的沟沟壑壑，经过无数个日夜的数据分析，悉心钻研，李保国拿出了帮助岗底村村民致富的计划，其中包括人均2亩苹果，平均收入2万元的目标。

目标明确了，接下来就需要将一切变为现实。李保国在岗底村亲自做示范，讲解果树栽培和管理技术。给果树刻芽正确的做法是在芽前刻伤，而村民却刻在了芽后，效果适得其反。李保国手把手教授正确方式，可村民常常是前边听、后头忘。为了让果农尽快掌握技术，李保国请村干部先制定一套果树管理工序，自己利用业余时间，通过实地考证和认真分析，对工序再进行订正、细化、完善。最终，科学规范又通俗易懂的128道苹果标准化生产管理工序出炉了。村民人手一册，一年

---

① 中国人民大学课题组编《党的十八大以来教育脱贫攻坚总结（典型案例汇编）》，2020。

365 天，什么时候管什么、不管什么、管到什么程度，都清清楚楚。岗底村果农靠这一"金刚钻"，不仅生产出绿色、有机苹果，还避免了苹果"大小年"。按工序生产的富岗苹果，果型、着色、个头像一个模子刻出来的。

截至 2018 年，经李保国精心改良培育出的"富岗苹果"已成为中国驰名商标，连锁基地遍及太行山区 369 个村，种植面积 5.8 万亩，产量超过 1 亿公斤，因此也带出了一大批农村脱贫致富带头人，7 万多名村民因此脱贫致富。同时，李保国示范推广了 36 项标准化林业技术，累计应用面积 1826 万亩，增加农业产值 35 亿元，举办不同层次的培训班 800 余次，培训人员 9 万余人次，许多果农成了真专家。太行山上，世世代代在荒山上"刨食"的农民真正甩掉了"穷帽子"。①

（二）如何通过高等学校科研优势带动产业发展

要从根本上解决贫困问题，必然要让贫困地区产业得到大发展，而高等学校有科研优势，可以在支持地方产业发展中发挥重要作用。为帮助最贫困地区的产业发展，2012 年以来，中国政府安排直属中央政府的 44 所综合类和以理工科为主的高校承担了 44 个国家扶贫开发工作重点县的定点扶贫任务。2019 年，又增加 20 所高校采取"1+1"模式，即由 1 所已承担定点扶贫任务的直属高校与 1 所尚未承担扶贫任务的直属高校共同定点扶贫一个贫困县。各省属高校也在各省政府统筹领导下，积极参与扶贫工作。

1. 案例：浙江大学挂职干部助力云南省景东县脱贫致富

云南省普洱市景东彝族自治县位于滇西南中部、普洱市最北端，全县贫困人口较多，13 个乡镇中有 7 个是贫困乡镇，其中有 4 个是建档立卡贫困乡镇。当地贫困人口多为少数民族群众，集中分布在哀牢山、无

---

① 《时代先锋："凡人"李保国》，《人民日报》2016 年 6 月 1 日。

量山周边的山区、半山区、边远高寒山区、干旱缺水地区和地质灾害隐患区，居住环境恶劣，处于整体贫困状态。在景东，90%以上建档立卡贫困户的主要生计就是养殖乌骨鸡。景东无量山乌骨鸡是"云南六大名鸡"之一，因生长周期长、成本低、肉质佳、口感好、生态健康而出名，早在2010年就被列入中国《国家畜禽遗传资源品种名录》。然而，乌骨鸡产蛋率低、苗鸡成活率低，村民缺乏系统选育，哪怕守着"金凤凰"，村民也没能富起来。

自2013年起，浙江大学定点扶贫景东县，浙江大学农业技术推广中心副教授尹兆正作为畜禽养殖专家来到景东的任务就是带动景东群众精准脱贫奔小康。一到景东，尹兆正就直接进了养鸡场，挨家挨户察看鸡舍和鸡种。说是鸡舍，其实就是贫困户在门前屋后自搭的原始鸡窝，又窄又矮，有的干脆建在柴火堆下、羊圈里。每到一处，尹兆正都要俯下身子、趴在地上才能观察每一只鸡的体质和生长情况。生长环境不佳，鸡苗也好不到哪去。尹兆正进到贫困户家里，爬上土炕伸手一抓，土法炕道式保温培育的苗鸡不是病恹恹的就是湿漉漉的，体质差，成活率自然低。浙江一些经选育后的乌骨鸡品种一只母鸡年产蛋可达100只以上，而景东乌骨鸡一只种鸡每年产蛋只有60只左右，有的甚至只能生产40来只，这无形中大大增加了景东乌骨鸡苗鸡的生产成本，当务之急便是要开展种质提纯。经过调研考察，尹兆正和他的团队决定，景东乌骨鸡产业化，必须搞良种选育，科学养殖，让村民摒弃原有的养殖传统，不仅要改变思维，还要增加设施等方面的投入。尹兆正先从几家企业入手，指导当地建设种鸡场，结合市场需要开展种鸡不同羽色整理分群工作，进行性能测定和持续选育。同时，他还针对企业和养殖大户进行了从种鸡选育、人工授精、机器孵化、育雏脱温到商品鸡养殖、销售等全过程技术指导和服务。

近年来，尹兆正每年至少在养鸡场、农贸市场里开设2次养鸡标准化培训课；他还动员浙江大学校友捐赠资金建起景东乌骨鸡遗传资源保护场；与景东县农科局方面共同编写了《景东无量山乌骨鸡养殖综合技术规范》，村民只要照着攻略，就能规范饲养乌骨鸡。尹兆正还在景东收了徒弟，哪怕自己不在景东，农户有了具体技术问题，也可以由徒弟教起来、帮到位，进而带动一批人掌握技术。在他的指导下，景东建起了一个个大型种鸡场，机械、立体的笼养模式逐渐形成，不同羽色和性能的高产种群建立了起来，种鸡繁殖性能和鸡只饲养成活率更是显著提升。现在，景东乌骨鸡现代规模种鸡场生产的优质种苗和商品鸡在市场上成了抢手货。2018 年景东乌骨鸡出栏 438.8 万只，比浙江大学定点扶贫前的 2012 年末提高了 200% 以上，产值达 3.65 亿元，帮助带动建档立卡贫困户 1.9 万户脱贫，带动 6.5 万人脱贫，乌骨鸡产业扶贫取得了显著成效，乌骨鸡成了名副其实的"金凤凰"。①

2. 案例：中国药科大学精准扶贫，发挥药学优势全力打造"巴山药乡"品牌

陕西省安康市镇坪县地处陕西最南端，位于陕渝鄂三省（市）交界处，区位独特，属《全国主体功能区规划》中的秦巴生物多样性生态功能区，森林覆盖率达 86.4%。中药材资源十分丰富，适宜种植的中药材有 420 余种，适宜种植中药材的土地有 40 万余亩。但是，受传统思维影响且缺乏有效的科技、人才等支撑，镇坪县长期以来在中药材资源开发利用上始终未取得实质性突破。

按照中央政府统一部署，中国药科大学定点帮扶陕西省镇坪县。2012 年以来，中国药科大学积极发挥人才、学科等智库优势，综合运用实地察看和数据分析等多种手段，帮助镇坪准确找出致贫原因，在提升中药材人力资源开发水平、助推镇坪中药材产业发展升级、支持镇坪社会事业发展以及提供多样化决策咨询服务等方面开展了一系列工作。在经费保障机制方面，学校每年从中央高校基本科研业务费中划拨 50 万元，

---

① 陈欣：《"一头扎进鸡窝里"，一位浙大教授的"致富经"》，央视网，2019，news.cctv.com。

立项资助镇坪相关课题研究，支持当地中药材产业科学发展。学校积极与当地政府沟通协调，支持镇坪开发设计药材发展项目，帮助建立镇坪药材产业发展的科研支撑平台、镇坪地道中药材品牌体系。推动中药食品、保健品、化妆品以及其他有机化工、肥料、饲料等相关产业发展，打造一套循环产业链。同时，开发休闲、保健、药膳等生态旅游商品，推动药材产业与生态旅游产业有机融合，积极帮扶镇坪打造美丽县区和生态县区。积极推介镇坪中药材的特色优势和需求信息等，协助联系引进知名医药企业来镇坪投资并建立生产基地，建立地道中药材种植园和标本馆，先后引进中科集团、广药集团、金陵制药、正大天晴等多家知名制药企业到镇坪考察，并组织镇坪中药产业发展相关人员赴江苏、重庆、成都等地的知名医药企业进行考察、交流等。2016年，在中国药科大学的帮助下，已停产8年的镇坪制药厂恢复生产，技改扩建年产5000吨中药饮片加工生产线，改造生产厂房和临时仓储场所4000平方米。在中国药科大学和镇坪县的共同努力下，该县已建成中药材种养基地14个，发展产业大户200余户、带动药农4000余户，中药材留存面积达18.1万亩，药材产业增加值占农林牧渔业增加值的比重达20%以上，药材产业带动贫困户户均增收1000元以上。2015年镇坪县实现生产总值13.6亿元，城镇居民人均可支配收入26941元，农村居民人均纯收入8088元，主要指标增速居安康市前列。[①]

（三）职业学校专业技能带动贫困地区产业发展

贫困产生的原因除外在环境的恶劣、资金的缺乏外，技能的缺乏往往也是关键。因此中国政府把在贫困地区进行广泛职业培训、广泛培养专业技能、支持当地产业发展作为减贫的重要手段。2019年，教育部等14部门启动《职业院校全面开展职业培训 促进就业创业行动计划》，鼓

---

① 中国人民大学课题组编《党的十八大以来教育脱贫攻坚总结（典型案例汇编）》，2020。

励职业院校积极面向农民工、建档立卡贫困劳动力、残疾人等重点人群开展就业创业培训。鼓励涉农职业院校深入开展职业技能扶贫，培养高素质农民和农村实用人才，服务脱贫攻坚和乡村振兴，实践表明其取得了良好成效。

1. 案例：甘肃省静宁县职教中心帮助贫困群众脱贫

地处六盘山西部的静宁县曾是甘肃省 23 个深度贫困县之一，也是国家扶贫开发工作重点县。劳务输出是当地群众脱贫增收的重要途径。随着外出务工的人越来越多，外出务工农民因缺乏技能而就业不稳定、收入难保障等问题日益增多。同时，当地苹果种植、建筑等富民产业在转型升级过程中也面临"本地人才干不了，外来人才不愿来"的尴尬局面。提高贫困群众就业创业能力问题成为脱贫路上绕不过的一道坎。

静宁县政府认为抓职教就是抓发展、抓职教就是抓经济、抓职教就是抓扶贫。截至 2017 年，静宁县统筹全县职业教育资源，投资 2.6 亿元为县职教中心建设新校区，建成理实一体化实训室 76 个，建成建筑专业实景实训室、静宁苹果产学研联盟基地和校外实训基地 16 个，并开设了数控技术应用、建筑工程施工、汽车运用与维修等 16 个专业。静宁县职教中心通过项目支持等多渠道筹措资金，58 个实训室和 10 个校内实训基地（实训中心）全天候面向学生开放。

宋京朋家住甘肃静宁界石铺，他是静宁县职教中心建筑专业就读的一名贫困学生，他还在全国职业院校学生创业创新技能大赛上获得三等奖，这意味着他毕业后可以找到一份收入不错的工作。如果没有进入职业院校，宋京朋很可能和村里的其他年轻人一样，在初中毕业后就走上外出打工的道路，很大可能遇到收入低、工作不稳定的困难，这让他深刻地感受到了知识改变命运的力量。就读于静宁县职教中心畜牧专业的张连成的家中养牛，但之前的养殖由于缺乏技术总卖不上价钱，他把课堂上学到的技术带回家里用于养牛，一头牛比上年多卖了 5000 元。王伏帅进入静宁县职教中心就读园艺专业后，家里在她的指导下盖起温室大棚，发展油桃、杏等多种果树种植，并通过低温诱导技术提前一个月上市，家里实现了靠技术吃饭。

为促进毕业生尤其是贫困家庭学生就业，静宁县职教中心与甘肃省内外30余家企业合作，采取"定人、定专业、定企业、定工种、定岗位、定工资"的原则，建立了贫困家庭学生就业援助机制，拓宽学生就业渠道，实现入学能入职、顶岗能上岗、毕业能就业。2015~2017年，静宁县职教中心毕业生一次性就业率达到99%，其中贫困家庭学生就业率达到100%。[①]

2. 案例：怀化职业技术学院将培训课堂办到田间地头帮助武陵山区脱贫

武陵山片区是中国政府确定的14个集中连片特困地区之一。近年来怀化职业技术学院发挥自身优势，开展职业教育与培训扶贫取得显著成效。

首先，怀化职业技术学院选派最好的老师参加扶贫工作。为了圆满完成每一次培训任务，该校每年从省级特色一流专业群中选拔40余名中级以上职称、专业技术水平高、教学经验丰富、教学评估质量好的教师参与扶贫培训，同时还从高等院校、市县农业局、畜牧局选聘一批实践经验丰富的技术人员组成校外专家队伍，共同承担培训任务。其中，学院教授、高级兽医师胡辉是动物科技系湖南省黄炎培杰出教师奖获得者、湖南省"三区"科技特派员、万名工程专家服务团成员，是一名深受广大农民学员喜爱的老师。她认为，学员来自农村，大多数文化水平不高，只有用通俗易懂的语言来传授知识，才能真正解决他们在生产中遇到的问题。每次培训，她都鼓励学员走进田间，参与实训。而为了真正让广大学员学以致用，每次培训结束后，胡辉都会将自己的联系方式留给学员，与学员保持紧密联系，热情地为他们解决问题。2018年，辰

---

① 宋喜群、蔺紫鸥：《甘肃教育改革助力脱贫攻坚》，《光明日报》2018年1月17日。

溪一名学养鸡的学员给胡辉打来电话，咨询解决养鸡过程中遇到的问题，胡辉通过微信诊断发现是温和型禽流感。随后，在胡辉的指导下，该学员采取了相应的措施，进行了紧急接种，有效控制了禽流感继续扩展。

与此同时，学院还通过科技下乡助力脱贫攻坚。借助农业科技人才优势，每年派出 20 余名优秀农业科技教师，组成扶农助农专业队伍，奔赴各个乡镇、村组，点对点进行种养技术指导及技能培训，扩大脱贫致富辐射面。杨世谦是省扶贫办怀化职业技术学院第 20 期农村科技骨干培训班学员。2009 年，他来到怀化职业技术学院参加培训，学会了黄牛的养殖技术和牧草种植技术。2016 年，他成立新晃辉煌牧业公司，公司现有 100 头以上肉牛的规模养殖场 12 个，为怀化市农业产业化龙头企业。2017 年，公司的 22 个合作社分布在新晃七镇一乡，调动了半个新晃县农民创业致富的热情，直接受益农户达 1250 户 5000 余人，年人均收入 2000 元以上。另外，他还发动下属合作社社员一对一扶贫，共帮扶贫困户 600 户 2130 余人。

麻阳谭家寨乡宋家湾村致富能手、村支部书记姚茂盛也是怀化职业技术学院的培训学员，是带动一方致富的能手。2009 年、2017 年，姚茂盛先后两次来到怀化职业技术学院安江校区求学，参加淡水养殖和家禽养殖培训班学习。随后，姚茂盛带领村民一起创办了宋家湾村"全民创业创新园"，搞农业综合开发利用，带领当地村民一起致富。

截至 2018 年，怀化职业技术学院用科技"武装"贫困地区群众的头脑，共培养具有大专学历的村干部 500 余名；组织省市农村科技骨干培训、基层农技人员培训、农村产业致富带头人培训等各类培训 54 期，共培训学员 1.7 万余人次。参训的学员把实用技术带回家乡，成为带领村民脱贫致富的"领头雁"。[1]

---

① 史琴：《播撒希望的种子——怀化职业技术学院办好扶贫培训助力脱贫攻坚纪实》，怀化新闻网，2019，www.0745news.cn。

五 多渠道共同推动教育脱贫

（一）动员社会力量为教育脱贫添砖加瓦

中国的脱贫攻坚不仅充分发挥了各级政府的强大动员力量，也汇聚了各类资源、动员各方面社会力量，鼓励支持各类企业、公益组织等投入资金和资源参与脱贫攻坚，从而形成了全社会广泛参与的减贫工作格局，在中国实现减贫目标的过程中发挥了重要作用。

1. 案例：友成企业家扶贫基金会，"青椒计划"支持每一个乡村青年教师成长、成功、成就

2017 年，友成企业家扶贫基金会、北京师范大学、沪江"沪 + 计划"联合 30 余家公益组织、学术机构、爱心企业发起"青椒计划"，目标是支持乡村教师培训与乡村教师教学能力提升。"青椒计划"从乡村青年教师培训入手，研发适合乡村青年教师的课程，采用线上直播、社群学习的方式定期培训。一是提高乡村青年教师的教学水平，激发他们自主学习与发展的力量，解决"教不好"的问题；二是提升他们的职业幸福感和认同感，解决"留不住"的问题。

该计划利用慕课，打破传统教师培训固定的空间、时间限制，在开展培训时让近 2 万名乡村教师在线学习，聆听国内顶尖教育专家、一线优秀教师的知识传授与经验分享。在课程体系设计方面，全国师范教育最高学府北京师范大学进行教育学专业课程研发，让每节课都力争解决乡村青年教师实践场景中面临的问题。"青椒计划"还开发了幼儿、小学、中学、综合四大模块共 18 个教育专题的选修科目，帮助乡村青年教师更精准地对接学科教学需求、更系统地理解全新的教学模式。在发挥社群力量方面，"青椒计划"鼓励乡村教师分享互动，通过网络工具架构学习共同体，形成相互信任和鼓励的社群，并在项目组内设立专

人管理，引导群成员就课程相关问题进行交流、研讨。在激励制度层面，"青椒计划"不仅有针对能力素质的培训，还设置了对青年教师的激励制度，每一年的培训结业，项目组都会评选出100名表现突出的优秀青年教师，带领他们到中国最顶尖的师范院校进行为期一周的暑期研训，提供与教育大咖、培训讲师、全国"青椒"同伴面对面学习交流的机会。

截至2019年，"青椒计划"已研发教师培训专业课程50讲，各分科课程144讲，专题研修课程60讲，为参与项目的乡村青年教师构建起了一套专业、系统的能力提升课程体系。"青椒计划"组建了近200个区域联络微信群，依托这些交流群，参与该计划的学员建立了近百个简书专题，总投稿字数超过千万，学员得以将课程学习内容结合自身教学实际，形成有深度、有思考的文章。在促进教师学习热情方面，2018年9月，由友成企业家扶贫基金会联合企业，通过众筹和定向捐赠为乡村教师募集奖励金，对参加"青椒计划"的优秀乡村教师进行资金奖励，促使"青椒"中的优秀教师成为各地乡村教育发展的"金种子"，带动更多乡村教师自我学习和提升。[①]

2. 案例：中国机械工业集团有限公司打造教育扶贫新模式

中国机械工业集团有限公司（以下简称"国机集团"）是世界500强企业，国机集团曾在河南省固始县、淮滨县和四川省广元市朝天区、山西省平陆县共4个贫困县（区）开展了定点扶贫工作。

一是投入资金支持贫困地区中小学改善办学条件。2016~2019年，该公司累计投入1476万余元，用于4个贫困县（区）改善中小学教学设施和学校生活条件。在广元市朝天区，国机集团累计出资近300万元，对原有鱼洞乡小学进行系统修缮和改造，建设"幸福国机小学"。目前该校已发展成为广元市"最美乡村学校"，近年来山区学生回流数量和教学质

---

① 中国人民大学课题组编《党的十八大以来教育脱贫攻坚总结（典型案例汇编）》，2020。

量连年上升。

二是支持扶贫县（区）教师培训。2017 年起，国机集团专门出资支持定点帮扶县（区）开展中小学教师培训。每年面向基层语文、数学、英语等学科教师和学校校长，分批组织 500 多人前往北京师范大学进行为期一周的专题培训，帮助他们提升学科教学和学校管理能力。

三是依托下属职业学校帮助贫困学生学技能和就业。面向朝天区建档立卡贫困户的应届高中毕业生，30 周岁以下的往届初、高中毕业生（或具有相当文化水平者）实行定向招生，对录取学生提供学制 3 年的职业教育（学费由国家承担），国机集团承担其在校期间的住宿费、管理费、书本费、实习费等各类费用。对完成学制、取得学历和职业资格的学生，学校负责帮助就业，国机集团下属企业优先录用。

四是面向贫困群众提供多样化技能培训。国机集团依托德阳安装技师学院培训中心，为朝天区建档立卡贫困户中 18~45 岁具备劳动能力、有技能培训或技能提升需求和创业需求的人员，提供 30 多个工种、15 天至 6 个月的免费技能培训，并为其推荐就业机会。2016~2018 年，国机集团累计投资约 120 万元，面向朝天区近 3500 名贫困人口开展了免费创业和技能培训。①

（二）国际组织力量参与中国教育扶贫事业

改革开放是中国的基本国策，因此，多年来，中国政府一直重视与国际组织的合作，在华国际组织和机构也积极参与了中国的教育减贫工作，并发挥了积极作用。

1. 案例：联合国儿童基金会"爱生学校"项目，助力农村教育更加公平、包容、有质量

2001 年，联合国儿童基金会与中国教育部教师工作司开始在中国西

---

① 中国人民大学课题组编《党的十八大以来教育脱贫攻坚总结（典型案例汇编）》，2020。

部地区三省七县的72所县中心校和村小学开展"爱生学校"试点项目，结合国家政策和国际理念，项目制定和实施了《中国爱生学校标准》，旨在引导学校改进创新，在入学、学习内容、学习过程、学习环境以及学习成果上保障每一名学龄儿童的最大利益，实施素质教育，促进学生的全面发展和健康成长。

结合当时新一轮基础教育课程改革，项目以教师培训为切入点，将"爱生学校"所倡导的以儿童利益为本、平等、全纳、参与和有效学习融入培训内容中，旨在推动学校实践以学生为本的新理念，改变教与学的关系，密切学校、家庭和社区的联系，为学生身心健康发展营造良好氛围，促进素质教育在西部农村地区的落实。

截至2005年年底，该项目已组织各类培训活动500多期，直接受益教师13000多人，其中很多人后来成为能够直接开展培训和指导"爱生学校"实践的基层培训者和骨干教师，使"爱生学校"的影响不限于最初的72所学校，为该项目在西部地区更大规模的开展奠定了基础。中国"爱生学校"项目遵循"让所有儿童入校就读，鼓励儿童参与学习并表达自我，尊重差异性和多样性，消除性别歧视，为所有儿童提供有质量的教育，确保每个儿童得到全面发展"的总目标，突出强调全纳与性别平等、有效的教与学、安全健康的校园环境以及校长的领导能力。学校环境、儿童的风貌和学习状态、教师的教学理念和方法、管理者的办学理念都发生了显著的变化。85%的项目学校能够围绕《中国爱生学校标准》改进学校。全纳、安全、儿童权利、儿童参与成为项目学校发展计划中的重要内容。

"爱生学校"试点和标准的实施，对中国西部地区特别是偏远贫困地区九年义务教育的全面普及起到了极大的促进作用，在国家和省级层面培养了一大批具有儿童观、性别意识敏感、能够开展参与式培训的技术骨干，使他们在不同的教育岗位上继续推广"爱生学校"的理念和实践。

2. 案例：云南探索民族农村地区多元文化背景下的社区学习中心多类型发展模式

云南省少数民族众多，呈现大杂居、小聚居的特点，各民族在自然环境、文化、人员结构、语言、风俗习惯等方面都有着明显的差异。针对民族农村地区的实际进行社区教育实践，引导当地居民自发组织、建立、管理并为社区发展服务，与其他地区相比存在诸多困难。

2005年以来，中国联合国教科文组织全国委员会、联合国教科文组织北京办事处和中国成人教育协会联合组织实施了农村社区学习中心（CLC）能力建设项目，在云南陆续建立了5个社区学习中心。这5个社区学习中心立足社区实际情况，根据自身特点积极参与项目的培训研究活动，不断开展学习教育活动，为当地村民提供培训，在创建和谐社区、提高社区居民生活质量、促进民族文化传承、促进农村经济社会发展等方面起到了积极作用。各中心逐渐形成各具特色的多类型发展模式。一是以政府部门主导建设的石林南门社区学习中心和开远小龙潭社区学习中心模式。依托乡镇、街道政府机构，协助开展部分社会服务和教育活动，在成人教育、妇女工作、政策宣传、生产技能培训、文明创建、社区自治等方面开展活动，下沉政府服务事项，丰富居民生活，维护社区和谐稳定。二是以家庭为中心建设的澜沧芒景村社区学习中心模式。围绕当地布朗族"末代王子"的居所进行建设，建有民族博物馆、各类民族文化建筑，以"王子"的个人威望和民族文化学识驱动，将民族文化中以茶为生的千年民族烙印、以茶叶保护为重点的和谐生态观作为社区成员的共同意识，通过将民族文化融入生产生活，加强生态环境保护，提升茶叶品质，进而提升生产生活技能和收入。三是以学校为中心建设的寻甸六哨乡社区学习中心和香格里拉仁安社区学习中心模式。六哨乡社区学习中心依托当地中心学校建立，致力于构建学校与社区和谐共生关系，将学校教育资源与社区资源相统一，通过建立社区图书室、建设脱毒马铃薯繁育实验基地、开展农业科技培训和各类民族文化活动，影响和带动社区成员意识的改变，将学校与社区深度融合，促进社区发展。仁安社区学习中心依托当地居民建设的公益免费幼儿园建立，以正规学前教育为基础，通过幼儿园的影响和辐射，"小手拉大手"，帮助社区成员改善陋习、参与学习、服务社区，促进社区和谐发展和民族文化传承。

5 个社区学习中心立足社区特点，探索多元文化背景下不同社区形态中的社区教育模式，既尊重社区成员发展需求，又融入现代社会生产生活体系，将民族文化中的先进思想与社区的经济活动相结合，吸引社区居民参与民族文化的保护传承，为云南各民族和谐共处和文化传承做出了重要贡献。

结　语

　　用不足 10 年时间，让超过 8000 万绝对贫困人口摆脱贫困，使拥有 14 亿人口的发展中国家消除了绝对贫困，实现全面建成小康社会的目标，是一项十分艰巨浩大的工程，其创造了人类减贫史上的奇迹。在这一过程中，必然有无数感人的故事可以作为典型经验与案例并给予启示。限于时间和可利用的人力资源，本书仅选取了部分案例，希望从侧面给这一人类创造的伟大业绩留下记录，为致力于人类减贫伟大事业的人们带来一点启示和借鉴。

　　对于中国来说，打赢脱贫攻坚战，如期实现脱贫攻坚目标任务，只是在创造美好生活、实现共同富裕的道路上迈出了坚实的一大步。中国并没有将消除绝对贫困作为减贫事业的终点。一方面，中国明确脱贫摘帽不是终点，而是新生活、新奋斗的起点。贫困人口、贫困村、贫困县退出后，在一定时期内原有扶持政策保持不变，摘帽不摘责任，摘帽不摘帮扶，摘帽不摘政策，摘帽不摘监管，留出缓冲期，确保稳定脱贫。另一方面，确立了解决发展不平衡不充分问题、缩小城乡区域发展差距、实现人的全面发展和全体人民共同富裕的新目标。持续巩固和拓展脱贫攻坚成果，做好同乡村振兴有效衔接，实现农业、农村和农民工作重心的历史性转移，以更有力的举措汇聚更强大的力量全面推进乡村振兴。

在教育方面，中国政府正深入推进巩固拓展教育脱贫攻坚成果同乡村振兴有效衔接，统筹做好乡村教育振兴和教育振兴乡村工作，促进乡村教育高质量发展，提升教育服务乡村振兴的能力和水平。

我们将继续对中国教育减贫经验的挖掘与研究，并将持续跟踪研究中国巩固教育减贫成果，通过教育支持乡村振兴的实践与经验，继续与世界分享我们的研究成果。

参考文献

1. 〔印〕阿马蒂亚·森:《以自由看待发展》,任颐、于真译,中国人民大学出版社,2002。

2. 戴岚:《新疆着力民生大事 让各族群众共享改革发展成果》,《人民日报》2010年5月18日。

3. 高建进:《福建宁化县:创新"三全三扶一档"教育精准扶贫机制》,《光明日报》2020年11月14日。

4. 廖其发:《当代中国重大教育改革事件专题研究》,重庆出版社,2007。

5. 刘盾:《发展特色产业,实施扶贫扩招,深圳职业技术学院推出一系列举措——精准施策为帮扶对象"拔穷根"》,《中国教育报》2020年6月15日。

6. 刘善槐、邬志辉:《"营养餐计划"推行5年 千万农村学生吃得怎么样?》,《光明日报》2017年1月12日。

7. 孟照海:《教育扶贫政策的理论依据及实现条件——国际经验与本土思考》,《教育研究》2016年第11期。

8. 汪三贵、殷浩栋、王瑜:《中国扶贫开发的实践、挑战与政策展望》,《华南师范大学学报》(社会科学版)2017年第4期。

9. 吴霓、王学男:《党的十八大以来教育扶贫政策的发展特征》,《教育研究》2017 年第 9 期。

10. 习近平:《摆脱贫困》,福建人民出版社,2014。

11. 习近平:《习近平谈治国理政》,外文出版社,2014。

12. 向雪琪、林曾:《改革开放以来我国教育扶贫的发展趋向》,《中南民族大学学报》(人文社会科学版) 2018 年第 3 期。

13. 薛二勇、周秀平:《中国教育脱贫的政策设计与制度创新》,《教育研究》2017 年第 12 期。

14. 袁利平、丁雅施:《我国教育扶贫政策的演进逻辑及未来展望——基于历史制度主义的视角》,《湖南师范大学教育科学学报》2019 年第 4 期。

15. 袁利平、张欣鑫:《教育扶贫何以可能——多学科视角下的教育扶贫及其实现》,《教育与经济》2018 年第 5 期。

16. 郑芃生:《甘肃省静宁县职教瞄准特色产业开展精准扶贫——职教扶贫,有"职"不贫》,《中国教育报》2018 年 11 月 15 日。

17. 中共中央文献研究室编《十六大以来重要文献选编》(下),中央文献出版社,2008。

18. 中共中央宣传部编《习近平总书记系列重要讲话读本》,学习出版社、人民出版社,2016。

19. 中国教育科学研究院课题组编《知识改变命运 教育奠基未来——中国教育脱贫攻坚的成就与经验》,教育科学出版社,2021。

20. 中华人民共和国国务院新闻办公室:《人类减贫的中国实践》白皮书,人民出版社,2021。

21. 中华人民共和国国务院新闻办公室:《中国的农村扶贫开发》白皮书,人民出版社,2005。

22. 中华人民共和国国务院新闻办公室:《中国农村扶贫开发的新进展》白皮书,人民出版社,2011。

23. 《安徽大学生村官扎根农村7年 带领村民脱贫致富》，《安徽日报》2020年5月5日。

24. 《百姓心中的"科技财神"——记河北农业大学教授李保国（上）》，《人民日报》2016年2月9日。

25. 《第三届省属高校精准扶贫精准脱贫典型项目扫描》，《中国教育报》2020年10月19日。

26. 程浩：《一段跨越2600公里的情谊》，新华网，2020，www.yn.xinhuanet.com。

27. 韩晓彤、彭辰辰：《海南巾帼励志中专班9年记：从思想扶贫，八千女生免费学技术》，澎湃新闻，2019，www.thepaper.cn。

28. 黄雪梅、王光庆、黄海：《万亩"福州林"，打造陇中"生态扶贫样本"》，人民网，2020，gs.people.com.cn。

29. 李伟民、严小娟、吴克发：《东西部职业教育合作助力精准扶贫》，央广网，2020，country.cnr.cn。

30. 李自良：《"一个不能少"，让辍学的孩子重返校园——云南脱贫攻坚总攻中"控辍保学"记略》，新华网，2020，www.xinhuanet.com。

31. 连振祥：《东西部协作共同推进我国职业教育发展》，中国政府网，2020，www.gov.cn。

32. 刘昌：《扶贫先扶智，海南省精准扶贫促进教育均衡发展》，中国网，2017，www.china.com.cn。

33. 王洪峰、孙铁翔、王昆：《追记共产党员、河北农业大学教授李保国》，新华网，2020，www.xinhuanet.com。

34. 韦美兰、冉涛：《巾帼脱贫奔小康（三十九）｜广西乐业罗美烈：非遗手艺引领致富路》，广西妇女网，2020，www.gxwomen.org.cn。

35. 魏倩：《云南：为控辍保学难题开出"药方"》，腾讯网，2020，new.qq.com。

36. 吴丹、曹征：《改善薄弱学校办学条件 促进教育公平》，人民网，

2016，edu.people.com.cn。

37. 郁静娴、李茂颖、苏滨：《4000 万农村娃吃上了营养餐》，人民网，2020，people.com.cn。

38. 曾维伦、谢卓芝：《习近平扶贫开发战略思想的丰富内涵》，求是网，2020，www.qstheory.cn。

39. 赵叶苹：《海南"扶贫巾帼班"为贫困女孩打开希望之门》，人民网，2014，people.com.cn。

40.《国家资助 燕园领航 助我成长》，中华人民共和国教育部，2013，www.moe.gov.cn。

41.《河南省成人教育教学改革实验学校工作会镇平召开》，镇平网，2020，yuxiangshequ.com。

42.《教师队伍建设典型工作案例一：农村义务教育阶段学校教师特设岗位计划实施工作优秀案例》，中华人民共和国教育部，2017，www.moe.gov.cn。

43.《教育部：全面改薄工作总体进展顺利实现时间过半任务过半》，中国政府网，2017，www.gov.cn。

44.《教育部办公厅 财政部办公厅关于做好 2018 年农村义务教育阶段学校教师特设岗位计划实施工作的通知》，中华人民共和国教育部，2018，www.moe.gov.cn。

45.《教育部办公厅 国务院扶贫办综合司关于印发〈贯彻落实《职业教育东西协作行动计划（2016—2020 年）》实施方案〉的通知》，中华人民共和国教育部，www.moe.gov.cn。

46.《教育精准扶贫显实效，贵州乡村教师迎春天》，人民网，2018，edu.people.com.cn。

47.《介绍农村义务教育学生营养改善计划实施进展情况》，中华人民共和国教育部，2022，www.moe.gov.cn。

48.《李保国：开创山区扶贫新路的"太行山愚公"》，共产党员网，

2020，www.12371.cn。

49. 《农村义务教育营养改善计划助推"精准脱贫"》，央广网，2020，country.cnr.cn。

50. 《实行"两免一补"政策》，中国政府网，2020，www.gov.cn。

51. 《脱贫攻坚进行时 中组部典型案例之——甘肃静宁县职业教育保就业的探索实践》，平凉市人民政府，2020，www.pingliang.gov.cn。

52. 《浙大扶贫干部变身主播"带货"10分钟卖出豌豆3000斤》，浙江新闻，2020，zj.zjol.com.cn。

53. Banerjee, A.V., Duflo, E., *Poor Economics: A Radical Rethinking of the Way to Fight Global Poverty*, Public Affairs, 2011.

54. Conceição, P., *Human Development Report 2019: Beyond Income, Beyond Averages, Beyond Today: Inequalities in Human Development in the 21st Century*, United Nations 2019.

55. Cremin, P., Nakabugo, M. G., "Education, Development and Poverty Reduction: A Literature Critique," *International Journal of Educational Development*, 2012, 32(4).

56. Gamawa, A. I., "The Role of Home Economics Education in Alleviating Poverty for Sustainable Development and Human Capacity Building in Nigeria," *Journal of Emerging Trends in Educational Research and Policy Studies*, 2015, 6(7): 325-330.

57. Hicks, R., "The Capability Approach: Insights for A New Poverty," *Journal of Social Policy*, 2012, 41(2).

58. Majumder, S., Biswas, S. C., "The Role of Education in Poverty Alleviation: Evidence from Bangladesh," *Journal of Economics and Sustainable Development*, 2017, 8(20).

59. Omoniyi, M. B. I., "The Role of Education in Poverty Alleviation and Economic Development: A Theoretical Perspective and Counselling

Implications," *British Journal of Arts and Social Sciences*, 2013, 15(2).

60. Sen, A., "Capability and Well-Being," in *The Quality of Life*, ed. Nussbaum, M., Sen, A., Oxford University Press, 1993.

61. Sen, A., "Human Rights and Capabilities," *Journal of Human Development, 2005*, 6(2).

62. Sen, A., *Development as Freedom*, Oxford University Press, 1999.

63. Zhang, Y., Chen, S., "Analyzing the Cause of Left-Behind Children by Bourdieu's Practical Theory," *American Journal of Industrial and Business Management*, 2018, 8(6).

64. Alkire, S., Santos, M. E., "Multidimensional Poverty Index," 2010, www. ophi.org.uk.

65. Bhattacharya, D., Khan, T. I., Rezbana, U. S., & Mostaque, L., *Moving Forward with the SDGs Implementation Challenges in Developing Countries*, Center for Policy Dialogue (CPD), 2016, www.researchgate.net.

66. Food and Agriculture Organization of the United Nations (FAO), International Fund for Agricultural Development (IFAD), United Nations International Children's Emergency Fund (UNICEF), World Food Programme (WFP), & World Health Organization (WHO), *The State of Food Security and Nutrition in the World 2020: Transforming Food Systems for Affordable Healthy Diets*, 2020, www.fao.org.

67. Foster, J., Seth, S., Lokshin, M., & Sajaia Z., *A Unified Approach to Measuring Poverty and Inequality: Theory and Practice*, World Bank, 2013, openknowledge. worldbank.org.

68. International Domestic Workers Federation, *ILO Monitor: Covid-19 and the World of Work*, 2020, www.ilo.org.

69. International Food Policy Research Institute, *2020 Global Food Policy Report: Building Inclusive Food Systems*, 2020, ebrary.ifpri.org.

70. Kharas, H., Hamel, K., & Hofer, M., " Rethinking Global Poverty Reduction in 2019," 2018, www.brookings.edu.

71. Kharas, H., *The Impact of Covid-19 on Global Extreme Poverty*, Brookings, 2020, www.brookings.edu.

72. United Nations Development Programme (UNDP), Oxford Poverty and Human Development Initiative (OPHI), *Global Multidimensional Poverty Index 2019: Illuminating Inequalities*, 2019, hdr.undp.org.

73. United Nations Development Programme (UNDP), Oxford Poverty and Human Development Initiative (OPHI), *Creating Pathways out of Multidimensional Poverty: Achieving the SDGs*, 2020, hdr.undp.org.

74. United Nations Economic and Social Council (UNECOSOC), *Progress towards the Sustainable Development Goals: report of the Secretary General*, 2018, sustainabledevelopment.un.org.

75. United Nations Educational, Scientific and Cultural Organization (UNESCO). 2013. *Educational Attainment and Employment Outcomes: Evidence from 11 Developing Countries*, 2013, unesdoc.unesco.org.

76. United Nations Educational, Scientific and Cultural Organization (UNESCO), *Education for All 2000-2015: Achievements and Challenges. EFA Global Monitoring Report 2015*, 2015, unesdoc.unesco.org.

77. United Nations Educational, Scientific and Cultural Organization (UNESCO), *Education 2030: Incheon Declaration and Framework for Action for the Implementation of Sustainable Development Goal 4*, 2015, uis.unesco.org.

78. United Nations Educational, Scientific and Cultural Organization (UNESCO), *Global Education Monitoring Report 2016: Education for People and Planet: Creating Sustainable Futures for All*, 2016, unesdoc.unesco.org.

79. United Nations Educational, Scientific and Cultural Organization (UNESCO), *Reducing Global Poverty through Universal Primary and Secondary*

Education, 2017, uis.unesco.org.

80. United Nations Educational, Scientific and Cultural Organization (UNESCO), *Global Education Monitoring Report 2019: Gender Report: Building Bridges for Gender Equality*. Paris, 2019, unesdoc.unesco.org.

81. United Nations Educational, Scientific and Cultural Organization (UNESCO), *Meeting Commitments: Are Countries on Track To Achieve SDG4?* 2019, uis.unesco.org.

82. United Nations Educational, Scientific and Cultural Organization (UNESCO), *Beyond commitments – How countries implement SDG 4*, 2019, unesdoc.unesco.org.

83. United Nations Educational, Scientific and Cultural Organization (UNESCO), *Global Education Monitoring Report: Inclusion and Education: All Means All*, 2020, unesdoc.unesco.org.

84. United Nations Educational, Scientific and Cultural Organization (UNESCO), *Act Now: Reduce the Impact of Covid-19 on the Cost of Achieving SDG 4: Policy Paper 42*, 2020, en.unesco.org.

85. United Nations International Children's Emergency Fund (UNICEF), *The Investment Case for Education and Equity*, 2015, www.unicef.org.

86. United Nations International Children's Emergency Fund (UNICEF), Save the Children, *Technical Note: Impact of COVID on Child Poverty*, 2020, data.unicef.org.

87. United Nations, *Financing for Sustainable Development Report 2020: Report of the Inter-agency Task Force on Financing for Development*, 2020, developmentfinance.un.org.

88. United Nations, *Report of the Secretary-General on SDG Progress Special Edition*, 2019, sustainabledevelopment.un.org.

89. United Nations, *The Sustainable Development Goals Report 2019*, 2019, unstats.

un.org.

90. United Nations, *The Sustainable Development Goals Report 2020*, 2020, unstats. un.org.

91. United Nations, *The Sustainable Development Goals Report 2021*, 2021, www. un.org.

92. World Bank, *Ending Learning Poverty: What will it take?* 2019, openknowledge. worldbank.org.

93. World Bank, *Global Monitoring Report 2014/2015: Ending Poverty and Sharing Prosperity*, 2015, pubdocs.worldbank.org.

94. World Bank, *Poverty and Shared Prosperity 2018: Piecing Together the Poverty Puzzle*, 2018, openknowledge.worldbank.org.

致　谢

在本书完成的时刻，我们首先要致敬多年来战斗在扶贫攻坚第一线的千千万万基层教育工作者和社区工作者，是他们的聪明才智和辛勤的汗水灌溉成就了本书所展示的内容与成果。

在本书编写的各个阶段，中国联合国教科文组织全国委员会秘书处给予了大力指导、帮助和贡献，我们对它的支持表示衷心的感谢。感谢联合国教科文组织国际农村教育研究与培训中心的依托单位北京师范大学的大力支持。我们也要感谢教育部发展规划司、财务司、基础教育司、职业教育与成人教育司、教师工作司，中国教育科学研究院，全国学生资助管理中心，国家开放大学，联合国教科文组织北京办事处、联合国儿童基金会驻华办事处等机构和部门对本书提出的宝贵意见和建议。

本书中文版的撰写由王力先生牵头，并获得了一批专家和农教中心员工的支持，他们是：Min Bista、Robert Parua、王迪、王雅雯、方圆安、任超、齐志勇、齐新建、李小平、李兴洲、李阳、李磊、张铁道、陆一帆、孟鸿伟、侯小雨、姚骥坤、黄琳珈、崔建民、董建红、谭焱卿、潘昆峰等。很多同事为本书提供了相关案例，他们是：刘风雷、李劲松、杨文明、吴延磊、沈鹏、陆和杰、金燕、郑刚强、蒋根兴等（上述人名按姓氏笔画排序）。秦昌威、王力、贾楠、张淞云、郭志军、王咏乾、沈凯文、夏靖轩等同事研究起草了本书框架，对本书进行了最后的文字修改并定稿。

本书英文版由农教中心副主任赵玉池博士领头的团队完成，成员包括刘静博士（北京师范大学教育学部国际交流与合作办公室主任）、刘芮希女士和江竹君女士。王力等同事也为英文版做出了贡献。尼泊尔特里布文大学（Tribhuwan University）前教授和联合国教科文组织退休教育专家 Min Bista 先生对文稿进行审阅并润色。

感谢农教中心主任黄荣怀教授、执行主任曾晓东教授自始至终对本书编写提供支持和帮助。

联合国教科文组织

国际农村教育研究与培训中心

This book is supported by the Secretariat of
Chinese National Commission for UNESCO and UNESCO Beijing Office

TOWARDS 2030

Practices of Poverty Alleviation through Education in China

UNESCO International Research and Training Centre for Rural Education/Edit

社会科学文献出版社
SOCIAL SCIENCES ACADEMIC PRESS (CHINA)

Preface

Poverty is a chronic affliction of human society and a common challenge faced by the whole world. Eliminating poverty is the persistent goal of humankind, and the history of human development is a journey of fighting against poverty. In 2015, poverty reduction was included as the first goal of the *United Nations 2030 Agenda for Sustainable Development*. Since the launch of the *2030 Agenda*, the international community has worked together to make continuous progress.

However, difficulties and challenges remain serious, and the outbreak of the COVID-19 pandemic exacerbated poverty around the world. The *Sustainable Development Goals Report 2021* launched by the UN shows that the number of people falling into poverty globally increased by around 120 million in 2020. The extreme poverty rate rose to 9.5% from 8.4% in 2019 and it is estimated that 7% of the global population will still live in extreme poverty by 2030. In this regard, it is urgent to take stronger and more innovative measures for poverty reduction.

China is the largest developing country in the world. In the early stage since the founding of the People's Republic of China in 1949, it was facing challenges of abject poverty, weak economic foundation and unbalanced development, and suffered from poverty for a long time. Since its founding, China has carried out large-scale socialist reconstruction, committed to getting rid of poverty and improving people's lives.

1978 marks a new era as China launched the policy of reform and opening up. Enlightened by the new policy, China has implemented large-scale, planned and organized programmes for poverty alleviation and development, with the poverty reduction process greatly accelerated and many people lifted out of poverty. According to China's current poverty standard, the number of rural population living in poverty still exceeded 770 million in 1978, with the incidence of rural poverty reaching 97.5%. With over 30 years of efforts, rural population in poverty decreased to 98.99 million and poverty incidence decreased to 10.2% by 2012, which shows significant achievements in the cause of poverty

reduction. However, most of the remaining poor people live in the 14 contiguous extremely poverty-stricken areas with fragile ecological environments, frequent natural disasters, and inconvenient transportation and lagging-behind infrastructure and social development, where the task of poverty alleviation is extremely challenging.

Since 2012, China has highly prioritised poverty reduction in its agenda of national governance, taking targeted poverty alleviation and the elimination of absolute poverty as the bottom-line task of achieving moderate prosperity in all respects. President Xi Jinping was dedicated in person to strategically planning the cause and all levels of government across the country have been fully mobilized, launching the largest campaign against poverty unprecedented in human history. Although the sudden outbreak of COVID-19 pandemic has brought some disruptions to poverty alleviation, the Chinese government did not waver its determination and the goal as well. Moreover, the country launched a final attack against the absolute poverty with the nation of one mind and more firmly mobilized all available resources.

Chinese President Xi Jinping announced on February 25, 2021 that China has scored a "complete victory" in its fight against poverty and absolute poverty has been eradicated in the world's most populous country in a conference held to mark the country's accomplishments in poverty alleviation and honour its model poverty fighters. Under China's current standard, all 98.99 million rural poor people, all 832 poverty-stricken counties have been lifted out of poverty, and all 128,000 poverty villages have been removed from the list. The absolute poverty that has plagued the Chinese nation for thousands of years has been historically ended, creating a miracle standing out in the history of humankind.

China has made a significant contribution to the global poverty reduction. Since 1978, 770 million rural population have been pulled out of poverty, according to current national poverty line. The reduced population in poverty in China accounts for more than 70% of the world's total in the same period according to the World Bank international poverty standards. In particular, against the context that the global poverty situation is still severe and the intensified differentiation between the rich and the poor in some countries, China has achieved the UN 2030 Agenda's goal for poverty reduction 10 years in advance, and actively participated in international cooperation in poverty reduction efforts and become the advocate, promoter and contributor of the world poverty reduction cause.

Education is the fundamental way for human beings to pass on civilization and knowledge, nurture the younger generation and create a better life. Sustainable Development Goal 4 (SDG 4) of the 2030 Agenda which aims to "ensure inclusive and equitable quality education and promote lifelong learning opportunities for all" by 2030 is both an integral part of the 17 SDGs and a key foundation for achieving the other goals, especially crucial to the goal of poverty elimination. Universal access to equitable

and quality education can end the intergenerational transmission of poverty, and further remove its root causes. Poverty is the greatest obstacle to achieving universal access to equitable and quality education. It is strongly believed that eradicating poverty will contribute significantly to the implementation of the Education 2030 goals.

Unfortunately, the progress towards Education 2030 was not satisfactory, with more than 200 million children still out of school and only 60 percent of students completing upper secondary education. At the current rate of progress, the world will not meet the development goals by 2030. The outbreak of COVID-19 pandemic in 2020 brought great challenges to global development, with the total number of people living in poverty increasing for the first time in decades. More than 71 million people have been pushed into extreme poverty, schools have been temporarily closed in more than 190 countries, and more than 500 million students have been denied access to distance learning. It is evident that combining education with poverty reduction, which not only boosts the development of education, but also enables the poor to develop capacity through the provision of education, is an important way to accelerate the development of education and poverty reduction, eventually to achieve the 2030 Sustainable Development Goals.

In the process of fighting against poverty, China always adheres to the principle of "ending ignorance before eliminating poverty, and educating the poor before helping them" and education has played a fundamental and leading role. In addition, it has established a coordination, leadership and decision-making system that integrates central and local efforts on education for poverty alleviation, and also a responsibility fulfilling system, a financial guarantee system, an assessment system and paired-up cooperation mechanisms to underpin the fight against poverty through education. All these mechanisms will continue to function towards the subsequent comprehensive rural revitalization in the post-poverty reduction era.

Meanwhile, it has also contributed to the fulfilment of China's 2030 education goals. The most remarkable achievement is the historical breakthrough on the access to schooling for children from poor rural households through targeted support, and all kinds of schools in poverty-stricken areas have been greatly improved. All these have worked towards employment, income generation and a decent quality of life for the poor households, with skills acquired by education and training. A solid foundation has been laid to block the inter-generational transmission of poverty.

In order to explore the interlinks between education and poverty reduction and to promote the implementation of the *UN 2030 Agenda for Sustainable Development*, especially its Goal 1 and Goal 4, with the support of the Ministry of Education of the People's Republic of China, the Chinese National Commission for UNESCO, and the UNESCO Beijing Office, the UNESCO International Research and Training Centre for Rural Education (INRULED) has selected a number of cases of poverty reduction

through education from the variety of practices in China for global sharing.

This publication includes three chapters, with the first chapter reviewing the relationship between education development and poverty reduction from an international perspective, and the current global implementation of the United Nations Sustainable Development Goals, especially Goal 1 and 4.

Chapter Ⅱ provides an overview of the history of China's poverty reduction in and through education, with a focus on the implementation of targeted poverty alleviation since 2012, including the overall strategy, policy framework, the specific strategies for targeted poverty alleviation through education, as well as the remarkable results achieved.

Chapter Ⅲ selects a number of cases of China's poverty alleviation through education which showcases the specific policies and practices in five aspects:

- Ensuring the Universality and Equity in Education;
- Improving the Quality of Education in Poverty-stricken Areas;
- Empowering poor families in China through technical and vocational education and training (TVET) and skills development;
- Boosting rural industrial and economic development by higher education institutions and vocational schools;
- Cross-sector collaboration for poverty alleviation through education.

We believe that China's experience in the practice of education for poverty alleviation belongs to both China and the world, and it can be the reference for the international community committed to education for poverty alleviation. However, it needs to be stressed that all countries in the world have different contexts and development status quo, and that poverty reduction standards, methods and paths will inevitably be different. In this regard, strategies and approaches that work are those relevant to national context and drawn out from local practices.

The editors of this publication aspire to strengthen exchanges and cooperation in education for poverty alleviation with relevant institutions in various countries, accumulate concerted efforts towards the United Nations 2030 Sustainable Development Goals, and make greater contributions to building a global community with a shared future and pursuing common development.

UNESCO International Research and Training Centre for Rural Education
November 2022

Contents

Chapter I The International Context of Poverty, Poverty Reduction and Education

Chapter II China's Targeted Poverty Alleviation through Education: Actions and Results

Chapter Ⅲ   Poverty Alleviation through Education: Case Studies from China

Chapter I

The International Context of Poverty, Poverty Reduction and Education

I. Conceptualization of Poverty

Poverty is a complex issue. Although its initial focus was on material deprivation, the conceptualization and classification of poverty have evolved as people's understanding toward poverty has deepened over the years. According to different criteria, poverty can be further categorized into relative and absolute poverty, existential, substantial, and developmental poverty. The University of Oxford has developed a global Multidimensional Poverty Index (MPI), complementing traditional monetary poverty measurement by capturing the acute deprivations in three dimensions that a person faces simultaneously, namely health (nutrition, child mortality), education (enrolment rate, educational attainment), and living standards (drinking water, electricity, cooking fuel, housing, sanitation, and assets).

In recent years, poverty has evolved into a multidimensional concept consisting of economic, social, political and environmental perspectives. It is viewed as a denial of choices and opportunities, a violation of human dignity and human rights, as well as a deprivation of capabilities and skills. *The Human Development Report 2019* has further extended the understanding of capabilities and grouped them into two categories: basic capabilities and enhanced capabilities (see Figure 1-1). It argues that although basic capabilities are important for survival, they are not enough, and the enhanced capabilities play an indispensable role for living in dignity. The report highlights that it is imperative to transform from basic to enhanced capabilities to improve people's capabilities and skills, so as to solve poverty-related problems and achieve sustainable development goals.

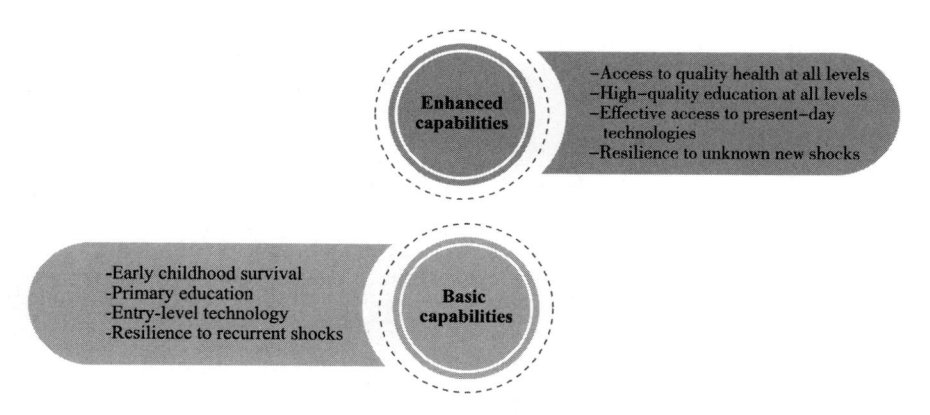

Figure 1-1 Human Development: From Basic to Enhanced Capabilities

Source: Conceição, P., *Human Development Report 2019: Beyond Income, Beyond Averages, Beyond Today: Inequalities in Human Development in the 21st Century*, 2019.

II. Education, Capacity Development and Poverty Reduction

Education is the fundamental key and the most significant path to skills acquisition and advancement. The deprivation of the right to education is both a manifestation of poverty and major cause for chronic poverty. Hence, universal education is a critical approach for human capital accumulation, poverty elimination and social inclusion, which helps lay a solid foundation for all-around human development and sustainable social development. The denial of the right to education is a prominent manifestation of "educational poverty", and protecting this right is the most effective means to break the vicious circle of "underdeveloped economy-educational poverty-lack of human capital-worsening the backwardness of economy". In this regard, alleviating "educational poverty" can remove the root causes for poverty.

Education and skills training can help poor families to shake off poverty by developing knowledge and skills and increasing productivity, so that they will be less vulnerable to poverty, hunger, exclusion and other risks. Education also provides rural households with the option of working in non-agricultural sectors, increasing their ability to generate income and thus diversifying their sources of income. In addition to knowledge and skills enhancement, education delivers values, beliefs and attitudes that are essential for people to participate effectively in social transformation.

From a human capital perspective, the human resource development has the potential to lift people out of poverty and accelerate economic growth. Investments in human capital through lifelong learning that targets the most vulnerable groups can play a pivotal role in breaking the intergenerational transmission of poverty. Evidence

suggests that the higher one's education level is, the lower the poverty severity will be. If all the students in low-income countries gained basic reading skills, there would be 171 million fewer people living in poverty in these countries. Similarly, a strong correlation has been observed between the average years of schooling for people aged 25-34 and their poverty severity, measured at less than $2 per day. The UNICEF Investment Case for Education and Equity has shown that poverty rates were 9 percentage points lower for each additional year of schooling.

Educational attainment is also highly correlated to people's abilities and opportunities to escape from poverty. According to a report by UNESCO Institute for Statistics (UIS) in 2012, which examined the average effects of education on growth and poverty reduction over the period 1965-2010 in developing countries, two more years of schooling for adults would help to lift nearly 60 million people out of poverty. Likewise, universal secondary education for all the adults would help to lift more than 420 million out of poverty, thus reducing the number of people living in poverty worldwide by more than half. Furthermore, one more year added to the average schooling years would lead to a reduction of the Gini coefficient by 1.4 percent, based on data from 114 countries for the 1985-2005 period.

Upgrading women's education level can effectively improve children's well-being, and it is crucial for gender equity and women's empowerment. "Investing in women and girls is a powerful driver of development," Asha-Rose Migiro, former UN Deputy Secretary-General, stressed at the 55th session of the United Nations Commission on the Status of Women in 2011. She emphasized that education was the best and most correct investment because it was not only a major impetus of economic growth but also a catalyst for women's empowerment. Through education, women would have more access to paid work, stay healthy and participate in all spheres of social life, thus significantly increasing their financial income as well as the well-being of their children and families.

UNICEF reported that if all women in low and middle-income countries completed secondary education, the chances of a child receiving immunizations would increase by 43 percent. UNESCO indicated that in low-income countries, if all women completed primary education, the number of stunting children would reduce by 1.7 million. Moreover, girls' education is associated with late marriages and late childbirth. A projection carried out by UNESCO showed that if all girls had a secondary level of education in South and West Asia and sub-Saharan Africa, the number of child marriage would decline from 2.9 million to 1 million (decreased by 65.5 percent). Likewise, the early fertility would fall from 3.4 million to 1.4 million (decreased by 59 percent).

It is evident that universal education and skills training is particularly important for the poor and disadvantaged people to escape from poverty. The key to poverty

alleviation is to empower people with basic skills and competencies that are required for a dignified job and productivity, so as to reduce the risks of financial setbacks and break the chain of discrimination.

Studies show the linkage between education, the prospect of skills acquisition and employment opportunities. More education opportunities lead to better and well-paid jobs. The difference is evident between those who have attained secondary education and those who have not, as well as between those completing secondary level and those enjoying tertiary level education. Higher education graduates are more likely to be employed than others. Under difficult economic circumstances, education is generally a good insurance against unemployment.

Ⅲ. Education and Poverty Alleviation in the 2030 Agenda for Sustainable Development

1. The 2030 Agenda for Sustainable Development and Global Poverty Reduction

The 70th session of the United Nations General Assembly was convened in New York in September 2015. Heads of the states, governments and high-level representatives from 192 member states gathered at the UN headquarters to set the new global development goals, known as the *2030 Agenda for Sustainable Development*. The agenda stressed that the elimination of poverty in all its forms and manifestations, including extreme poverty, was the greatest challenge for the world and was essential for the achievement of sustainable development. Therefore, the Goal "to end poverty in all its forms everywhere" ranks first among the 17 sustainable development goals (SDGs). With its 7 specific targets, including, "by 2030, eradicate extreme poverty for all people everywhere", "by 2030 reduce at least by half the proportion of men, women and children of all ages living in poverty in all its dimensions according to national definitions", the Goal shows the vision of the international community for global development.

The SDGs seeks to address the global challenges that the world is facing, including poverty (SDG1), hunger (SDG2), good health and well-being (SDG3), education (SDG4), gender equality (SDG5), clean water and sanitation (SDG 6), decent work and economic growth (SDG 8), reduced inequalities (SDG 10) and responsible consumption and production (SDG 12), which are all crucial for poverty reduction. Although each goal has its significance and responds to specific global challenges, the 17 goals as a whole are closely intertwined. This means the stagnant progress in any of the goals will impede the development of others.

Hence, a holistic and comprehensive approach is needed for the transition to a sustainable, peaceful and prosperous society, fully recognizing intricate mutual relations of the SDGs. One example is the synergy of poverty alleviation (SDG1), good health and well-being (SDG3), education (SDG4) and some other sustainable goals. Meanwhile, the progress of other goals will contribute to the development of poverty alleviation, good health and well-being, and education. The interconnected and integrated nature is critical to the realization of sustainable development, including poverty reduction. Education, in particular, has been recognized as the foundation of all other goals and the backbone of tackling human development challenges.

Shortly after the adoption of the SDGs, the United Nations (UN) System in China launched the new *United Nations Development Assistance Framework (UNDAF) for the People's Republic of China 2016-2020*, which marks a strong partnership between the UN and China for a new 5-year period. As a result of consultations involving the Government of China, the UN System and other stakeholders, the new UNDAF is a strategic document that provides an integrated response to assist in addressing national development priorities and challenges in China. Three priority areas were then identified: (1) poverty reduction and equitable development; (2) improved and sustainable environment, and (3) enhanced global engagement. The significance of the Framework is not only to address China's own development challenges, but also to engage China more in global development, including poverty reduction.

Over the past decades, remarkable progress has been achieved in poverty reduction thanks to the joint efforts of all countries, especially China and other emerging economies. In 2018, the UN Secretary-General António Guterres submitted a report to the UN High-level Political Forum on Sustainable Development (HLPF), outlining the global progress concerning the implementation of the 17 SDGs. The report noted that extreme poverty has greatly been reduced over the past few decades. The proportion of workers living on less than $1.90 per person per day has fallen dramatically over the past 17 years, from 26.9 percent in 2000 to 9.2 percent in 2017, and many parts of the world have made significant progress in expanding social security.

In recent years, however, the global rate of poverty reduction has shown a downward trend and the driving force for poverty reduction is insufficient. Predictions show that, due to the slowing-down economic development, the number of people lifted out of poverty per second has fallen from 1 person in 2017 to 0.8 person in 2018, and 0.6 person in 2019. From a regional perspective, the proportion of Africans in the global poor has raised from 60 percent in 2016 when the SDGs were initially implemented to 70 percent in 2019. And it is still rising. Thus, the challenges of global poverty reduction are still daunting, and Africa is likely to be the last region to end global extreme poverty. It is predicted that by 2030, around 600 million people will still be living in extreme

poverty.

The sudden outbreak of COVID-19 pandemic has devastated the global economy, with immediate and long-term negative impacts on people around the world. The number of people living in extreme poverty worldwide increased for the first time since 1998, with 119 million -124 million people living in extreme poverty; inequalities have increased; 255 million full-time jobs were lost in 2020; 101 million children and teenagers were under the minimum literacy level; and an additional 10 million girls will be at risk of child marriage in the next decade. The pandemic has had a great impact on both developed and developing economies, while the poor and vulnerable groups in developing countries will suffer from the rising extreme poverty. The pandemic has undone all the progress made in poverty reduction since the launch of SDGs in 2015.

Table 1-1 shows the pre-COVID poverty estimates compared to the estimates made in October 2020. The first row represents the poverty estimates that were made in 2019, which indicated that in 2019 a total of 650 million people was in extreme poverty.[1] It is noted that the poverty rate according to the 2019 estimates was on a trajectory of steady decline from 2019 through 2030, with 8.4% in 2019, 8.0% in 2020, 7.6% in 2021 and 6.3% in 2030. On the contrary, according to the 2020 projections, it is estimated that in 2020 the percentage of people living in extreme poverty would rise to 9.9%, and then drop to 9.3% in 2021 and 7.0% in 2030 eventually.

Table 1-1　Changes in Poverty and Policy Responses Due to the Outbreak of COVID-19 Pandemic

		2019	2020	2021	2030
End of 2019 (before COVID-19)	Absolute numbers	650433712	621931609	598347067	536923904
	Percentage of world population	8.4%	8.0%	7.6%	6.3%
October 2020 (after COVID-19)	Absolute numbers	646806659	766032180	726524822	597902578
	Percentage of world population	8.4%	9.9%	9.3%	7.0%

Source: Kharas, H., Hamel, K., & Hofer, M., *Rethinking Global Poverty Reduction in 2019*, Brookings 2018, www.brookings.edu.

The COVID-19 pandemic is still evolving, which has caused an economic, health and educational crisis globally, exposing the vulnerabilities and inequalities within and between countries. One of the groups most affected by the COVID-19 pandemic

---

[1]　Extreme poverty is defined as households spending less than $1.90 per capita per day on 2011 purchasing power parity (PPP) terms.

outbreak is the "low-skilled" population in the developing world. Due to the slowing-down or even falling-back economic development caused by the pandemic, a large number of low-skilled people are unable to get jobs or are unemployed, and the poverty caused by the lack of regular income is widespread. This reflects an urgent need for people to acquire skills and capabilities, as well as the importance of empowering people through education and using education as a means to reduce poverty.

2. The Launch of Education 2030 Agenda

There is a growing international consensus that measures such as ensuring the right to education, reducing illiteracy and promoting the development of education can change the plight of poor people in underdeveloped areas. Since the dawning of the 21st century, countries around the world have made great efforts to promote education for all, eliminate illiteracy and improve the quality of education.

In April 2000, the international community adopted the *Dakar Framework for Action "Education for All (EFA): Meeting Our Collective Commitment"* in Dakar, Senegal. The Framework reaffirmed the global vision of the *World Declaration on Education for All* adopted in 1990 at Jomtien, Thailand. It is committed to meeting the learning needs of all children, youths and adults by 2015, reflected in its six goals. These goals range from improving early childhood care and education and universalizing primary education to reducing adult illiteracy, ensuring gender equality in education and improving the quality of education. In September 2000, the *Millennium Declaration* was adopted at the United Nations in New York that set out to achieve eight goals known as *Millennium Development Goals (MDGs)*, two of which were related to education: universalization of primary education and gender equality in education.

2015 was the ending year of the global journey towards achieving EFA and education-related MDGs, and it was the time to comprehensively assess the achievements and experiences made by countries since 2000 to reflect on national, regional and international strategies adopted. In April 2015, UNESCO launched the final *EFA Global Monitoring Report*. Mr. Ban Ki-moon, the then UN Secretary-General, addressed in his remarks for the launch of the report that, the international community had made much progress over the past 15 years in promoting EFA:

- 50 million more children were enrolled in primary school than ever before;
- the number of children and adolescents that were out of school had been reduced by nearly half; and
- many countries had made great progress in increasing primary school enrolment rate, including that for girls.

The report pointed out that in 2015, 47 percent of the total countries across the

globe were able to achieve the first goal of the 6 EFA goals—improving early childhood care and education, and that 52% of the countries had achieved the second goal—ensuring all the children especially girls complete quality, free and compulsory primary education by 2015.

Nevertheless, the report indicated that EFA was still "an unfinished business". While there had been substantial progress in terms of the number of boys and girls attending schools, by and large, the six EFA goals and the MDGs were not reached by the 2015 deadline, with the following persistent challenges,

- education systems around the world continued to be beset with poor quality of learning;
- education disparities based on gender, ethnicity, language and disability were further widened;
- illiteracy, low levels of skills, limited or no access to TVET and tertiary education were easy to be noted;
- children and youths were not equipped with the knowledge, values, competencies and attitudes to function in a globalizing world and contribute to the creation of an inclusive, peaceful, civilized and sustainable society.

Obviously, the world needs a new education agenda that would not only attend to the unfinished business of EFA goals and the education-related MDGs but also effectively address the current and future global and national challenges.

It is within this context, the international community convened the World Education Forum in May 2015 in Incheon, the Republic of Korea (ROK). Heads of the states, governments and representatives from international organizations participated in the Forum. The Incheon Declaration was adopted by the Forum. In September of that year, the *2030 Agenda for Sustainable Development* was adopted at the 70th session of the UN General Assembly, recognizing that education was the key to achieving all the 17 Sustainable Development Goals. The educational goals established in the Incheon Declaration constitute an integral part of the 2030 Agenda. In November the *2030 Framework for Action* on Education to implement SDG 4 of the 2030 Agenda was adopted at the UNESCO's 38th General Conference, which provides a blueprint for governments and partners to translate their commitments into action. The Framework adheres to the following fundamental principles:

- Education is a fundamental human right and an enabling right. To fulfil this right, countries must ensure universal and equal access to inclusive and equitable quality education and learning, which should be free and compulsory, leaving no one behind.

- Education is a public good, of which the state is the duty bearer.
- Gender equality is inextricably linked to the right to education for all.

3. Challenges for Education 2030 Agenda

Seven years into the implementation of the Education 2030 Agenda, countries around the world have taken efforts to advance quality learning, inclusion, gender equality, skills and competencies, lifelong learning, teachers' professional development and other fields that are highly related to the realization of the SDG 4. However, challenges still remain on the way towards Education 2030.

(1) Big Number of Out-of-School Children

The number of out-of-school children is still big, with the majority of them in developing countries, and securing their right to education is facing great challenges. A report by UNESCO-UIS has indicated that the progress in education has stagnated in recent years, particularly since 2008. It was reported that around 264 million children, adolescents and youths stayed out of school in 2015. As Figure 1-2 shows, the proportion of out-of-school children has remained almost stagnant since 2008, with 9 percent for primary school, 16 percent for lower secondary school, and 37 percent for upper secondary school throughout 2000-2015.

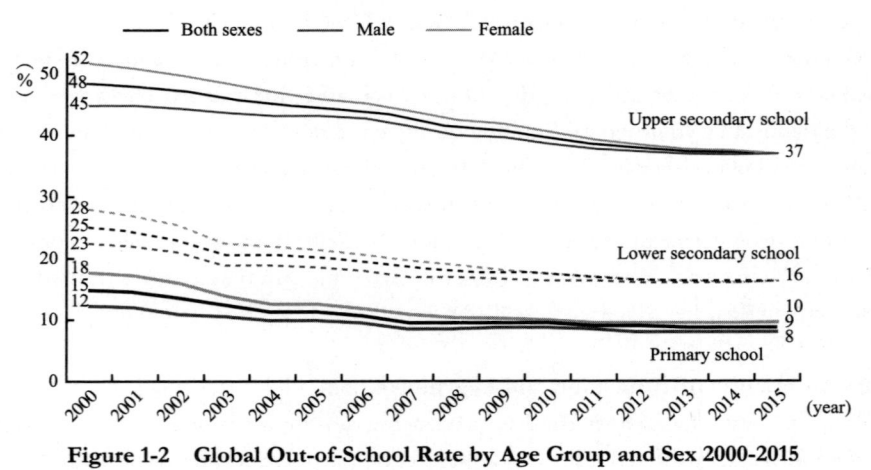

Figure 1-2   Global Out-of-School Rate by Age Group and Sex 2000-2015

Source: United Nations Educational, Scientific and Cultural Organization (UNESCO), *Reducing Global Poverty through Universal Primary and Secondary Education*, 2017, uis. unesco. org.

According to *UNESCO Global Education Monitoring Report 2020*, an estimated 258 million children, adolescents and youths were deprived of access to education due

to social status, family background, personal capabilities and other factors, and the outbreak of COVID-19 pandemic has further exacerbated educational exclusion. It is estimated that about 40% of low and middle-income countries worldwide failed to provide any support to vulnerable students when schools were closed due to the pandemic.

Moreover, students' attendance gap due to disparities in wealth of their families is large. For the 65 low- and middle-income countries, the average gap in attendance rate between the poorest and the richest 20 percent of households was 9 percentage points for primary school-age children, 13 percentage points for lower secondary school-age adolescents and 27 percentage points for upper secondary school-age youth. As the poorest are more likely to leave school earlier, wealth gaps are even wider in completion rates: 30 percentage points for primary, 45 percentage points for lower secondary and 40 percentage points for upper secondary.

The incidence of dropping-out of school is associated with the poverty or income level (see Table 1-2, Table 1-3 and Table 1-4). Data show that out-of-school rates are significantly higher in low-income countries than that in lower-middle-income, middle-income and high-income countries. For instance, the primary out-of-school rate is 19.1% in low-income countries against 9.7%, 4.3% and 2.8% in lower-middle-income, upper-middle-income and high-income countries respectively. The lower secondary out-of-school rate of low-income and high-income countries is 38.5% and 1.5%, and the upper secondary out-of-school rate is 62.3% and 7.1% respectively.

Gender, ethnicity, language, geographic location, migration status and other factors further widen the disparities in education, exacerbating the existing challenges faced by the disadvantaged group in acquiring quality education. In view of these trends, the High-Level Political Forum thus concluded that the world was not on track to achieve SDG4 and should these trends prevail over the next ten years, 220 million children and youth would remain excluded from school by 2030. If the youth fails to complete secondary education and achieve effective learning outcomes, it will impede the achievement of other SDGs.

(2) Low Quality of Education and Learning Crisis

High quality education is the foundation for development, growth, and poverty reduction. Low quality education is almost equal to no education at all and the less developed countries and regions are facing a learning crisis. As the International Committee of the Red Cross (ICRC) notes on its website, "access to education does not necessarily lead to quality education and learning outcomes; facilitating access to a school where learning outcomes are poor do the pupils and students little good and raises the possibility of their dropping-out."

Table 1-2   Out-of-School Rates and Numbers of Primary School Age by Income Level in 2015

	Out-of-school rates (%)				Out-of-school numbers (millions)		
	Both sexes	Male	Female	GPIA	Both sexes	Male	Female
Low-income countries	19.1	16.7	21.4	1.28	19.9	8.8	11.1
Lower-middle-income countries	9.7	9.0	10.6	1.18	31.0	14.8	16.2
Upper-middle-income countries	4.3	4.1	4.5	1.10	8.4	4.2	4.2
High-income countries	2.8	3.0	2.6	0.87	2.2	1.2	1.0
World	8.8	8.1	9.7	1.20	61.4	29.0	32.4

Data Source: United Nations Educational, Scientific and Cultural organization (UNESCO), *Education for All 2000-2015: Achievements and Challenges. EFA Global Monitoring Report 2015*, 2015, unesdoc.unesco.org.

Table 1-3   Out-of-School Rates and Numbers of Lower Secondary School Age by Income Level in 2015

	Out-of-school rates (%)				Out-of-school numbers (millions)		
	Both sexes	Male	Female	GPIA	Both sexes	Male	Female
Low-income countries	38.5	35.7	41.3	1.16	19.4	9.1	10.3
Lower-middle-income countries	19.2	20.4	17.9	0.87	33.7	18.6	15.1
Upper-middle-income countries	7.1	7.3	7.7	1.05	8.2	4.1	4.1
High-income countries	1.5	–	–	–	0.6	–	–
World	16.4	16.4	16.3	0.99	61.9	32.1	29.8

Data Source: United Nations Educational, Scientific and Cultural organization (UNESCO), *Education for All 2000-2015: Achievements and Challenges. EFA Global Monitoring Report 2015*, 2015, unesdoc.unesco.org.

Table 1-4   Out-of-School Rates and Numbers of Upper Secondary School Age by Income Level in 2015

	Out-of-school rates (%)				Out-of-school numbers (millions)		
	Both sexes	Male	Female	GPIA	Both sexes	Male	Female
Low-income countries	62.3	58.2	66.4	1.14	24.6	11.6	13.0
Lower-middle-income countries	46.8	45.6	48.0	1.05	91.0	46.1	44.9
Upper-middle-income countries	21.6	23.9	19.2	0.80	22.4	12.9	9.5
High-income countries	7.1	7.7	6.4	0.83	3.0	1.7	1.3
World	37.1	36.7	37.5	1.02	141.0	72.3	68.7

Data Source: United Nations Educational, Scientific and Cultural organization (UNESCO), *Education for All 2000-2015: Achievements and Challenges. EFA Global Monitoring Report 2015*, 2015, unesdoc.unesco.org.

In developing countries, many children cannot receive schooling for diversified reasons, and their enjoying education does not necessarily lead to good learning outcomes, which reflects the common problem of "educational poverty" (low level of education quality). Low quality education means poor quality of teachers, low teaching quality, insufficient infrastructure and teaching facilities, inappropriate education and teaching and assessment methods, as well as the unbalanced regional education development. It leads to the fact that hundreds of millions of young people leave schools without acquiring basic skills, let alone learning skills for life and employment.

Low-quality education and the learning crisis can also be detrimental to social prosperity. Data from UIS shows that more than 617 million children and adolescents of primary and lower secondary school age—more than 55 percent of the global total—have not achieved the minimum levels in reading and mathematics in 2015. This is most common in sub-Saharan Africa, followed by Central and Southern Asia (see Figure 1-3).

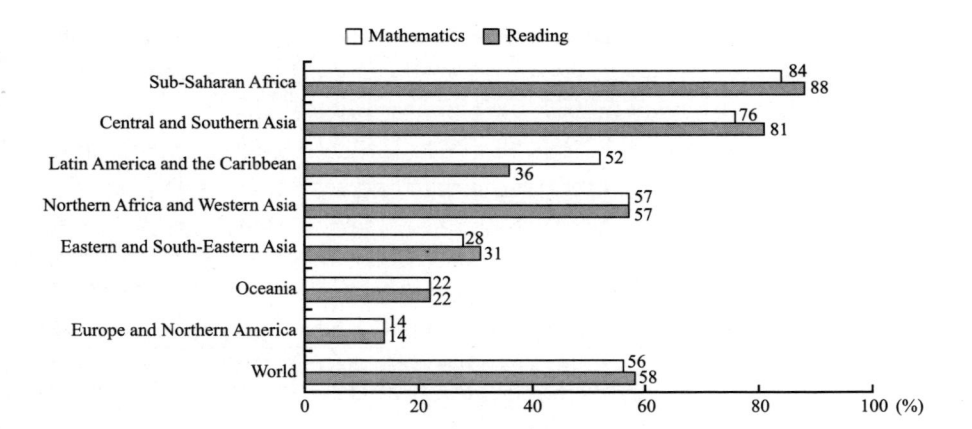

Figure 1-3   Percentage of Children and Adolescents Who Do Not Meet Minimum Passing Levels

Data source: United Nations, *Report of the Secretary-General on SDG Progress Special Edition*, 2019, sustainabledevelopment.un.org.

The results are similar to those of the international assessments. The PISA for Development (PISA-D)[1], an international programme that examines student performance in low- and middle-income countries, also reported low learning levels in 2018. The test involved 15-year-old students who are in school. Although only 7 countries participated in PISA-D, it revealed that only 12% of children tested met the minimum levels for math, and 23% for reading. This is sharply against the 77% and 80% in the OECD (Organization for Economic Co-operation and Development) countries for the two subjects respectively.

Children's failure to achieve minimum levels is a global learning crisis. The World Bank has introduced the concept of "learning poverty" to highlight the rising phenomenon of children not learning. The term in particular refers to the inability to read and understand a simple text by age 10. World Bank argues that just as income poverty excludes people from economic, social, and political opportunities, a lack of basic reading skills or learning poverty also prevents people from living a productive and fulfilling life in the modern world. Poor quality education and learning crisis would not only lead to a person's ability to shake off poverty but also impede economic prosperity. Therefore, in order to reduce and eradicate poverty, the challenges of "educational poverty" and the learning crisis must be solved.

---

[1]   Launched in 2013 by the OECD and a number of partners, the PISA for Development (PISA-D) initiative aims to facilitate the participation of low and middle-income countries in PISA assessment. It uses the same scales as the main PISA assessment but assessment instruments are particularly designed to make them relevant for the contexts of middle-and low-income countries.

(3) Shortage of Qualified Teachers in Underdeveloped Areas

Teachers are one of the key factors affecting the development of education in poverty-stricken areas. They are also key to teaching quality and play a pivotal role in helping students acquire knowledge and skills. However, in many underdeveloped regions around the world, especially those in extreme poverty, many students are short of basic literacy or numeracy skills even when they complete their education, and this can be attributed to a lack of trained and qualified teachers.

The shortage of qualified teachers is a global challenge, and it is especially serious in sub-Saharan Africa. According to UIS, 70% of sub-Saharan African countries face a severe shortage of teachers, even up to 90% at the secondary education level; at the primary level, the average pupil-teacher ratio is 42:1, and in some countries, it is higher than 60:1. In 2020, there was a shortfall of 9 million qualified teachers in secondary and primary education in sub-Saharan Africa and 32 million worldwide. It is estimated that the number will reach 17 million and 69 million respectively by 2030.

Addressing the deficiency of qualified teachers requires a comprehensive policy covering all aspects concerning teachers, including preparation and training, recruitment and deployment, social status, working conditions and salary. In many countries that lack teachers, teacher training institutions do not have the capacity to train enough qualified teachers, and a large number of institutions encounter a temporary closure due to the COVID-19 pandemic. Hence the training of high-quality teachers is severely hampered, which adds more challenges to the underdeveloped areas.

(4) Insufficient Investments in Education in Poverty Areas

It is estimated that, to achieve the SDG4, global spending on education must rise annually from $1.2 trillion per year to $3 trillion by 2030. And the investment of domestic resources is crucial. *The Global Education Monitoring Report 2016 (GEMR)* themed on "Education for People and Planet: Creating Sustainable Futures for All" indicated that the education spending in many countries, especially in less developed countries, fell far below the target of 4% of GDP or over 15% of total public spending, as recommended by the Education 2030 Action Framework. Relevant plans or strategies cannot be implemented without adequate financial input. The serious funding gap was an important reason why EFA did not make enough progress between 2000 and 2015.

(5) Violation of Vulnerable People's Right to Education

People with disabilities often fall into income poverty as they lack survival skills caused by their inadequate education and poor working ability. People with disabilities and income poverty are confronting the biggest challenges of getting out of poverty

and have the highest rate of returning to poverty. Guaranteeing their right to education can help them quickly acquire the survival, productivity and life skills that meet their needs. How to provide targeted assistance to people with disabilities so that they can better integrate into society and live a dignified life is a challenge for poverty reduction globally.

(6) Education Disrupted by the Covid-19 Pandemic

The outbreak of COVID-19 pandemic has exacerbated the challenges in education in low and middle-income countries, affecting around 1.9 billion learners in more than 190 countries. It is estimated that some 94% of the world's student population was impacted because of the closure of schools and educational institutions, and it was as high as 99% in low and lower-middle-income countries. Countries that suffer the worst recession would cut public expenses, including those on education. Learning losses, both short-term and long-term are estimated to be severe, affecting learners from poor households, whose educational opportunities have been seriously disrupted. A UN estimate suggests that some 24 million children and youths from pre-primary to tertiary will drop out of school permanently. Without necessary and appropriate actions to mitigate disruptions caused by the pandemic, the world will see a generational catastrophe due to the global failure to achieve SDG4 targets.

Achieving SDG1 of the 2030 Agenda for Sustainable Development—to eradicate poverty worldwide—is a challenge for all governments. Facts and researches have indicated that poverty remains a constant obstacle to realizing the 2030 educational goal and education plays a key role for poverty reduction through enhancing individuals' knowledge, skills and competence. Therefore, there needs coordinated implementation of SDG 1 and SDG 4, by mobilizing more public resources to increase government investment, protecting the right to education and improving the quality of education. This is fundamental and overarching to effectively promote poverty reduction, and finally achieve the goals of the 2030 Agenda.

Education at all levels should be advanced. Pre-school education, higher education, vocational education, adult education, special education and education for sustainable development are all important for poverty reduction. For example, vocational education and skill training can help people acquire skills, which can assist their families getting rid of poverty through employment. Through continuing and adult education, people's production and life skills can be improved. The purpose of special education is to empower children with disabilities through acquiring relevant skills, which will help them better integrate into society and live a fulfilling life. Finally, concerted efforts joined by multiple partners is the foundation for effective poverty alleviation through education.

Poverty has multi-dimensional causes and education needs a multi-stakeholder approach. Therefore, effective implementation of the global agenda, which is broad, interconnected and integrated, requires coordination and joint efforts from government, society and family. One of the lessons learned from the implementation of the MDGs and EFA, coordinated actions from different sectors, different government branches and layers of the government at the national and local levels are needed to promote poverty alleviation through education and the implementation of development goals.

Chapter II
China's Targeted Poverty Alleviation through Education: Actions and Results

China is the largest developing country in the world and has long been beset by poverty due to its massive population, weak economic foundation and unbalanced development. It is the persistent aspiration for the Chinese nation and its people to get rid of poverty and build a moderately prosperous society in all respects.

I. China's Targeted Fight against Poverty

The People's Republic of China (PRC), facing extreme poverty and collapsing businesses after its founding in 1949, carried out large-scale socialist construction to build an independent and relatively wholistic industrial system and national economic system. China actively advanced the social undertaking, especially in the field of education, and carried out a wide range of campaigns to eradicate illiteracy, which has built a solid foundation for poverty alleviation and improving the quality of living for all.

1978 marks a new era as China launched the policy of reform and opening up. Enlightened by the new policy, China has implemented large-scale, planned and organized programmes for poverty alleviation and development, with the poverty reduction process greatly accelerated and many people lifted out of poverty. According to China's current poverty standard, the number of rural population living in poverty still exceeded 770 million in 1978, with the incidence of rural poverty reached 97.5%. With over 30 years of efforts, rural population in poverty decreased to 98.99 million and poverty incidence decreased to 10.2% by 2012 (see Figure 2-1).

This shows significant achievements in the cause of poverty reduction, which was

well recognized by the international community. In October 2005, Paul Wolfowitz, then-president of the World Bank, visited China and said: "In the span of a few decades, East Asia has experienced the greatest increase in wealth for the largest number of people in the shortest time in the history of mankind. It is an incredible fact, and of course, without this growth in China, it wouldn't have happened."[①]

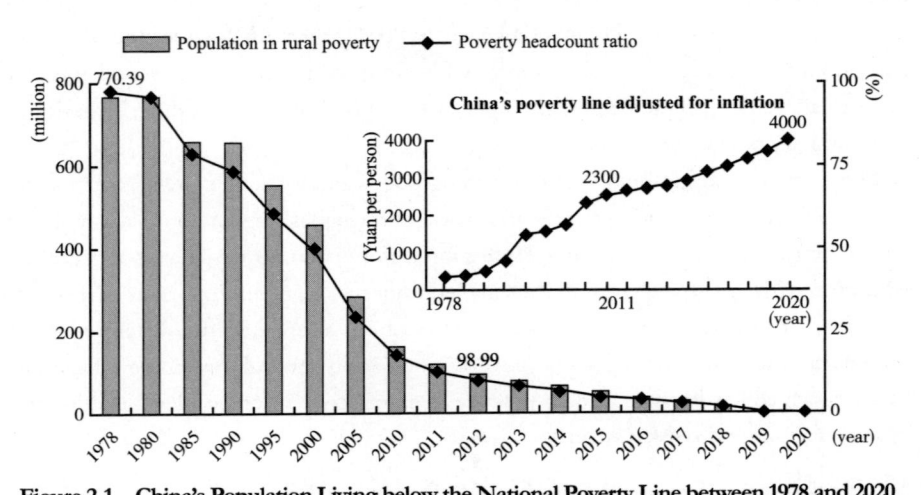

Figure 2-1   China's Population Living below the National Poverty Line between 1978 and 2020

Source: " Targeted Poverty Relief: China's Way to Achieve Prosperity," CGTN, 2021, news.cgtn.com.

In 2012, the remaining 98.99 million poverty population in China were located across 832 poverty-stricken counties, among which 50.67 million lived in Liupan Mountain Area, Qinba Mountain Area, Wuling Mountain Area, Wumeng Mountain Area, Yunnan-Guizhou-Guangxi Rocky Desertification Area, West Yunnan Border Mountain Area, the South Great Khingan Mountains Area, Yanshan-Taihang Mountain Area, Lüliang Mountain Area, Dabie Mountain Area, Luoxiao Mountain Area, Tibet, and part of Qinghai, Sichuan, Yunan and Gansu and four regions in Southern Xinjiang. These areas are called 14 contiguous impoverished areas.

The above poverty areas suffer from stagnated development of infrastructure and social undertaking, fragile ecological environment, frequent natural disasters, and inconvenient traffic. These areas also share the characteristics of having complex causes of deep poverty, weak self-development capacity and high rates of relapse to poverty. Conventional economic growth is unable to effectively drive development in these regions, and conventional approaches for poverty alleviation are difficult

---

① "World Bank President to Visit China," 2022, www.china.org.cn.

to produce fruitful outcomes, making the mission of poverty alleviation extremely arduous. In addition, the longer this mission is left behind, the higher the cost and more difficult it becomes.

Facing the poorest population and the most difficult task, Chinese government places the targeted fight against poverty top on its priorities in state governance and considers ending extreme poverty as the bottom-line task of building China into a moderately prosperous society in all respects in 2021. Since 2012, under the leadership and advocacy of President Xi Jinping, Chinese government has initiated targeted poverty alleviation, implemented the fight against poverty, and introduced a series of extraordinary policies and actions.

These initiatives have built well-functioning policy and working systems, formulating a Chinese pathway towards poverty alleviation and establishing an anti-poverty theory with Chinese characteristics. One of the most important approaches is to combine education with poverty alleviation and take education as both an important part of and a means for poverty alleviation. This approach both supported the development of the education sector, and aided the poverty population through providing educational services, which has been proved by practice as an effective means to develop education in poor regions and reduce poverty.

1. Proposing a Targeted Strategy for Poverty Alleviation

At the end of 2012, shortly after the Eighteenth National Congress of the Communist Party of China, President Xi stressed that "to achieve initial prosperity in the countryside, it is essential to raise rural living standards and particularly those of impoverished villagers" and promised that "no single poor area or single poor person should be left behind in achieving this goal." In 2013, during his inspection visit to impoverished area in Xiangxi, Hunan Province, President Xi proposed for the first time the idea of "giving differentiated guidance for targeted poverty alleviation in line with local conditions by seeking truth from facts". This marks China's transition from development-driven poverty alleviation to targeted poverty alleviation.

In June 2015, President Xi during his visit to Guizhou Province further proposed "Targeted Efforts in Six Aspects", which refers to identifying the poor accurately, arranging targeted programmes, utilizing the funds efficiently, taking household-tailored measures, assigning government officials to be based in villages, and valuing the effectiveness. To implement this new strategy, China has established a poverty alleviation information system, identifying the poorest people and establishing portfolio for each. This system aims to identify "whom to help" and clarify "who offers help" by strengthening leadership and the team building. The issue of "how to help" is solved

through tailored measures. Finally, strict criteria were adopted to decide when and how to deregister those who have been lifted out of poverty, and follow-up monitoring is conducted to ensure that people stay out of poverty.

Targeted poverty alleviation and its targeted strategies are a holistic approach covering aid, poverty alleviation and post-poverty development. This reflects core ideas of poverty alleviation and it is China's strongest weapon in its final battle to secure the victory against poverty, and it is also a breakthrough in the theory and practice of poverty alleviation.

2. Proposing and Implementing the Fight against Poverty

At the end of 2015, President Xi attended the Working Conference on National Poverty Alleviation and Development, and stressed that "we should be determined, target oriented and work hard towards the goal", launching the final attack on extreme poverty. In order to ensure that all impoverished areas and poor people are completely lifted out of poverty and achieve moderate prosperity in all respects, the central government issued the *"Decision to Win the Battle Against Poverty"*. The overarching goal of the initiative was that "by 2020, the rural poor have no worries about food, clothing; and compulsory education, basic medical care and housing safety are guaranteed." Figure 2-2 shows five measures for poverty alleviation.

Furthermore, the new policy aims to ensure the growth rate of farmers' per capita disposable income in poverty-stricken areas is higher than the national average; and the quality of basic public services is close to the national average. It aspires that by then, all rural poor people, under China's current standards, will be lifted out of poverty; all poor counties will be removed from the poverty list. This requires governments at all levels to implement series of development projects on expanding production, promoting relocated immigration, offering ecological compensation, developing education, and providing social security under the guidance of the "Targeted Efforts in Six Aspects".

In 2017, the 19th National Congress of the Communist Party of China made a comprehensive plan for targeted poverty eradication, which reinforced the goal of building a moderately prosperous society in all respects and gathered the force for the cause of poverty alleviation. In 2018, the central government issued the *"Three-Year Guideline on Winning the Battle Against Poverty"*, further enhanced the efforts and its effectives. In 2020, in order to mitigate the disruptions caused by COVID-19 pandemic, the central government re-allocated and re-mobilised resources for the cause of poverty reduction, and encouraged more determination and efforts to accelerate the progress towards the ultimate goal.

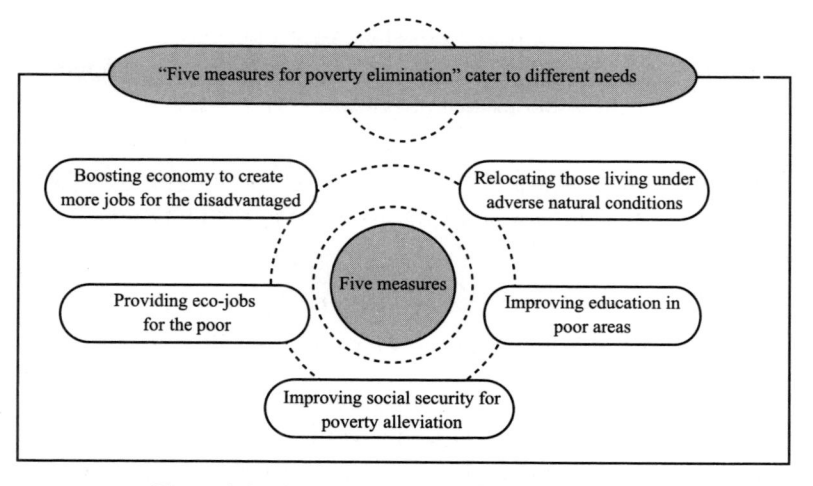

Figure 2-2   Five Measures for Poverty Alleviation

This cause has won the strong support from President Xi. During the 8 years from 2012 to 2020, President Xi chaired seven national seminars on poverty alleviation, made over 50 survey trips, covering all the 14 contiguous poverty areas. He reviewed the annual reports on poverty alleviation for 5 consecutive years; attended important events or issued directives on the National Poverty Alleviation Day for 7 consecutive years; and included a message on the fight against extreme poverty in his New Year address for 7 consecutive years. In addition, he was committed to discussing the issue of poverty reduction with representative of the "Two Sessions" [①]; answering letters to encourage the grassroots officials and community leaders to engage in the great cause.

China upholds the coordinated leadership of the central government on the fight against poverty, with it included in the *Five-Sphere Integrated Development Plan*, which aims to accelerate the improvement in economy, politics, culture, social undertaking, and ecological civilization. The fight against poverty is also a part of the *Four-pronged Comprehensive Strategy*, which refers to China's comprehensive strategic plan to: build a moderately prosperous society in all respects; further advance the reform; enhance the national governance following the rule of law; strengthening the Party's self-governance.

These plans ensure the establishment of a poverty eradication management system with the central government acting as the core leadership and coordinator, provincial governments taking overall responsibility, and city and county governments overseeing implementation. Meanwhile, a working mechanism is built, adopting tailored measures

---

① "Two sessions" refers to the annual sessions of the National People's Congress and the Chinese Political Consultative Conference (NPC & CPPCC).

for the targeted areas, villages and households; an accountability system formulated, with the heads of 5-layers (provincial, city/prefecture, county, township, village) of administrations leading the work. Furthermore, working teams and officials were assigned to provide support on site. Since 2012, a total of 255,000 working teams and more than 3 million officials had been dispatched to be based in the villages, fighting on the front line of poverty alleviation alongside nearly 2 million township officials and millions of village heads.

China mobilizes the forces of all people and the society to fight against poverty to form a paradigm of poverty alleviation with government-sponsored projects, sector-specific programmes, and corporate and societal assistance supplementing each other. It is a social poverty alleviation framework with the full participation of multiple players from different regions, sectors, departments and businesses. China has strengthened collaboration and paired-up assistance between the eastern and western regions at provincial, city and county levels. Assistance for poverty alleviation has been directed to designated targets.

The Communist Party and government departments, people's organizations, state-owned enterprises and public institutions, and the military have aided poor counties or villages. Various industries have been encouraged to offer assistance through professional and technological support, improving education, cultural undertakings and healthcare, and boosting consumption. Private enterprises, social organisations, and individual citizens have actively participated in development-driven poverty alleviation and initiated public benefit activities for poverty alleviation. The poor population is motivated to be active, proactive, creative, and to rely on their own power to escape from poverty.

Government investment is the major financial source and plays a leading role in financing the fight against poverty. Nearly RMB 1.6 trillion of fiscal funds has been invested into the cause of poverty alleviation over the past eight years from central, provincial, city and county levels, of which RMB 660.1 billion comes from the central government. Over RMB 710 billion for microcredit, RMB 668.8 billion for re-loan, and RMB 9.2 trillion of targeted financial loans for poverty alleviation were offered. In addition, nine provinces and cities from the East invested over RMB 100.5 billion of financial aid and social support to its paired-up areas in the West for poverty alleviation, and enterprises from the East accumulatively invested one trillion yuan to their poverty alleviation collaboration regions.

China adopts refined management for the targeted poverty alleviation by accurately allocating resources, conducting targeted assistance to the poor population and establishing national registration system for households living under the poverty line. This ensures that the resources for poverty alleviation are used to support the targeted

population and the poor regions. China takes the effective approach to eradicate poverty through improving the conditions and capacity for development, aiming to transition from the poverty reduction model of "giving fish" to "teaching them to fish". China also implements strict assessment and evaluation, addresses any corruption and misconduct in poverty alleviation with rigor, and establishes a comprehensive monitoring system against formalism and bureaucracy, to ensure poverty reduction really happens and benefits people in need.

By the end of 2020, while effectively responding to the disruptions caused by COVID-19 pandemic, China had achieved a complete victory in the fight against poverty. All the 98.99 million rural residents living below the current poverty line in China had been lifted out of poverty. In the past eight years (2012-2020), over 10 million people rose and remained above the poverty line every year, which is equivalent to the population of a medium-sized country. The income level of the poverty-stricken population has increased significantly, and the goal "by 2020, the rural poor have no worries about food, clothing, and compulsory education, basic medical care and housing safety are guaranteed" has been achieved, with safe drinking water also secured.

Millions of children from impoverished households have enjoyed better access to quality education, and they do not need to travel by "climbing hills and crossing rivers" to school, as they can board on campus and have meals in the school canteens. All the 832 counties and 128,000 villages classified as poor had been lifted out of poverty. The issue of absolute poverty, which had plagued the Chinese nation for thousands of years, has been solved, which is an outstanding and historically landmark achievement.

China also made a significant contribution to global poverty reduction. Since 1978, 770 million of China's rural population living below the current poverty line have been lifted out of poverty. Against the World Bank's international poverty line, the number of people out of poverty in China accounts for more than 70 percent of the world's total during this period. China realised its poverty reduction goal 10 years ahead of the target year of the UN 2030 Agenda for Sustainable Development, especially when the global poverty is still severe and the gap between the rich and the poor in some countries is widening. Meanwhile, China has actively participated in international cooperation on poverty alleviation, acted as an advocate for, facilitator of and contributor to the international cause of poverty alleviation, and worked with other countries to build a global community of shared future that is free from poverty and pursues common prosperity for humankind.

The *National Human Development Report 2019: China* issued by the United Nations Development Programme in 2019 introduced P.R.China's extraordinary development since its founding, especially that after the reform and opening up in 1978. China's human development index (HDI) rose from 0.410 in 1978 to 0.752 in 2017. With this

achievement, China is recognised as the only country that has leaped from the low human development group to the high. This report points out that China has now become a major economy and a source of international investment and aid. From 2000 to 2018, the income of the bottom 40% people had grown at a staggering rate of 263%, which has contributed to the rapid reduction of extreme poverty. United Nations officials pointed out that targeted poverty alleviation is an important practice from China, achieving its overarching goal through tailored measures in response to the needs of each village and household. "The Chinese experience provides an important reference for the global poverty reduction work".

Ⅱ. Major Actions of Education for Targeted Poverty Alleviation in China

Since 2012, the Chinese central government has established a refined management system[①] for poverty alleviation within and outside the education system, covering multi-level administrations and multi- institutions. Relevant mechanisms and policies have been formulated to ensure the strategies are implemented and the goals can be achieved.

1. A Clear Responsibility System

The Ministry of Education (MoE) of China established a leading group to coordinate the promotion of poverty alleviation in education. A responsibility system has been established, with different layers of education administrations taking different responsibilities and roles to coordinate and implement relevant policies and practices. In addition, the MoE signed a *"Memorandum of Cooperation in Winning the Tough Battle for Poverty Alleviation"* with the 13 provincial governments with challenging poverty alleviation tasks, clarifying the responsibilities of the Ministry and each province, and making joint efforts to overcome difficulties.

To leverage the technological and talent advantages of higher education institutions

---

① China's governmental system consists of five levels: central government, provincial government, prefectural and municipal government, county government, and township government, with compulsory education under the leadership of the State Council, coordinated and implemented by the provincial governments, autonomous regions, and municipalities directly under the central government and managed by the people's governments at the county level. The central departments involved in education include the Ministry of Education, the Development and Reform Commission, the Ministry of Finance, the Ministry of Human Resources and Social Security, the Ministry of Science and Technology.

(HEIs), since 2012, MoE has taken the lead in organising universities under the direct administration of the central government and universities jointly established by ministries and provinces to undertake paired-up assistance for poverty alleviation, with written pledges signed, performance and effectiveness regularly monitored and assessed. MoE effectively fulfilled its paired-up support to poverty alleviation in western Yunnan, through establishing a communication mechanism with 26 ministries and a ministerial-provincial consultation mechanism with Yunnan Province, and mobilizing multiple resources.

During the COVID-19 Pandemic, MoE has effectively coordinated the work to mitigate the disruptions and accelerate the cause of poverty reduction in and through education, adopting video conferences, information technology and other methods to promote paired-up assistance on poverty alleviation between western Yunnan and MoE affiliated universities. Meanwhile, it actively supported the programmes and projects on poverty reduction in the contiguous poverty areas initiated by other ministries and cooperated with them to carry out poverty alleviation through education.

2. A Targeted and Problem-Oriented Working Mechanism

In response to the severe dropout problem in poor areas, the government carried out an initiative to address school dropout problem and ensure attendance. It has established comparison and verification mechanism to identify each poor student, through triangulation of the data from the national information system for primary and secondary students, national population information database, and targeted households' database for poverty reduction. A "dropout control and prevention management platform" was created to accurately identify each dropout due to poverty and a checklist is developed to ensure their re-entry into schools.

Furthermore, the local governments established a multi-departmental and multi-agency prevention and control mechanism to ensure that dropout children and adolescents in poverty-stricken areas can return to school. In accordance with the principle of "one person, one solution", each drop-out would have the option of continuing their education through various measures, no matter why they discontinue their education (haven't attended school; have learning difficulties; be tired of schooling; or have dropped out due to family reasons, physical disability or other reasons). They can either return to classrooms, attend secondary vocational colleges, or receive education through home tutoring and/or other means. Appropriate arrangements have been adopted to ensure that the learning needs of all drop-outs have been adequately addressed.

Considering the weak foundation and uneven development of compulsory education in poor areas, the central government has made efforts to support the improvement

of the disadvantaged schools by strengthening conditions and capacity. Starting with the infrastructure development, the government has focused on improving the schooling conditions, leveraging the national public service platform for educational resources to divert quality resources to poverty-stricken areas. As a result, the quality of education and teaching in impoverished rural areas in China has been significantly improved.

Regarding the lack of quality education resources and teachers, and inadequate structure of the teaching force in poor areas, the government continues to implement "Special Post Plan" [①] and launched the Teacher Chapter Talents Programme Supporting "Three Regions"[②]. Under these schemes, quality teachers and educational personnel are deployed to teach in schools in remote poor areas and ethnic group regions. This has effectively addressed the issue of insufficient quality teachers in poor areas and contributed to the improvement of teaching quality and management capacity of local schools. Meanwhile, the "National Training Programme" for primary, and secondary, and kindergarten teachers has been implemented to provide large-scale in-service training for rural teachers in central and western China, with a total investment of more than RMB 20 billion, training teachers more than 17 million times, covering all rural teachers in poor areas, and significantly enhancing the professional development of rural teachers.

To support children in poverty, the central government has established a student funding system that covers all education levels, both public and private schools, to reach all students facing financial difficulties. Further to expanding the targeted groups of funding and raising the funding standards, the "National Student Funding Information System" has been fully aligned with the information systems of the State Council's Poverty Alleviation Office, the Ministry of Civil Affairs and other departments, aiming for data comparisons. A five-layer student funding management mechanism covering the central government, provinces, cities, counties, and the school has been established,

---

① The "Special Post Plan" is a special policy for improving rural compulsory education in poverty-stricken areas in the central and western regions, implemented by the Central Government. Through open recruitment of college graduates to teach in rural schools below the county level in the central and western regions, the government aims to guide and encourage college graduates to engage in rural compulsory education, innovate the supply mechanism for rural school teachers, and gradually solve the problems of insufficient teacher resources and its unreasonable structure in rural schools, improve the overall quality of rural teachers, and promote balanced development of urban and rural education. Recruitment of special-post teachers reached 101,400 nationwide in 2020.

② "Three Regions" refers to: remote and poor areas, ethnic group area in the borderland and old revolutionary base areas in China.

which strongly supports the identification and targets financial aid to students in need and ensures no one drop-out due to financial difficulties.

It is worth noting that the Communist Party of China, as the ruling party, has advocated gender equality since its founding. China has established a legal system guaranteeing equality between men and women, including the Constitution, the Law on the Protection of Rights and Interests of Women, and the Law on Maternal and Infant Health Care. The labour participation rate of women in China is among the highest in the world. China has also achieved gender parity in terms of enrolment rates at all levels of education. The fight against poverty in education also follows the basic principle of gender equality. Both boys and girls must enjoy equal education opportunities under the framework of law and policies both on education and poverty alleviation to ensure equal rights to education.

3. A Multi-Level Unified and Coordinated Policy System

The Chinese central government has issued a series of guiding policy documents, which highlights the strategies and implementation modalities of education for poverty alleviation for various government departments at all levels. These policies range from overarching policies to drop-outs control, school conditions improvement, rural teachers, and finance of education for poverty reduction.

(1) Overarching and General Policies
- *Guidelines on Implementing Poverty Alleviation Project through Education* , as the first guiding document for poverty alleviation in the education sector, 2013.
- *Thirteenth Five-Year Plan for Poverty Alleviation by Education* (2016-2020) , 2016.
- *Implementation Plan for Educational Poverty Alleviation in Deep Poverty Areas (2018-2020)*, 2017.
- *General Plan on Securing the Final Victory of the Poverty Alleviation through Education*, 2020.

(2) Drop-Outs Control
- *Notice on Further Strengthening the Control of Dropouts and Schooling Guarantee to Consolidate Compulsory Education*.
- *Guidelines on Further Strengthening the Work of Controlling Dropout and Improving the Guaranteed and Long-term Mechanism for the Completion of Compulsory Education*.

(3) School Conditions Improvement
- *Guidance for Comprehensively Improving the Basic Conditions for Running Schools in Compulsory Education in Poverty-stricken Areas*.

- *Guidance for Effectively Improving the Weak Links of Compulsory Education and Capability Building.*
- *Implementation Plan for Building an Effective Mechanism to Use ICTs to Expand the Coverage of High-Quality Educational Resources.*
- *Action Plan for Informatization of Education 2.0.*

(4) Rural Teachers

- *Rural Teacher Support Plan (2015-2020).*
- *Guidelines on Strengthening the Construction of Rural Teachers in the New Era*, guiding local governments, education authorities and higher education institutions, to build up a stronger teaching force for rural schools.

(5) Finance

- *Guidance on Further Adjusting and Optimizing the Structure and Improving the Effectiveness of the Use of Education Funds*, providing a mechanism to ensure fund support and optimized investment.
- *Guidelines on Further Strengthening the Management of Financial Investment and Reducing Poverty through Education in "three regions and three prefectures".*
- *Notice on Further Increasing Support for Poverty-stricken Areas and Promoting Completion of Compulsory Education.*

Meanwhile, the central government has issued a series of policy documents covering student funding, pre-school education, high school education, ethnic education, vocational education, preferential policy for enrolment, and employment assistance. Apart from these, local education departments have formulated and implemented the strategies, plans, and guidelines related to poverty alleviation through education in their provinces, prefectures and counties. All these have jointly formulated a policy system that helps push forward the cause of poverty alleviation through education.

To ensure the implementation of the policies at all levels, the central government has established a regular working mechanism that combines task assignment at the beginning of the year, promotion in the middle, and annual review at the end, while relying on various training sessions to improve institutional and personnel capacity to implement the policies. Furthermore, the Ministry of Education of China has commissioned independent evaluations since 2018 to understand the effectiveness and impacts of key projects, such as the nutrition improvement plan for rural compulsory education and the overall improvement of fundamental conditions for running compulsory education schools in poverty-stricken areas. This has improved the overall

capacity of identifying problems during implementation, adjusting policies, and ensuring the effectiveness.

4. Multi-Source of Funding, Talents and Intelligence

Since 2012, the central government has adjusted several national policies on financial transfer for education development, following the fiscal and taxation system reforms and the poverty alleviation task to guarantee the development of compulsory education. The fiscal policy system has been continuously enhanced for supporting poverty alleviation through education. For example, the government has established a unified urban and rural compulsory education financing mechanism that prioritizes rural areas, adopting the same benchmark standard for public expenditure per student in urban and rural areas. The MoE has also established a team of outstanding young cadres and university leaders to be assigned to targeted areas for poverty alleviation tasks. Since 2012, more than 3 million cadres have been deployed to work in the frontline of anti-poverty work in poor areas of China.

The MoE is increasing its support for human resource development in poverty-stricken areas. Relying on higher education institutions, a series of education and training projects have been planned and implemented. Through training programmes for educational administration staff, and professionals and technicians, a large number of outstanding cadres and talents have been cultivated for poverty alleviation.

In terms of intellectual input, higher education institutions in China continuously implement the scientific and technological innovation action plan for rural revitalization. Relying on the key laboratories of the state and MoE, major original innovations and key technological breakthroughs have been made in agricultural fields, such as genetic breeding and soil improvement, providing scientific and technological support for the development of industries in poverty-stricken areas. A variety of new methods designed to promote agricultural technology have continuously transformed the innovative research outcomes of universities into new driving forces for industrial development towards poverty alleviation.

5. Responsive and Individualized Assistance from Higher Education Institutions

Since China's HEIs started their targeted assistance to poverty alleviation, they have been closely working with impoverished counties to adopt poverty alleviation measures responsive to local conditions, by leveraging their advantages. The assistance is grounded in local realities, achieving major breakthroughs and overall improvement. In terms of poverty alleviation through education, attempts were made to ensure alignment between hardware construction and software upgrading. Assistance was

provided in the form of donations, teacher and student deployment to targeted schools, teacher training, resource sharing, student funding, and paired care. These common actions of HEIs have been critical in helping poverty-stricken areas to effectively overcome difficulties of weak foundation, shortage of teachers, and insufficient resources for education development. This has led to quality improvement in teaching and learning in poverty-stricken counties.

HEIs play an important role in supporting industry-driven poverty alleviation, taking advantage of their knowledge and skills in various disciplines, in particular science and technology, intelligence, and human resources. In so doing, HEIs have explored to formulate industrial plans, introduce professional forces, commercialize scientific and research findings, develop multi-functional agriculture and new forms of agriculture, and invite and promote investment. These actions have helped improve the variety, quality, and branding of agricultural products in poverty-stricken areas. The integrated development of rural primary, secondary and tertiary industries has been accelerated. Many poor counties and villages have developed their first collective industries or enterprises, and continuously grew them stronger, functioning towards poverty reduction driven by industrial development.

In response to the entrenched problems faced by the impoverished areas, especially the deeply impoverished areas, HEIs in China have also put forward targeted solutions for poverty reduction. The Open University of China has continuously implemented the "One College Student Per Village" programme, to train technically skilled talents for rural areas. The university has set up county-level teaching sites in nearly a thousand counties in poverty-stricken areas in central and western China, which has effectively promoted the cultivation of human resources with practical agricultural skills, income-generation leaders and rural management personnel.

China's HEIs have always prioritized the employment of students from poverty-stricken areas and poor families when promoting graduates' employment. In 2020, the university graduates faced tough challenges in employment due to the Covid-19 pandemic. HEIs gave top priority to assisting the employment of registered poor graduates, through a range of measures including training for further education, setting up special posts, and organizing tailored job fairs. Those measures have helped provide hundreds of thousands of jobs and job information for students from poor areas. To this end, HEIs have introduced practices of "one portfolio for each poor student" and "one poor student, one solution" to implement targeted assistance. In the past five years, with the joint power of supportive policies, the employment rate of Chinese graduates with economic difficulties has registered 1 to 4 percentage points higher than the national average, effectively easing the economic difficulties of families in poverty-stricken areas.

Actions have also been taken to enhance vocational education in impoverished areas. The poverty-stricken counties with no secondary vocational schools have adopted following measures: building new schools, training students in nearby vocational schools, and opening vocational classes in general secondary schools, which have effectively bridged the gaps in vocational school enrolment in poverty-stricken areas. In counties with secondary vocational schools, following supportive measures have been introduced to accelerate the quality improvement of vocational education: improving school conditions, promoting school-enterprise cooperation, and strengthening guidance for employment.

6. Social Mobilization with Extensive Participation

The Central Government of China has implemented the *East-West Cooperation Action Plan for Vocational Education (2016-2020)*, to enhance the collaboration through financial assistance, skills training, and labour cooperation among vocational colleges and schools in the eastern and western regions. This has comprehensively upgraded the quality of vocational education in poverty-stricken areas and improved the employment of people in poor areas. In 2020, 27 vocational colleges offering undergraduate programmes have been mobilized to provide paired-up support to vocational schools in ethnic group areas.

HEIs from eastern China collaborate with their counterparts in the west for paired-up and targeted assistance, with 119 eastern high-ranking universities supporting 103 universities in central and western China, formulating a comprehensive, multi-level and all-around support system. The "Action Plan in MOOCs for the West" launched in 2018 has mobilized more than 10 online course platforms to open their high-quality courses and resources for areas, such as Xinjiang, Tibet, Qinghai, Shaanxi, Guizhou, etc., and promoted the sharing of teaching resources among universities in the east and west. This has helped improve the quality of teaching and learning in the western regions.

HEIs have mobilized high-quality resources to support teacher development in poor rural areas. Relying on its sub-program on training leading expert teachers and principals, the "National Training Program" has deployed teaching support teams consisted of principals, heads of teaching research, and backbone teachers, to offer "one-to-one" assistance to deep-poverty areas, such as Liangshan Prefecture and Nujiang Prefecture. This innovative teaching support model simultaneously drives the overall improvement of the school management, capacity building of backbone teachers, and teaching research teams in poverty-stricken areas.

Social resources have also been mobilized for the cause of poverty reduction through education. The central government coordinates with non-profit organizations, foundations, enterprises under the supervision of the central government, private

education institutions and other social forces for this purpose, mobilizing big investment to support students from families with financial difficulties and teachers, and to improve the school facilities and conditions in poverty-stricken areas. This has strongly underpinned the healthy development of students, the development of ICT in education and the improvement of digital education resources, in poverty-stricken areas.

7. Overall Monitoring and Inspection

The central government has prioritized poverty alleviation through education as the focus of the national inspection and supervisory visits. Actions would be taken based on feedback from the inspection: formulating implementing measures, working out the rectification plan, establishing the problem list, the task list and the responsibility-distribution list, translating the tasks into specific measures and setting a deadline for each task.

An Inspection Committee has been established at the national level and it coordinated relevant departments, to monitor and inspect the implementation of compulsory education policies. It required and pushed local governments to formulate remedy measures when there is an issue, to ensure everything is on track and each task can be completed in a timely manner. A special inspection was commissioned to investigate the implementation of "disadvantaged schools' improvement" project and strengthen the supervision of the funds for poverty alleviation through education, with a focus on the 20 "bottom-line requirements" of basic school-running conditions.

The government organized annual inspections for poverty alleviation, strengthened daily feedback and handling of issues related to poverty alleviation, and ensured that various educational poverty alleviation policies at all levels were fully implemented and achieved positive results.

8. Performance Review and Evaluation

Since 2016, the central government has gradually developed an evaluation system, to review the effectiveness of poverty alleviation actions by governments at all levels, cooperation between the east and the west, and the effectiveness of national agencies paired-up support for poverty alleviation. The format includes inter-provincial comparison and assessment by a special working group, independent evaluation, and the cost-effectiveness review of the funds used. The comprehensive and in-depth evaluations are critical in improving the efficiency of problem identification and problem-solving during the implementation, which has laid a solid foundation for consolidating the outcomes of poverty alleviation and the future rural revitalization.

III. Achievements of Education for Targeted Poverty Alleviation in China

From 2012 to 2020, China has made remarkable strides in education for targeted poverty reduction, obtaining the following achievements.

1. The Goal of Ensuring Compulsory Education for the Poor Fully Realized

In 2020, the retention rate of nine-year compulsory education in China was 95.2%. This rate in the poor counties reached 94.8%, enjoying an increase of nearly 5 percentage points from 2015 and it is very close to the national average. By the end of 2020, there was 145 million students enrolled in China's compulsory education, and the number of dropouts decreased from more than 600,000 to 682. Among them, over 200,000 dropouts from registered poor households have been cleared off, and the long-existing problem of poor students' drop-out has been resolved as a landmark in the history.

2. Comprehensive Changes in Schools from Poor Areas

School conditions in poor areas in China have been greatly improved. Schools as the best buildings in poor areas is the best demonstration for the results of poverty elimination. Since 2013, 760 poor counties have passed the national evaluation and achieved the goal of basically balanced development of compulsory education within the counties, and 99.8% of compulsory education schools (including teaching points) nationwide have met the basic requirements for school running conditions. In addition, the Internet access rate of primary and secondary schools (including teaching points) nationwide has increased from 25% in 2012 to 100%, and the proportion of schools equipped with multimedia classrooms has increased from 48% to 95.3%.

The overall quality of the rural teaching force has been improved. As a result of a range of projects under the framework of poverty alleviation to build a stronger teaching force, China's schools in poor areas are now staffed with teachers who are "retainable and teach well". The "Special Post Project" has recruited 950,000 teachers for rural schools since its implementation, and 40,000 graduates from government-funded teacher education programmes in local teachers' colleges have been deployed to rural schools, and the "National Training Programme" has trained more than 17 million teachers and principals in rural schools in the central and western regions. In addition, the living allowances for rural teachers in contiguous poverty-stricken areas benefited nearly 1.3 million teachers in 80,000 rural schools, and the governments have

assigned 190,000 quality teachers to support the development of teaching and learning in poverty-stricken and border areas. All these efforts have led to the improvement of the rural teaching force, and teachers with a bachelor's or higher degrees account for 51.6%.

3. Remarkable Achievements in Poverty Elimination through Developing Education

The impact of vocational education on poverty alleviation is rapidly emerging. Since 2012, more than 8 million students from poor families have received secondary and higher vocational education, among which over 1 million have been recruited from Western China through the East-West Cooperation Programme. Currently, 70% plus of those enrolled in vocational colleges and schools come from rural areas, with vocational education functioning as the catalyst for employment and poverty alleviation of the household. The vocational colleges and schools in the West have witnessed significant improvement in the following aspects: the overall educational quality, basic schooling conditions such as the training equipment, teachers' teaching for practical courses and their capacity of providing technical service, and students' practical skills in response to the needs of local economy and industry.

Higher education facilitates a wider path for the upwards mobility of poor students. Since 2012, around 5.14 million registered poor students have received higher education, and millions of poor families have the first generation of college students. Supportive policies have created more equitable education and employment opportunities for students in poverty-stricken areas. The targeted enrolment programme for poverty-stricken areas has enrolled 700,000 students from rural and poor areas. And over 70,000 undergraduate medical students have been trained for rural areas in central and western China, in average preparing two for each township hospital. In addition, the "One College Student Per Village" programme has trained a total of 600,000 village cadre and entrepreneurship leaders for the villages.

A sound financial assistance system for students builds a solid safety net for all. Led by the government and actively participated by schools and the society, the student subsidy has covered all stages of education from preschool to postgraduate. The system guarantees that no one will drop out of school due to his/her family's financial difficulties. The Nutrition Improvement Plan at the compulsory education stage has reached 136,300 schools in 1,643 counties, benefiting more than 40 million students every year. Data from monitoring shows that in 2019, the average height of boys and girls of each age group in the pilot areas of the Programme increased by 1.54 cm and 1.69 cm respectively, and the average weight increased by 1.06 kg and 1.18 kg respectively, which was higher than the national average growth of rural students.

Promoting standard Mandarin learning has helped enhance the effectiveness of poverty alleviation efforts. The ethnic youths in poverty-stricken areas have low capacity in communicating in Mandarin, which has posed additional challenges for them to get rid of poverty. Thus, the state launched a national common language popularization project to help them learn Mandarin while protecting their ethnic languages. Over 3.5 million rural teachers, young and middle-aged farmers and herdsmen have received relevant training.

Meanwhile, an App on "Language Learning for Poverty Alleviation" was developed and has accumulated 884,000 users, with the support of social partners. The idea of "poverty alleviation through capacity building on language competency" has been deeply rooted in the mind of the people. While promoting Mandarin to help alleviate poverty, the government also attaches great importance to protecting the languages and cultures of ethnic groups, safeguarding local intangible cultural heritage, and leveraging the power of education in this regard. Support to local people is provided to transform traditional culture into products and services, making it a means of getting rid of poverty and achieving prosperity. With these efforts, the willingness and capacity of people in poverty-stricken areas to communicate in Mandarin and to get rid of poverty have been significantly enhanced.

4. Multi-Layer and Multi-Stakeholder Strategy of Poverty Alleviation through Education Formulated

The cause of education for poverty alleviation has received strong support from administrative agencies, education institutions, enterprises, and social organizations at all levels. The special plans under the framework of China's poverty alleviation programme has recognized education as an important part of poverty alleviation. For this purpose, there has been a substantial increase of inputs in human, material and financial resources. Gradually, the modalities of inputs have transformed from donations, school construction and financial support for students to building teaching force and developing quality education resources. As a result, a comprehensive "three-in-one" campaign against poverty has been implemented, including special projects, industry-driven poverty alleviation, and social mobilisation-based poverty alleviation.

Within China's education system, the mechanism for coordinated development has been continuously improved. From 2016 to 2020, there was an investment of RMB 1.82 billion (according to incomplete statistics) for the East-West collaborative project on vocational education, with 683 vocational education programmes, over 1,000 training bases established, and 400,000 plus people trained. The assistance fund reached over RMB 130 billion for education development in Tibet, Xinjiang, and Qinghai, which are key targeted areas of national poverty alleviation and development. Some 119 eastern

high-level universities directly under the supervision of the MoE have increased their support for the development of 103 universities in the central and western regions, covering all the 12 western provinces and autonomous regions. The sub-programme on teachers of the "Three Regions" Talent Support Programme has assigned a total of 170,000 teachers to 1,272 counties to support local teaching, covering all the poor counties. All these actions have joined together to form a multi-layer and multi-stakeholder strategy for poverty alleviation through education, and it has become the pillar of eradicating extreme poverty and laid a solid foundation for the continuing fight against poverty and the rural revitalization.

Chapter III
Poverty Alleviation through Education: Case Studies from China

Over the years, China has made significant progress in poverty reduction through education, contributing to the achievement of the goals of the 2030 Agenda for Development, in particular Goal 4 (Education) and Goal 1 (Poverty Reduction). This chapter presents case studies from China that illustrate the practices and experiences in promoting education for targeted poverty alleviation in China, focusing on five core themes of Education 2030 Agenda that demonstrate cases from various contexts involving all levels and types of education. It is intended that lessons drawn from these case studies will provide a reference for the international community in implementing the 2030 Development Agenda, especially SDG 1 and SDG 4.

I. Ensuring the Universality, Inclusion and Equity in Education

1. No Drop-Out Because of Poverty

The main priority of poverty reduction through education in China is to help children from poor families to transform their future through equal access to quality basic education and increase opportunities to enter vocational schools or universities. In this regard, the Central Government issued the *Guidance on the Three-Year Action Plan for Poverty Elimination* in 2018, aiming to ensure that all children from poor families are able to go to school and receive a quality nine-year compulsory education. Accordingly, the government of China has established a financial aid system for economically disadvantaged students which supports students at all levels of education attending both public and private schools. Table 3-1 shows financial aid mechanisms in place in

education sector to ensure access for all.

The efforts have made a considerable impact towards the attainment of goals laid out in the Action Plan. A number of comprehensive financial aid mechanisms have been in place to ensure access for all at different levels of education. According to the *2020 Report on Financial Aid for Chinese Students*, the government has annually funded RMB 240.82 billion yuan serving a total of 146,175 million students.

Table 3-1   Financial Aid Mechanisms in Place in Education Sector to Ensure Access for All

Level of education	Policy / Mechanism/ Practice
Preschool education	• Government: Local governments shall provide financial assistance to children from poor households, orphans, and children with disabilities. • Kindergarten: Kindergartens allocate some funds from their income to subsidize the needy children. • Society: Social organizations, enterprises and individuals are encouraged to make contributions to the financial aid to needy children.
Compulsory education	• "Two Exemptions and One Subsidy" Policy: The government shall exempt tuition and miscellaneous fees for students receiving compulsory education both in urban and rural areas. Textbooks shall be distributed free of charge to all students, while living subsidy shall be provided to students from poor households. • Free meals shall be provided to rural students in areas that are identified as least developed, including contiguous areas with extreme poverty, key targeted counties of poverty alleviation at national and provincial level, ethnic minority counties, border counties, etc.
Secondary vocational education	• National scholarships, national student aid grants, and exemption of tuition fee. • Financial aid provided by local governments, schools, and the society.
General senior secondary education	• National student aid grants, exemption of tuition and miscellaneous fees for students who have registered poverty profiles. • Financial aid provided by local governments, schools, and the society.
Undergraduate education	• National scholarship, national student aid grants, and national student loans; • Tuition partly returned and loan repaid by government for university graduates who choose to work at the grassroots level; • National subsidy for students who choose to take military services; • Publicly funded teacher preparation programmes; • Work-study programme, school scholarship, hardship allowance, meal allowance, tuition waivers and "green channel" for freshmen.
Graduate education	• National scholarship, academic scholarship, national student aid grants, and national student loans; • Tuition partly returned and loan repaid by government for university graduates who choose to work at the grassroots level; • National subsidy for students who choose to join the military services; • University level scholarship and aid grants, and "green channel" for freshmen.

The following four cases demonstrate the way the various financial aid mechanisms and other support services were implemented, including the impact of these initiatives in ensuring the equitable and inclusive access to education for all in China.

(1) Case: Mechanism to Promote Equitable Access to Education: A Case of Ninghua County, Fujian Province

An innovative mechanism of targeted poverty alleviation through education has been introduced in Ninghua County, Fujian Province, with the following considerations:

- Ensuring the full participation of stakeholders, covering all levels of education, and enhancing the process management and providing holistic care to targeted students for learning, life and emotional well-being;
- Assisting students to build up confidence and motivation for transforming lives, improving learning, and addressing economic difficulties;
- Establishing profiles of students from poor families which continues throughout their education, including their higher education level, in order for individualized assistance, tracking and follow-up support.

BOX 3-1　Teachers Help to Improve Students' Confidence, Learning Achievements and the Financial Situation

At Ninghua No.1 High School, Zhang Yuanyuan is a senior grade-two student from a family registered for targeted poverty alleviation. When she was admitted to No.1 Middle School last year, she was worried about the financial difficulties she may encounter in her new schooling life. Upon entering the school campus, she didn't have to worry any longer and felt like being at home, because the school assigned three teachers to assist her in many aspects.

Mr. Wang Shenglian was one of the mentors. He told the reporter that when Zhang Yuanyuan came to study at senior middle school, she was comparatively slow in the learning of science subjects, especially mathematics and physics. He said, *I taught her some practical learning methods in science and took her to relevant teachers for tutoring. Soon she made quite an improvement in the learning of mathematics and physics.*

Meanwhile, Mr. Zhang Bin worked as a mentor for her psychological and emotional improvement. He encouraged Zhang Yuanyuan to make good use of the schooling time and study hard with self-confidence.

Mr. Zhang Weibin, another mentor, guided Zhang Yuanyuan in applying for tuition waiver and living subsidy, so that she could be devoted to study with all her heart.

With this help, both financially and mentally, Zhang Yuanyuan has become a happy and optimistic student who enjoys her progress in science learning. She expressed her satisfaction in the following manner:

The volunteer teachers' care and support have made me more confident. I learned effective methods and improved my learning steadily.

Like Zhang Yuanyuan, there were 97 students from families with financial difficulties who received all-around assistance from 2019 to 2020 in the school.

Source: Innovative Mechanism of An Education Management System Created for Poverty Alleviation-Ninghua Online, available at www.sohu.com.

Since 2016, the coverage of financial assistance has expanded reaching out to students attending institutions from pre-school to higher education. In pre-school education, the County Finance Bureau has provided subsidies to kids from the households registered under the implementation of targeted poverty reduction policy. In the 2018-2019 school year, a total of 140,800 yuan was provided benefiting 332 children. In higher education, the County has provided the targeted youth students with subsidies each school year (4,000 and 8,000 yuan respectively for diploma level and bachelor level students who study in the province, and 5,000 and 10,000 yuan respectively for diploma level and bachelor level students who study out of the province), with a total of 6.996 million yuan granted, reaching 972 students.

BOX 3-2   A Student Receiving National Aid Subsidy

Xiao Cao, who graduated from Ninghua No.1 High School in 2017 is from an impoverished household. When studying in high school, he was supported with tuition-free and a national aid subsidy of 3,000 Yuan per school year. After entering Peking University as a student in clinical medicine, he continued to get a subsidy of 10,000 Yuan per school year supported by the County Government.

Source: Innovative Mechanism of An Education Management System Created for Poverty Alleviation-Ninghua Online, available at www.sohu.com.

(2) Case: Balanced Urban-Rural Education Development through the "Two Exemptions and One Subsidy" Policy: A Case from Henan Province

The policy of "Two Exemptions and One Subsidy" has played an important role in the universalization of nine-year compulsory education in China. It requires that the Chinese governments at all levels exempt the miscellaneous fees, provide free schooling materials and boarding subsidies to primary and junior middle school students who are in financial difficulties. The policy has been part of the national-local co-sharing financial system, which has been implemented and continuously improved since 2006.

With continuous urbanization in China, a large number of rural surplus laborers move to the developed cities and provinces in the East as migrant workers. The protection of the right to education, especially compulsory education, for the children of migrant workers in the cities has become a priority for the Chinese government, which is the foundation for breaking the vicious circle of intergenerational transmission of poverty. In this context, in 2015, the government issued the *Notice of the State Council on Further Improving the Financial Mechanism for Ensuring Urban and Rural Compulsory Education Development*, unifying the urban- rural "Two Exemptions and One Subsidy" policy to ensure that the children of migrant workers are subsidized in urban compulsory education schools.

In addition, a national Education Management Information System (EMIS) for

students at primary and middle schools and a National Financial Aid Information System for students have been established to monitor the status of all students at compulsory education level. Through these systems, the education funds, including the funds for "Two Exemptions and One Subsidy" and the benchmark public expense per student can be redistributed for their resettlement and it is "portable with the mobility of students". The policy has made significant contributions to ensuring the right to education for nearly 14 million children of migrant workers who move to cities across China, reducing the financial burden of the masses and promoting balanced urban-rural education development. In 2020, the central government provided 169.59 billion yuan in subsidies for compulsory education in urban and rural areas, with an increase of 13.06 billion yuan or 8.3% over 2019.

In Henan, 13.3 billion yuan was allocated in 2016 for students' subsidy, benefiting around 1.03 million students from poor families. Starting from the spring semester of 2017, the policy of "Two Exemptions and One Subsidy" has been fully carried out for all students at compulsory education level both in urban and rural areas of the Province.

BOX 3-3   A Child of Migrant Worker Receiving Subsidy in an Urban School

Li Cheng is a fourth-grade student at a primary school in the New Zhengdong District of Zhengzhou Municipality, the capital city of Henan Province. His parents moved to work in Zhengzhou from the countryside of Zhumadian four years ago. They said:

Our household will be re-registered in the city quite soon, and our income is improving. We are happy to see that our children can still enjoy the benefits of the policy 'two exemptions and one subsidy' in Zhengzhou, which has relieved us from some financial burdens.

The 13.44 million Henan students who are receiving compulsory education, just like Li Cheng, can enjoy the same policy of "Two Exemptions and One Subsidy" starting from 2016, regardless whether they live in rural or urban areas.

Source: 13.3 billion for "Two Exemptions and One Subsidy" to Promote Balanced Development of Urban and Rural Education, available at hn.cnr.cn.

(3) Case: Integrated Financial Aid Policy System for Higher Education

With the implementation of the *Notice on Further Implementation of Financial Aid Policies for Higher Education Students* and the *Notice on Further Strengthening and Standardizing the Work of Identifying Students with Financial Difficulties in Colleges and Universities*, the scope of financial aid for higher education students in China has expanded significantly. Besides, by leveraging the power of big data, Chinese colleges and universities are able to provide more timely and targeted financial aid for students under difficult

circumstances.

The financial aid system of Chinese higher education supports students through numerous schemes such as "awards", "loans" and "grants", and they are often supplemented by "work-study", "subsidies" and "exemptions". It has formed a tripartite structure of financial support led by the government and complemented by the universities and the society. Additionally, it adopts a mixed model with the combination of universal financial support, hardship allowance, financial support as reward and compensatory financial support. It has introduced a range of aid modalities, including national scholarships, national inspirational scholarships, national aid grants, national student loans, free teacher preparation, work-study, green channels and so on.

BOX 3-4   "Green Channels" Benefitting Freshmen with Financial Difficulties

Ma Yu, who was a student in the School of Economics and Management at China Agricultural University, registered for the university in 2014 through a green channel. In the national student loan programme he chose a campus-based loan.

I borrowed a total of more than RMB 20,000 yuan, which will be repaid in ten years and it is interest-free during the four years of schooling. The process was very smooth and convenient, said Ma Yu.

Student loan is currently one of the key ways aiding students financially from poor families at the higher education level, and the state guarantees college students' right to education and allows them to complete their studies with a peace of mind through financial subsidies.

Source: Financial Aid Policies Allow the Poor Students to Go to College without Further Concern, available at xgb.shnu.edu.cn.

In 2020, a number of financial aid policies for general higher education students set up by the government, universities and society collectively subsidized a total of 36,782,200 students nationwide, with the total financial aid of RMB 124.379 billion. Of this amount, RMB 65.304 billion was allocated from the government revenue, accounting for 52.50% of the total. The banks approved RMB 37.812 billion of national student loans, accounting for 30.40% of the total. The financial aid funds expended by colleges and universities from their income is around RMB 18.362 billion, accounting for 14.76%. The funds donated by social organizations, enterprises and institutions and individuals (referred to as social funds) amounted to RMB 2.901 billion yuan, accounting for 2.33% of the total. These diverse subsidies favorably protect the right to education of students from poor families.

BOX 3-5   Integrated Financial Aid Removes Students' Concerns about Missing Education

I was able to get out of my predicament and enter university for further education, thanks to the supportive policies of the state. I will doubly cherish the hard-won learning opportunities and learn to repay the society.

Liu Xiaohua (a pseudonym), a student at Xi'an Medical College, burst into tears after receiving a grant of 2,000 yuan from the Bank of China's financial aid programme supporting students from national contiguous poor counties in early 2018. Liu Xiaohua, from Chunhua County, Xianyang City, Shaanxi Province, whose family is poor and father is suffering from a malignant tumor, was torn between "seeing the doctor" and "going to school" when she received her college admission letter in August 2017.

With the help of the Student Financial Assistance Centre of the County Education Bureau, Liu Xiaohua received RMB 5,500 through a loan, RMB 7,000 through social donations, and RMB 6,000 yuan of financial aid from the college. This helped Liu Xiaohua get rid of the shackles of poverty and rekindle her confidence for a better future.

Source: More Precise and Effective Student Financial Aid—A Review of the Continuous Progress of National Student Financial Aid Work, available at www.moe.gov.cn.

BOX 3-6   Tsinghua University Provides Support to a Student with Disability

Wei Xiang, a candidate in Dingxi City, Gansu Province, suffers from congenital *spina bifida*, intraspinal cysts, and loss of motor function in both lower limbs after birth. Unfortunately, Wei's father died early and only his mother accompanied him all the way through school. After being admitted to Tsinghua University, he hoped that the school would provide him and his mother a dormitory to facilitate his studies. On June 28, Tsinghua University wrote back to Wei Xiang,

We would provide a two-room apartment for you and your mother. The university will provide financial support. A number of alumni of Tsinghua University also took the initiative to sponsor and assist you in your treatment when they saw the news... Please believe that there is enough support inside and outside the university, Tsinghua will not miss any outstanding students.

I was thrilled that this letter touched me with all caring details. I just envisioned that there would be a positive answer for providing support, but I didn't expect a letter of response in such way, said Wei Xiang.

There are many other students like Wei Xiang who are in poverty because of illness and other reasons. Financial support is not only a matter of money, but also a major livelihood project, bearing the hope that education will transform their futures.

Source: Allow More Students from Poor Families to Go to Key Universities, available at www.xinhuanet.com.

Moreover, Chinese higher education institutions set up a "work-study" mechanism, which allows students from poor areas to work part-time in libraries and school cafeterias to increase their income during their schooling so as to inspire them to fight against poverty through their own efforts and build up their aspiration to drive their families and communities out of poverty after graduation.

(4) Case: Supporting Students from Poor Areas through Multiple Ways: Practices of Peking University

In March 2012, the Chinese government issued the *Notice on the Implementation of the Special Programme for Targeted Enrollment in Poverty-stricken Areas*, which aims to increase the access to quality higher education for students from poverty-stricken areas. It requires top domestic higher education institutions to allocate a certain number of quotas to enable students from contiguous poor areas to enroll at universities. It also guides and encourages students who have benefited from these enrolment programmes to return to poverty-stricken areas after graduation for employment and entrepreneurship.

As of 2020, the programme has covered all remote, poor and ethnic areas, such as concentrated contiguous areas in extreme poverty, national targeted counties for poverty reduction. As a result, enrollment has increased from 10,000 in 2012 to 117,000 in 2020, with a total of over 700,000 students from areas in extreme poverty having received quality higher education since the launch of the programme.

BOX 3-7   Peking University Implements the Targeted Enrollment Programme for Students from Poverty-Stricken Areas

For more than 30 years since 1978[①], in Weng'an county (Guizhou Province, located in southwest China) with a population of 480,000, only 22 people have been admitted to Peking University and Tsinghua University (the top two universities in China). However, since the implementation of the programme of targeted enrollment in Guizhou Province in 2012, Weng'an county has been able to have an average of one person admitted to Peking and Tsinghua University each year.

Peng Yuheng, a student in geology at Peking University's College of Earth and Space Sciences, entered the University in 2014 with a score of 649. She ranked the first in science in Weng'an county, and the ninety-ninth in science in the province. Although the lowest admission score of Peking University in Guizhou that year was 667, Peng Yuheng was lucky to be admitted to Peking University under the targeted enrollment programme.

I was very lucky to benefit from this favourable policy, said Peng Yuheng.

Source: Allow More Students from Poor Families to Go to Key Universities, available at www.xinhuanet. com.

Besides financial aids, other means of support are in place in higher education institutions to help students from poor families to deal with the challenges they encounter in their studies and lives.

---

① From around 1978, China has resumed the National Higher Education Entrance Examination.

BOX 3-8   A Mentoring Programme Inspires Students to Grow and Succeed in Peking University

In 2010, Peking University established a mentoring programme named as "Yan Yuan Navigator", which invites scholars, social entrepreneurs and outstanding graduates who have received financial support to serve as mentors for the university students with financial difficulties, through pairing up. Within the ten years since its launch, the programme has reached around 20,000 students from financially disadvantaged families.

Luo Shuangshuang, a student at Peking University said,

When a swallow from the countryside flew into the Swallow Garden (the name of the university campus), everything was so strange and fresh. With the financial support policies of the state and the university, especially under the guidance of the mentors, I have transformed from a rural girl who was less knowledgeable to a confident girl. During these days in Yan Yuan, I not only learned academic knowledge, but also improved my interpersonal skills. The caring of mentors has built up my confidence. I have learned to take charge, cooperate, and contribute.

Source: State-funding and Yan Yuan Navigator Help Me Grow and Succeed, available at www.moe.gov.cn.

2. Reducing Dropout and Retaining Students in Compulsory Education

Although China has achieved the universalization of compulsory education across the country, several challenges regarding school dropouts continue to persist in many poor areas. In order to help out-of-school children return to school and complete the whole cycle of compulsory education, the Chinese government has established a portfolio for each student and carried out data verification on a regular basis, especially in poor rural areas. Furthermore, targeted measures have been taken to reduce school dropouts that occurs due to different causes. In July 2017, China's central government issued *the Notice on Further Strengthening the Prevention of Dropouts and Improving the Completion Rate of Compulsory Education,* which calls for additional efforts to control the drop-out rate and to ensure that the completion rate of nine-year compulsory education reaches 95% by 2020. *The Notice* highlights that the government shall practice classified guidance and implement tailored measures to fit the local and individual situation, with the following guiding principles:

- The quality of education should be improved to make schools more attractive to students so that they will not leave school because of learning difficulties or weariness;
- Poverty reduction should be enhanced to prevent students from dropping out of school due to financial difficulties;
- Educational investment, school construction and facilities improvement, and boarding school development should be enhanced to solve the transportation problems of rural students as well as related barriers.

The following cases show efforts made at different levels to tackle issues of school dropout in compulsory education.

(1) Case: Successful Measures to Reduce School Dropouts in Yunnan Province

Yunnan is an ethnically diverse province situated in border and mountainous areas in southwestern China. Due to its harsh geographic environment, low level of socio-economic development, persistent traditional ethnic, cultural customs and norms, etc., some children, especially those who live in remote, poor, and ethnic minority areas, are not enrolled in school or drop out of school early without completing schooling. Yunnan Province planned and implemented systematic measures (see Table 3-2) to address this challenge, which have helped 16,058 drop-outs to re-enter the school, with a return rate of 97.10%, including 4,512 students from poor families, as of May 2020.

Table 3-2   Measures Adopted to Reduce Dropouts and Increase Re-entry Students in Yunnan Province

Leadership and coordination	The Provincial Department of Education set up a working group to strengthen the leadership, guidance, and supervision of the work related to the prevention of dropouts and the retention of children and youths in school. Sub-working groups have been established and coordinators have been appointed by local governments.
Information	A full-scale survey is conducted to accurately identify the baseline of dropouts and out-of-school children. The survey collects a large variety of data covering diverse aspects of the student, family and community. A systematic data verification process is adopted as part of which the data on out-of-school children is verified through the comparison between the information of household registration and student registration, between the files of student registration and the actual students in school, and between the data of dropout students and the registered households for targeted poverty reduction.
Accountability	County governments are responsible and accountable for the prevention of dropouts and the retention of children and youths in school. Targeted programmes have been designed according to the needs of the individual county, school, and student. The governments shall legally obtain support from the communities to encourage students to return to school.
Legal protection	Where necessary, legal means are applied to protect the children's right to education.
Education	Local authorities coordinate funding, teachers and the provision of accommodation and other resources to provide tailored educational programmes for dropout students to continue their learning. The programmes integrate general and vocational education to equip them with subject knowledge and practical skills for employability.

BOX 3-9 Integrated General and Vocational Education Program in Jinping County, Yunnan Province

Xiaomei, a student in Jinping County, Honghe Autonomous Prefecture of Hani and Yi ethnic minorities, Yunnan Province, dropped out from a non-governmental school after one semester. She was overaged when she was enrolled in the school at the age of 12.

Jinping County government identified Xiaomei's case after a meticulous investigation when implementing the campaign to reduce dropouts in compulsory education. Subsequently, a task force consisting of government staff, teachers, and village leaders initiated dialogues with her parents regarding Xiaomei's re-entry to school. Xiaomei had been out of school for a long time and had almost "zero" foundation for learning, and she was encouraged to take the integrated general and vocational education programme.

Through the programme, she could acquire basic literacy and numeracy, and technical and vocational skills. In addition, a one-to-one tutor was appointed for her in the school to provide psychological and life support.

These supports have helped students like Xiaomei in Jinping County to mitigate the negative impacts caused by dropping out of school early. As of 2020, 106 students who dropped out from compulsory education have been enrolled in the integrated general and vocational education programme in Jinping County. After finishing the programme, they will be able to enter vocational high schools or technical schools, so that they could become economically productive and lift themselves out of poverty.

Source: Yunnan Prescribes "Medicine" for Controlling School Dropout, available at new.qq.com.

BOX 3-10 An Open Court on Children's Right to Education in Lajing Town, Lanping County, Yunnan Province

On November 24, 2017, the People's Government of Lajing Town, Lanping County, Yunnan Province, took five parents to court, demanding that the parents immediately send their children to school and complete their compulsory education as required by *The Compulsory Education Law of the People's Republic of China*. The court was open for public and attracted hundreds of villagers. This happened after the parents had refused to fulfill their obligation to send their children to school to receive compulsory education after repeated urges and mobilization of the Lajing Town government.

Through the court-directed mediation, the plaintiff (Lajing Town government) and the defendant (the parents) exchanged views on the actual situation of each defendant's family based on court investigations and discussed legal ways of resolving the disputes. The defendants acknowledged the legal obligations of parents to protect children's right to education and the punishment for violating national laws. Two parties reached consensus on the time limit for the children to return to school. The court issued a mediation letter on the spot. The parents responded that they did not know *"not allowing their children to go to school is illegal"* before, and indicated they did not pay enough attention to the children's learning which caused them to drop-out.

The court's verdict also popularized the general knowledge of the law among the villagers, who expressed that they will fully respect the children's right to education and ensure that their children can enroll in school and complete compulsory education according to the law.

Source: Lajing Town People's Government Took the Parents of 5 Students to the Court, available at www.sohu.com.

(2) Case: No One Left behind—Promoting Girls' Equal Access to Compulsory Education in Dongxiang County, Linxia Autonomous Prefecture of Hui Ethnic Group, Gansu Province

Basuchi village in Dongxiang County, Linxia Autonomous Prefecture of Hui Ethnic Group, Gansu Province, is a poor village with critical education challenges. Children of compulsory school age, especially girls, are not enrolled in schools in time due to various reasons, including the harsh natural environment and traditional gender norms.

To address these challenges, the poverty alleviation official assigned to the Basuchi village has been working meticulously and responsibly to enable many school-age children from poor families to enter school. In addition, full exemption of tuition, boarding and lodging fees have been provided for all female students from elementary school to university. Moreover, female "role models" from local communities, such as the staff of the county government and the school principals, have been invited by the County government to share their success stories with local villagers, which helps increase local villagers' awareness of the role of education in alleviating poverty.

Through collaborative efforts, the issue of school-age children's access to education has largely been resolved. In 2017, the retention rate of compulsory education in Linxia Prefecture reached 95.11%, while Dongxiang County achieved a successful clearing up of all dropouts in 24 townships under its jurisdiction in 2019.

BOX 3-11   Poverty Alleviation Coordinator in Basuchi Village Mobilized Parents to Send Girls back to School

Zhang Xuehong is a poverty alleviation coordinator assigned by Linxia Education Bureau to Basuchi village. Having worked in education for many years, he is particularly concerned about children's timely access to school, especially rural girls, which has become his prioritized work.

During a visit to the village, Zhang Xuehong found that the 10-year-old daughter Ma Baigeiye of a local poor household Ma Haru was once enrolled in Basuchi elementary school, but immediately dropped out of school without continuing her education. From the home visit to Ma's family, he learned that the child had dropped out of school due to the long distance to school and the parental indifference to education. To ensure that the girl returns to school, Zhang Xuehong and his poverty alleviation colleagues repeatedly visited Ma Baigeiye to promote education policies and the significance of education, which finally led to Ma Baigeiye's re-entry to the school.

Source: Stories of Poverty Alleviation Cadres in Linxia, Gansu Province, available at www.chinalxnet. com.

(3) Case: Educational Miracle in the Mountainous Area: Zhang Guimei and Her Free Girls' High School

Zhang Guimei, a female principal at Huaping Senior High School for Girls in Lijiang, Yunnan Province, has been teaching in the poor mountainous area of Yunnan for more than 40 years. She founded the first free high school for girls in China and is the "mother" of more than 130 orphans at the Huaping Children's Home which is a welfare organization. She devotes herself to the education and welfare of children in the remote ethnic regions. She has been a light of hope illuminating children's life that inspires them to pursue their dreams.

In 1997, Zhang Guimei, then 40 years old, was re-assigned to teach in Huaping County Ethnic High School. As time went by, she noticed that many girls living in extreme poverty were dropping out of schools, leading to early marriage and pregnancy. They were repeating the life of their parents who experienced poverty all their life. She was deeply concerned about this situation and realized that this can be corrected through education. She has complete faith in the power of education as she believed, *"Educating a girl can influence at least three generations. If we can cultivate educated and responsible mothers, children in the mountains will not drop out of school or become orphans."*

She was determined to make a difference by building a free girls' high school in this barren mountainous area so that girls in Huaping County could receive a better education. When she first started the school, she went door-to-door to "beg" for funds, went over the mountains to look for children who had dropped out of school, and managed to have six teachers by her glorified educational ideas and beliefs.

During the 13 years since its opening-up, Huaping Senior High School for Girls has successfully educated 11 batches of graduates and helped more than 1,800 poor girls in the mountainous areas enter higher education. Principal Zhang Guimei's free high school for girls has become a local educational miracle, breaking the vicious circle of inter-generational poverty.

(4) Case: Free Meals Programme to Retain Poverty-Stricken Rural Students in Schools: a Case from Huishui County, Guizhou Province

In early 2000s, child malnutrition was a severe problem that mainly occurred in the central and western rural areas of China. Many rural students went to school without having enough food. In 2002, the highest rate of growth retardation among school children aged 5-12 was in the nationally recognized poor counties of southwest China, with 38.0% for males and 38.2% for females respectively. The corresponding figures for boys and girls aged 13-17, were 40% and 36.5% respectively. The rate of retardation

in the poor counties of northwest China was also high, with 15.4% and 20.9% for males and females aged 5-12, and 27.4% and 11.4% for males and females aged 13-17, respectively.

Adequate nutrition is not only essential for children's healthy development, but also an incentive for families to send their children to school and help keep them in school. Much research on mid-day school meal has shown that it improves the quality of student learning in poor areas and narrows the learning gap between the urban and rural children. Evidence suggests that that it has great significance in reducing poverty.

Realizing the nutritional and educational value of school meal, the Chinese government issued *The Recommendations on Implementing the Nutrition Improvement Programme for Rural Students in Compulsory Education* (hereinafter referred to as *Recommendations*) and launched a pilot nutrition improvement programme for rural students in compulsory education in contiguous impoverished areas.

In May 2012, the Ministry of Education and other 15 national departments issued five supporting documents, including *The Implementation Guidelines of the Nutrition Improvement Programme for Compulsory Education Students*, to further promote the implementation of the policy. The Recommendations stipulates that the standard for free meal subsidy in contiguous impoverished areas is RMB 3 per student per day (calculated based on 200 days of schooling for the whole year), and all the funds required are borne by the central government. In 2015, the state further raised the standard to RMB 4 per student per day. Accordingly, local governments have adopted localized measures to ensure that free meals are rapidly promoted for the welfare of rural students.

BOX 3-12   Adequate Meal Subsidies and Meal Options Available for All Students

In the Fourth Middle School in Changshun County, Guizhou Province, the student free meal allowance increased from RMB 4 to RMB 5 per student per day from the fall semester of 2021. An additional subsidy of RMB 7 has been provided for boarding students with financial hardships so that they can have three meals a day for free in the school canteen.

The school canteen provides standard three dishes and one soup per meal and changes the menu once a week. The recipes of the canteen are designed by the Nutrition Office of the County Education Bureau based on consulting experts' advice.

Source: Guizhou Province: School and Farmers Help Nutrition Improvement Programme to Make Children "Eat Enough" and "Eat Better", available at www.moe.gov.cn.

BOX 3-13   Information Platforms and Networks to Monitor Food Security and Canteen Management

In Tongren City, Guizhou Province, a cloud-based smart management platform for student nutritious meals has been established to supervise the quality of services provided by the school canteens. The platform has multiple functions, such as supporting the procurement and management of meal ingredients, analyzing the quality of the meal ingredients, and issuing early alarm for ingredients with a preservation period of only one day. Besides, city, county, and school managers can conduct online inspections of school canteens through the mobile application of the platform at any time. This has helped improve the conditions of school canteen management.

Source: 7 Years of Implementation of the Nutrition Improvement Programme for Rural Students in Compulsory Education, available at edu.people.com.cn.

China's nutrition improvement programme for rural students in compulsory education covers schools in most of China's less economically developed areas. According to a national report by the Ministry of Education in June 2020, 1,647 counties in 28 provinces nationwide have implemented the free meal programme, covering 137,200 rural schools at the compulsory education level, accounting for 81.7% of the total number of rural schools, benefiting 37,283,000 students. This accounts for 39.6% of the total number of rural students in compulsory education.

The programme has played a significant role in promoting children's healthy growth, and in supporting students to complete compulsory education. Based on the tracking and monitoring data from the Chinese Center for Disease Control and Prevention in 2019, the average height of boys and girls in all age groups in the pilot areas of the free meal programme increased by 1.54 cm and 1.69 cm respectively compared to 2012, and the average weight increased by 1.06 kg and 1.18 kg respectively, which is higher than the national average for rural students. Meanwhile, the completion rate of compulsory education in China has increased from 90.8% in 2009 to 95.2% in 2020. There is evidence to suggest that the nutrition programme also helped increase learning achievement of children.

3. Developing Early Childhood Education in Poor Areas in China

The Chinese government attaches great importance to the expansion of early childhood development (ECD) across the country. The central government supports the expansion of pre-school education through proper policy and planning, leadership and coordination and financial support. ECD has a critical role in promoting the universalization of post-compulsory education. The government has adopted a range of measures to advance the development of pre-school education, as follows.

- **Policy and planning**

    In 2010, the central government launched the *Outline of the National Medium- and Long-term Education Reform and Development Plan* (hereafter referred to as the *Outline*), aiming to achieve universal access to preschool education in China within 10 years.

The outline recognizes the social benefits of pre-school education and its role in inclusive development. It proposes a number of implementation measures such as resource mobilization, structural adjustment, well-established mechanisms, and quality improvement. The governments shall implement three consecutive action plans for preschool education development at the county level.

- **Leadership and coordination**

China has established a management and implementation mechanism, with the State Council as the lead, provincial and municipal authorities as coordinator, and county authorities as the main implementer. Local governments at all levels are expected to vigorously develop public kindergartens and standardize private kindergartens through the work in the areas of construction, investment, personnel management, and supervision. Additionally, collaboration shall be ensured across departments of education, finance, construction, health, and others.

- **Finance and projects**

Increased financial investment shall be allocated for major projects. The central government has set up a special fund for ECD, with a total investment of 151.98 billion RMB during 2011-2020. Local governments at all levels set the standard of public funding per student. Meanwhile, a pre-school student subsidy mechanism has been established, with a total investment of RMB 64.3 billion from governments at different levels, and RMB 55 million of subsidies benefiting millions of students from impoverished families.

Consequently, ten years of efforts have made remarkable progress in expanding access to preschool education. By 2020, the number of kindergartens in China has increased by 141,000, the number of children in kindergarten has increased by 18.416 million, and the number of full-time kindergarten teachers has increased by 1.769 million, with growth rates of 93.9%, 61.9%, and 154.6% respectively. And the gross enrollment rate in the first three years of preschool has increased from 56.6% in 2011 to 85.2% in 2020.

From 2011 to 2020, RMB 151.98 billion was spent to support the development of preschool education. A funding system was established to provide preschool education subsidies. Governments at all levels have invested a total of RMB 64.3 billion in the past ten years to subsidize 55 million children from poor families. Localities have introduced and implemented the standard for financial allocation per student to support students in public kindergartens, and the subsidy standard for inclusive private kindergartens.

Following cases provide effective practices of ECD from two provinces to increase access and quality of preschool education in rural areas.

(1) Case: "One Village, One Kindergarten" Project in Yi Ethnic Group Area, Leshan City, Sichuan Province

For many years, the status of development of preschool education in the Yi ethnic group

area in Leshan City, Sichuan Province remained low. In 2013, there were only 9 village kindergartens in the Yi area of Leshan City (including 1 public kindergarten), enrolling 417 children of school age with 20 teachers. The gross preschool enrolment rate in the Yi area was only 62.6%, which was 23.54 percentage points lower than the city average.

To fill this gap in ECD, in April 2014, the Leshan government issued the *Notice on Further Accelerating the Poverty Alleviation and Development in Xiaoliang Mountains*, which aimed to achieve universal access to preschool education for all school-age children in the Yi area in three years through a project called "One Village, One Kindergarten". The project aimed to build at least one kindergarten for one village in the Yi area in Leshan City. This initiative was a major breakthrough to accelerate the development of the province's preschool education, especially for Yi children. Following the first phase of the project in Leshan City, it is planned that the programme coverage would be expanded to all 51 counties in the province's ethnic autonomous areas.

This project has been successfully implemented. As a result, the objective of full access of school-age children to preschool education in the Yi Area has been largely achieved. By the end of 2017, 295 village kindergartens had been built in 286 villages in the Yi area of Leshan City, with 9,947 children in school.

Specifically, the following are major activities and achievements of the "One Village, One Kindergarten" project.

- **Infrastructure**

  To meet the requirements of classroom or physical space, the programme primarily used the existing non-used classrooms in village elementary schools and village-level activity centres. These non-used classrooms and activity centers provided a safe and secure space for the functioning of kindergartens. Among the 295 kindergartens operated under the project, 157 are running in renovated non-used village primary schools or classrooms, 63 in village activity centres, 56 are attached to the centre primary schools, and only 19 are newly built.

- **Finance**

  The programme is being financed by authorities at the national, provincial, city and county levels. Governments at all levels have made considerable efforts to ensure that substantial resources are available for the development of preschool education. The central financial authority has set up a special fund for preschool education development and taken measures to improve mechanisms of resource mobilization and investment.

  The provincial financial authority has funded the staff wages under the project with an annual investment of RMB 13.73 million The city financial authority invested a total of RMB 14.75 million as the start-up funds for the project,

following the standard of RMB 50,000 per kindergarten. Moreover, a total of RMB 2.35 million was invested to purchase teaching materials and tools, and security facilities, while RMB 6.864 million was spent annually to subsidize the salary of the staff. The county-level finance authority invested over RMB 30 million in the construction and upgrading of kindergartens established under the project, subsidizing the kindergartens at a rate of RMB 1,000-4,000/person/year, providing free meals for children at a rate of RMB 800/student/year, and offering the kindergartens with public expenses at the rate of RMB 100-200/student/year.

- **Faculty and their capacity building**

   Leshan City effectively solved the problem of shortage of health care and educational staff for the "One Village, One Kindergarten" project through job-transfer of current educational staff and open recruitment. Furthermore, the city and county-level education authorities organized annual capacity-building training for health care and educational staff deployed for the project.

- **Support system**

   Support system has been established to enhance the effectiveness of the project implementation, which includes the paired-up assistance between cities and counties, within counties and between kindergartens. Several stakeholders including government officials, ECD specialists, and teachers from different areas are invited to share experiences and resources.

In addition, kindergartens in three ethnic districts/counties, Jinkouhe, Mabian, and Ebian, have been incorporated into the preschool education groups established in Leshan City by the project, through which they adopt a more efficient management model and advanced educational philosophy to improve the quality of preschool education.

(2) Case: Paired-Up Assistance to Rural Pre-school Education in Anhui Province

Over the past decade, the universalization of preschool education in China has increased rapidly. However, the development has been uneven, especially in rural areas, due to issues of shortage of educational resources, insufficient investment, and inadequate teaching force and so on.

China has taken a number of measures to help rural preschools development by mobilizing support from cities. Many places have carried out twinning activities, pairing urban model kindergartens with rural kindergartens to expand high-quality preschool education resources and help rural kindergartens improve teachers' professional capacity and the quality of schooling.

The measures have produced remarkable results in promoting the development of rural preschool education. In October 2017, the Education Administration of Luyang

District, Hefei City, Anhui Province, launched its work on poverty alleviation through education in Linquan County. As of July 2020, a total of 156 experts on early childhood education from Luyang District and kindergarten directors have delivered lectures and training sessions in Linquan County, reaching more than 3,300 kindergarten teachers. The experiences of early childhood education in Luyang District, Hefei, have been shared and adopted in the 377 kindergartens in Linquan County, and professional capacity of 700 plus kindergarten teachers has been enhanced, benefiting more than 100,000 children. In general, the standardization of kindergartens in Linquan County has been greatly achieved, which contributes to the balanced development of urban and rural early childhood education.

BOX 3-14   Prominent Kindergarten Principal Guides the Development of Pre-School Education in Poor Areas of Anhui Province

Li Zheng is the chief principal of the Anqing Road Kindergarten Education Group in Luyang District, Hefei City, Anhui Province, who was recognized as a "prominent provincial principal of kindergarten". From 2018 to 2020, Li Zheng traveled between the Luyang District, Hefei City, and Linquan County, Fuyang City to help guide the building of kindergartens in Linquan County and carry out twinning activities between the two places.

In October 2018, when Li Zheng first visited the centre kindergarten of Chengdong Street, Linquan County, she found that many parents had bought into the false notion that early instruction with heavy academic focus would increase children's learning performance in the latter level of education, and they wanted kindergartens to increase teaching of subject knowledge. Li Zheng immediately called for a parent-teacher meeting with the participation of all parents and kindergarten teachers, in which she discussed with parents the trap of "primary schooling" in kindergarten, a phenomenon in which preprimary schools teach subjects that are taught in primary schools. A subsequent meeting was held to advocate the idea that preschool education should focus on the child's physical, social, emotional and mental development through the use of play-based methods, presentation of case studies and the introduction to the daily and weekly schedules of the kindergarten. Li Zheng also gave concrete and actionable suggestions on the construction of a true kindergarten environment. With the help of Li Zheng, the Centre Kindergarten in Chengdong Street of Linquan County was successfully classified as a first-class kindergarten in Fuyang City.

Like Li Zheng, many prominent kindergarten principals guided their counterparts at township level in poor areas to improve the quality of preschool education. In November 2018, Cui Lihong, the director of the Hefei Municipal Commission's Kindergarten Education Group mobilized the group's resources to support Yangqiao Township Centre Kindergarten in Linquan County to establish a "Fuyang City First-class Kindergarten". She translated the standards of the first-class kindergarten into detailed tasks in game areas creation, kindergarten management, teaching improvement, health care and safety, and materials development. In addition, a task force has been established, comprising professionals from the education group and educators of Yanqiao Township Centre kindergarten. Within three months, the kindergarten has made significant improvement.

In the heart of many principals in Linquan County, the support from prominent principals from Luyang District, Hefei City, and their teams, not only changed the outlook of kindergarten but also boosted the confidence of the teachers. *Local teachers understand that they are not babysitters, but kindergarten teachers with professionalism and confidence.* Liu Lingling, a township kindergarten teacher said. She felt that her biggest gain in the past two years is that she has learned to think from the perspective of a kid.

In the past, I always thought that the creation of kindergarten's physical environment, education corners, and games and activities is just as a show-off for adults. Now I realize this idea is wrong. Squatting down to the height of children and see the world with their eyes. Only then can we see the spotlights of our career. said Liu Lingling.

Source: Twinning Activities Help Preschools Cross the Threshold towards Quality Preschool Education - Luyang District, Hefei Province has Formed A Learning Community for Kindergarten Teachers Since the Launching of Poverty Alleviation in Education in Linquan County in 2017, available at www.jyb.cn.

4. Ensuring the Right to Education for Children with Disabilities

The Chinese government attaches great importance to ensuring the right to education for persons with disabilities in line with the Education 2030 goals and China's actions on poverty alleviation through education. The laws and regulations promulgated and implemented by the Chinese government, such as the *Education Law*, revised *Regulations on Education for Persons with Disabilities*, the *China Education Modernization 2035*, Five-Year Plan for the National Education, all set out development goals, including the targets and means for ensuring the education of persons with disabilities. Since 2014, two Plans for the Advancement of Special Education have been implemented consecutively. The governments at all levels have intensively issued detailed implementation guidelines. With these unprecedented efforts, China's special education has achieved rapid development in recent years as presented below:

- **Increased access to special education**

  The facilities of special education have been greatly expanded, which contributes to the achievement of universal access to compulsory education for children and adolescents with disabilities. In 2020, there were 2,244 special education schools nationwide, 191 more than that in 2015, with an increase of 9.3%. There were 880,800 students in 2019, 438,600 more than that in 2015, with an increase of 99%. Consequently, people with disabilities have increased access to preschool education, vocationally-oriented secondary education, and higher education for people with disabilities.

- **Improved financial support**

  From 2016 to 2020, the Central Government committed a special fund of RMB 2.05 billion, with an annual investment of RMB 410 million, to support the central and western regions to strengthen the development of special education. The average public funding standard for special education schools and students with disabilities attending non-special classes has been raised to RMB 6,000, which is 6-8 times higher than that of ordinary students and it has ensured the well-functioning of special education schools.

- **Strengthened capacities of the faculty**

  By the end of 2020, there had been 66,200 full-time teachers in special education schools nationwide, with an increase of 13,000 compared to 2015, which accounts for a growth of 26%. Meanwhile, the teachers' professional development standards have been constantly improved. More than 20 provinces (autonomous regions and municipalities) have introduced staffing standards for special education schools.

  All localities are required to raise the allowance of special education teachers by 15% on their basic salary, and over 18 provinces (autonomous regions and

municipalities) have raised the allowance standard.

- **Improved quality of special education**

China promotes integrated education and has taken measures to improve the working mechanisms of Learning in Regular Classrooms (LRC)[①] to provide support services for disabled students related to learning, living, and employment guidance.

The government has developed compulsory education curriculum standards for the special school for the blind, deaf, and mentally disabled students, which are under implementation. By the end of 2020, 239 volumes of ministerial textbooks based on the new curriculum standards have been developed, approved, and put into use.

Overall, China has been able to establish a special education system, which is characterized by an equitable distribution of resources, linkage between learning stages, integration of general and vocational education, and the combination of learners' medical care and special education. Besides, a special education support and service mechanism has been in place to ensure substantial financial and social assistance, as well as the full coverage and accessibility of services. Moreover, a strong cooperation system has been set up that underpins inter-sectoral collaborations and promotes a participatory and multi-stakeholder involvement.

(1) Case: Implementing Integrated Education in Xinfeng County, Jiangxi Province

A special education resource centre was established in 2016 in Xinfeng County, Jiangxi Province, as a pilot for special education reform, to provide a one-on-one assessment of children with special needs and ensure their access to education through diversified learning pathways such as special schools, LRCs, and home tutoring.

Based on the individual assessment of each child with disabilities by the Special Education Resource Centre, Xinfeng County adopted the LRC approach for 565 children with mild learning difficulties. Portfolios were established for each child, and funds were allocated to the non-special schools at a rate of RMB 6,000 per person per year. In addition, the ratio of teachers for LRC classes increased. In addition, teachers from the Centre pay regular visits and provide guidance to the schools and carry out researches on pedagogy for LRCs, and the Centre deploys assistant teachers according to students' needs.

---

① Learning in Regular Classrooms (LRCs) was officially proposed as an education pilot to promote special education for children with disabilities in the First National Conference of Special Education in 1988. The LRC aims to enable children with disabilities to gain access to education and to learn in mainstream classrooms with their non-disabled peers.

BOX 3-15   Lrc and Support from Xinfeng Special Education Resource Center

Li Xiaoqiang (pseudonym), eight years old, is now attending a LRC class in an elementary school in Xinfeng County. As he has a literacy difficulty, his teachers have set up a support group to assist him in studies and help him develop his social skills. With the accompaniment and support from the teachers and peers, he has made strides in his studies and integrated well into the class.

Furthermore, to implement the national *Plan for the Advancement of Special Education* which calls for relevant education for those with severe disabilities who cannot get access to schools, the Centre has developed a home tutoring model combining special education and general education. It also delivers tailored service to students from the nearest schools.

Currently, 171 teaching teams have been organized to deliver a home tutoring programme for students with severe disabilities from more than 300 villages and communities in Xinfeng County. Up to now, a total of 386 children have received individualized tutoring and more than 45,000 lessons have been provided.

BOX 3-16   Home Tutoring to Support Students with Severe Disabilities

Liu Jiayi, who lives in Jiudu Village, Zhengping Town, Xinfeng County, was identified as severely disabled at the age of four due to an accidental intracranial injury. Since Jiayi was six years old, a special education teacher and two general education teachers formed a teaching team to support her studies. In addition to weekly home visits, the team also provides training service to Jiayi's family through video-call and WeChat and guides her in daily physical rehabilitation and learning, forming a model of online and offline interaction and joint school and family participation. Jiayi's health condition and cognitive ability have been significantly improved.

Source: Xinfeng County, Jiangxi Province: 171 Home Tutoring Teams, available at tv.cctv.com.

(2) Case: Promoting Vocational Education for Students with Disabilities in Quanzhou City, Fujian Province

Quanzhou City, Fujian Province, has been implementing the *Plan for the Advancement of Special Education* and has developed the provision of vocational education to support the employment and entrepreneurship of people with disabilities and to help them integrate into society with skills.

The special education in Quanzhou City follows the idea that "special education should be vocationally oriented, and vocational education should be responsive to social needs", and is also driven by needs of the labour market. It utilizes south Fujian cultural resources, master craftsmen, and an e-commerce platform, and has set up five specialties in special education schools, including arts and crafts, cultural creativity, life service, massage by the visually impaired, and art performance, providing the students

with fifteen courses, such as ceramics, oil painting, painting and calligraphy framing, printmaking, shadow carving, massage, and others. It applies the 1+N vocational training model which enables students to choose more vocational courses in addition to their planning programme. This model provides individualized vocational education and platforms for each student to display their skill-sets, allowing better labor market access.

In addition, with the support of the earmarked fund for special education established by the Quanzhou Education Foundation, Quanzhou Special Education School has founded Jingtu Wenchuang Institute (or as Jingtu Cultural and Creative Institute), an employment and entrepreneurship cultivation base for students with disabilities, which provides internships, vocational training, vocational certification, pre-service training, and employment opportunities for students at vocational schools. Students with disabilities have not only improved their vocational and technical skills and entrepreneurial abilities, but also enhanced their confidence in becoming self-sufficient, thus integrating into society.

BOX 3-17   Success Stories of Graduates from Quanzhou Special Education School

Pingping is a Quanzhou Special Education School graduate with a hearing impairment. She is currently an employee of Quanzhou Jingtu Cultural and Creative Institute as a painter.

Pingping said, *I like working here. It's like my home. I'm especially happy when people like my work. It gives me a great sense of self-worth.*

During her studies at school, Pingping has participated in municipal art exhibitions organized for people with disabilities, and her paintings have won many awards.

There are also four interns from the Quanzhou Special Education School, who have been successfully employed by the Jingtu Wenchuang Institute through vocational education and have expressed satisfaction with their careers.

Source: Quanzhou City Promotes the Vocationalization of Special Education and Opens Channels of Employment and Entrepreneurship for People with Disabilities, *Quanzhou Evening News*, available at www. qzcns.com.

II. Improving the Quality of Education in Poverty-stricken Areas

1. Narrowing the Urban-Rural Gap in Education Quality

China achieved the goal of universalizing nine-year compulsory education in 2011. However, there are significant gaps in the education development of China, especially between the economically developed eastern regions, and the central and western regions, and between urban and rural areas, and in some cases even between schools.

To mitigate the gaps, the Chinese government has taken great efforts to advance

the balanced development of compulsory education, aiming to provide a fairer and better-quality education for children, with a focus on integrated efforts at the county level. In September 2012, the State Council document *Guidance on Further Promoting the Balanced Development of Compulsory Education* elaborated on the strategy of balanced development of compulsory education in the county.

One of the major measures concerns the implementation of the projects *Renovation Plan for Rural Low-performing Schools in Compulsory Education* and the *Renovation Plan of Middle and Western Rural Junior High School Premises*, aspiring to enhance the management of rural schools and low-performing schools, the quality of compulsory education, and ensure all school-age children have access to a quality school. To accelerate this cause, in January 2013, the Chinese Ministry of Education launched a supervision and evaluation scheme, which uses ten specific indicators, such as teacher-student ratio, the pass rate of full-time teachers' qualification, the average school space per student, the average school building space per student, and the adequacy of laboratory rooms and so on.

The work of balanced development of compulsory education has received substantial support and reached most of the counties in China. In 2020, the national investment in education was RMB 5303.4 billion yuan, with compulsory education receiving the largest share. By the end of December 2020, 2,809 counties have been supervised and their achievement towards the goal of balanced development of compulsory education has been validated. According to the statistics, 95.32% of the total counties located in central and western regions of China have achieved validation.

The following cases present exemplary practices of balanced urban - rural development of compulsory education in Hu'nan and Anhui provinces.

(1) Case: The Improvement of Disadvantaged Schools in Wugang City, Hunan Province

In December 2013, China launched " the Comprehensive Renovation of Disadvantaged Schools Programme", which aimed to improve the conditions of compulsory education in disadvantaged communities, and promote the equity of public education. The project mainly targets the poverty-stricken areas in the central and western regions, while covering some difficult areas in the eastern China and other poverty-stricken areas, such as the ethnic and border areas. The project includes six key tasks concerning the major challenges in compulsory education in poor areas:

- Guarantee basic conditions for teaching
- Improve living facilities in schools

- Build needed teaching points[①]
- Reduce the class size in county-town and township schools
- Promote the use of ICT in rural schools
- Improve the quality of teachers

The implementation of the programme has received considerable support and achieved significant results in Wugang City, Hu'nan Province. The city has advanced the construction of "standard rural school campus", through unified planning and design following the principles of "practicality, sufficiency, safety and frugality" and "what is missing, what to make up for". A total of RMB 110 million yuan has been invested, with 169 teaching buildings and students' canteens, 61 basketball courts newly built or rebuilt and expanded. All classes of small-sized schools[②] have been fully equipped with teaching and learning facilities.

In addition, the "Rural Teacher Support Programme" has been fully implemented, with special favour given to small-sized schools through full-time teacher deployment. More than 400 excellent teachers have been assigned to rural teaching points in the past three years. In addition, more than 800 apartments have been built for rural teachers' "better living, better teaching".

Besides, an innovative management model of small-sized schools was introduced in Wugang City, with the idea of "large schools supporting the small schools" . Thus 73 small rural schools were able to become satellite schools of nearby standard primary schools, adopting the integrated approach of school management, teacher deployment, allocation of education facilities, and use of educational funds, which has significantly promoted the quality of primary education as a whole.

By the end of 2020, all 73 small-sized rural schools had completed the construction of standardized campus and greatly improved the quality of teaching and learning. More than 700 rural students who moved to schools in the urban areas have returned to the small-sized schools in rural areas because of their improved teaching quality.

[①] "Teaching points" refers to small-sized primary schools not covering all 6 grades of a standard primary school, which are common in inaccessible, sparsely populated mountainous and economically underdeveloped areas, and are built as a solution to address the gap in the accessibility of compulsory education in these hard-to-reach areas.

[②] "Small-sized schools" mainly refers to schools below the township level and with fewer than 200 students. They are mainly distributed in rural areas. Most of them are primary and secondary schools and teaching points with a small number of students. The class size, number of teachers are limited. The faculty structure is imbalanced, and the teacher-student ratio is low.

BOX 3-18   Two Rural Primary Schools in Wugang City Improved the Quality of Education through "the Comprehensive Renovation of Disadvantaged Schools Programme"

The Tongwan Primary School in Wugang City, Hunan Province, was once closed due to poor teaching quality. In 2016, driven by the "the Comprehensive Renovation of Disadvantaged Schools Programme", Tongwan Primary School resumed its opening and operation. The old buildings constructed in 1970s have been turned into two-story school buildings, and each classroom is equipped with facilities connected to internet of more than 200, each class has access to online quality learning resources and each student can enjoy an online learning space. The school conditions have been completely upgraded, while the teaching quality has also been significantly promoted.

Liangshan Primary School in Chushutang township of Wugang city is a rural primary school serving for three villages. A few years ago, the school had just five students and was most likely to be closed. In 2017, Wugang city, with the support of the Programme, re-built the school in a location convenient for all the three villages. In September 2018, the new Liangshan Primary School was re-opened, with 76 students enrolled that year. One year later, the villagers were satisfied with the school and urged to open classes at the fifth and sixth grades. Today, Liangshan Primary School has covered all 6 grades of a standard primary school, with 132 students.

Source: The Previous "Pain Point" is Now a "Highlight Spot": Wugang Has Invested 110 Million Yuan to Build Small-sized Schools, available at www.sohu.com.

(2) Case: Smart Education Empowers Small-Sized Rural Schools in Anhui Province

Anhui province has achieved significant results by promoting information and communication technology to improve the quality of rural school education. It has prioritized the construction of smart schools in rural areas, especially small-sized schools in poor areas, as part of the provincial government's work plan and actions benefiting the public.

Jinzhai County has the largest area with the largest immigrant population due to construction of Dams. It is located in the Dabie Mountainous area, under the administration of Lu'an City, Anhui Province. There are 127 small-sized schools, most of which are located in mountainous area. The six teaching points attached to Tiantangzhai Centre Primary School, Jinzhai County are based remotely. There is a severe shortage of teachers, especially for subjects such as English, art, and music, due to which many schools are not able to teach these subjects.

In 2015, an online teaching programme was introduced in to the county, through which six schools were able to have simultaneous access to the teaching and teachers' professional development activities in the Centre Primary School. Thus, the children who attend the remote teaching sites can take English, art, music and other courses online. So far, the original online classroom has been upgraded as the smart cloud classroom 2.0 mode, which allows for the participation and interaction of teachers and students based in the teaching

points. The students in the teaching site can also synchronize classroom interaction and homework evaluation with the teachers of the Central Primary School. Students can use the intelligent classroom for self-study and homework after class. Teachers can recommend their students to view courses recorded by famous teachers.

Furthermore, a special plan has also been implemented to improve the applications of information technology for rural teachers in Anhui Province. The plan focuses on strengthening the ability of teachers in applying information technology in teaching. By January 2021, nearly 1,800 training sessions were held on smart school application in Anhui, and the ability to apply information technology has been included as one of the criteria for new teachers' promotion and career advancement. Besides, with the help of the online classroom platform, six teaching points realized the synchronization with the Centre Primary School classroom in teaching research.

2. Improving the Number of Quality Teachers in Remote Rural Schools

Poverty-stricken areas, especially those remote mountainous regions, are often unable to attract sufficient qualified teachers due to a number of factors, such as lack of transportation, geographical conditions, language barriers, financial difficulties, and others. These factors have prevented the improvement of teaching quality in rural schools and often lead to an outflow of students from rural to sub-urban or urban areas. Poor quality of teaching in rural schools may even encourage children to drop out of schools. The Chinese central government has formulated and implemented plans to establish a strong teaching force, which has effectively promoted the overall quality of teachers in poverty-stricken rural areas.

(1) Case: The "Special Post Plan" to Increase the Supply of Qualified Teachers for Rural Schools: the Practice in Guangxi Autonomous Region

With a view to addressing the problems of insufficient supply and quality of teachers in rural schools, the Ministry of Education, the Ministry of Finance, Ministry of Human Resources and Social Security, and the State Commission Office for Public Sector Reform, jointly issued *The Notice on The Implementation of the Special Post Plan for Teachers in Rural Compulsory Education Schools* in May 2006.

The Plan aims to openly recruit college graduates to teach in the compulsory education schools at the county level, which targeted counties of "Two Basics"[1] programme, counties on the borderline, autonomous counties of ethnic

---

[1] The "Two Basics" refers to two targets in education: basically universalize nine-year compulsory education, and basically eradicate illiteracy among young and middle-aged people. It is a national programmeme for education development in rural areas in western China, launched in 2003.

groups and counties in ethnic group regions in western China, and autonomous prefectures of ethnic groups in central China. The term of teachers to be appointed under the special post provision is three years, and the central government provides salary subsidies to special post teachers. Additionally, in June 2015, the General Office of the State Council issued *The Support Plan for Rural Teachers* (2015-2020), which specifies a package of support to rural teachers comprising the following: recruitment, living conditions and welfare, staff quota management standards, professional career ladder, teacher exchange, capacity building, and honor system.

The Special Post Plan has made remarkable progress in increasing the supply of teachers in rural areas. The recruitment scale has been gradually expanded from 16,000 in 2006 to 100,000 teachers in 2019. Between 2006 and 2019, a total of 850,000 teachers joined the Plan, teaching in more than 30,000 rural schools (including primary schools and teaching points) in over 1,000 counties, and the retention rate of special post teachers after three-year term has reached 90% plus.

Additionally, the quality of teaching staff in rural schools in the targeted counties has shown significant improvement. In 2006, only 53.61% of full-time teachers in rural primary schools had a college diploma and above, but that figure reached 86.49% in 2015 and 94.79% in 2019. Moreover, the average age of special post teachers is about 24 years old, which has addressed the ageing problem of rural teachers, especially those in remote villages and teaching points. In addition, the proportion of full-time teachers in subjects such as English, information technology, music, sports, and fine arts, has grown from 6.38% in 2006 to 11.54% in 2015 and 16.72% in 2019.

Tianyang County, Guangxi Autonomous Region of Zhuang Ethnic Group, has adopted a variety of measures to help special post teachers "come, stay, and teach well" in remote rural schools, as shown in Table 3-3.

(2) Case: Targeted Preparation of Outstanding Teachers for Poor Areas: Beijing Normal University's Ambition Programme

To prepare highly qualified teachers for rural schools, the Ministry of Education has launched a talent training programme in cooperation with China's top teachers' universities. One of these is the Ambition Programme implemented by Beijing Normal University in 2020. The programme is open to outstanding high school graduates from the remaining 52 national-level poor counties, aiming to train high-quality teachers with high aspirations, commitment to and right skill-sets for teaching, following the principle of targeted enrollment, targeted training, and targeted deployment.

Table 3-3   Measures to Support Special Post Teachers in Tianyang County, Guangxi Autonomous Region

Relocation	• Newly recruited special post teachers shall be preferentially deployed to township schools with better transportation and more students. • Schools shall give priority to providing a single dormitory for special post teachers, and the construction of teachers' temporary dormitory shall be arranged in township schools with special post teachers. • Schools with special post teachers shall set up a canteen for teachers.
Preferential salary package	• The county implements a living subsidy plan for rural teachers with an annual budget of over RMB 6 million yuan. The subsidies for special post teachers range from 500 to 700 yuan per month. • Annual performance bonuses are expanded by the county government to cover the special post teachers for their retention, which can reach a maximum of RMB 23,000 yuan. • The special post teachers who have well adapted to their new roles and have outstanding performance shall be promoted to the middle-level management positions. • Some quotas assigned specially to the special post teachers when honoring outstanding teachers on the occasion of annual Chinese Teachers' Day, with 52 special post teachers having received the honor during their term.
Professional development and retention	• Qualified teachers who can pass the assessment and aspire to continue their teaching in local schools will be recruited into the normal county-paid teaching staff positions when they complete the 3-year teaching. • Through the twinning projects, rural schools are paired with urban schools, receive expert teachers from paired schools, and establish mentoring arrangements between experienced and new teachers, including the special post teachers. • Newly recruited teachers must complete at least 120 hours of intensive pre-service training. Additionally, the county education bureau provides the special post teachers with training opportunities under the National Teacher Training Plan and Provincial Teacher Training Plan. • The county education bureau sets up a mechanism to showcase excellent teaching, such as teaching skills competitions at different levels.

Source: Excellent Cases of the Implementation of Special Post Plan for Teachers of Rural Compulsory Education, Ministry of Education, P.R.China, www.moe.gov.cn.

In 2020, the Ambition Programme enrolled 156 students from the seven western provinces/Autonomous Regions: Guangxi, Sichuan, Guizhou, Yunnan, Gansu, Ningxia, and Xinjiang. The programme offers three disciplines: Mandarin and Literature, Mathematics and Applied Mathematics, and English.

Graduates of the programme will be deployed by the provincial education authorities

to teach in primary and secondary schools in the nationally recognized poor counties in the province where they are appointed for at least 6 years, based on the students' will and aspirations. For those who fulfill the agreement, the Beijing Normal University will refund their tuition and accommodation fees for the four-year undergraduate programme. They will also be covered by the incentive scheme "Good Teachers with Four Qualities"[①], which aims to encourage outstanding university graduates to continuously teach in rural schools through a package of support, including cash reward, training opportunities and so on. Those who have completed one semester of service and meet the access requirements can be accepted free of examination to study for a professional master's degree in education at Beijing Normal University.

In addition, the graduates can have access to diversified opportunities and resources for teachers provided by Beijing Normal University during their term. These include in-service training programme for teachers in basic education, teaching resources such as demonstration courses and online educational resources, guidance from experts in subject teaching, and other learning opportunities for teaching improvement.

(3) Case: Recruiting Retired Teachers for Education Development in Poor Areas: Lecturing by Seniors Programme for Universities, Primary and Secondary Schools

Chinese government has introduced the initiative of recruiting qualified, retired teachers to support teaching in poor areas. In July 2018, the Ministry of Education and Ministry of Finance jointly issued *The Implementation Plan for the Lecturing by Seniors Programme*. The programme recruits outstanding retired principals, teaching researchers, expert teachers, and senior teachers to be lecturers in rural schools at the compulsory education level. It aims to leverage the intellectual support from outstanding retired teachers for rural schools to improve the teaching quality, enhance management capacity, address issues of the shortage of excellent teachers and unbalanced faculty composition, and ultimately promote the balanced urban-rural development of compulsory education.

---

① "Good Teachers with Four Qualities" was raised by President Xi Jinping when he spoke at Beijing Normal University, at the occasion of National Teachers' Day in 2014. It indicates that a good teacher should have four qualities: ideals and beliefs, moral sentiments, solid knowledge and a heart of benevolence. The incentive scheme is funded by the Beijing Normal University Education Foundation.

- **Programme scope:** The programme is implemented on a county-by-county basis, mainly in counties identified by the state as contiguous special hardship areas, targeted counties for poverty alleviation and development at the national and provincial levels, severely impoverished counties, and poor counties with ethnic peoples. The recipient schools are those located in the county town, townships, and rural areas.
- **Activities:** The recruited lecturers can deliver classroom-based lecturing, and organize activities in response to the needs of the recipient schools, such as observation of classroom teaching, demonstration lessons, seminars, or lectures, aiming to provide guidance for young teachers, school-based teaching research, and assist in school management.
- **Recruitment:** The recruitment is done by the provincial education department, following the principles of "openness, fairness, voluntarism, and selecting the best" and "designated county, designated school, and designated post". Lecturers are hired according to the needs of the schools in the recipient counties, and the subject expertise of the candidates. The recruitment takes the following procedures: (1) posting the job advertisement; (2) voluntary registration; qualification (3) check and selection; (4) public announcement; (5) signing the agreement; (6) deployment.

In principle, the term for the lecturers is not less than one academic year, and continuous teaching is encouraged for those who pass the assessment. The Education Bureau of the recipient county signs a contract on a yearly basis with the lecturer, specifying the rights and obligations of both parties. A physical examination report of the recruited lecturer within the past six months is required before signing the contract.

During the service period, the lecturer will be followed up and evaluated by the recipient county. The contract will be terminated if he/she does not fulfill the required obligations, or if he/she is unfit to work due to medical reasons. The lecturer's retirement benefits remain unchanged. Work expenses that include work subsidies, travel expenses, and accident insurance fee are paid on a monthly basis.

The programme was launched in 2018 and piloted in Hebei, Jiangxi, Hu'nan, Guangxi, Sichuan, Yunnan, Gansu, and Qinghai provinces/Autonomous Regions in central and western China. From 2018 to 2020, the programme has been expanded to 16 provinces/Autonomous Regions. It has recruited nearly 10,000 retired lecturers to teach in rural areas. The programme prioritizes the most hard-to-reach areas.

BOX 3-19   A Teacher's Testimonial of the Lecturing by Seniors Programme in Hubei Province

Zhang Baojun, one of the first group of lecturers for the Lecturing by Seniors Programme in Hubei Province, said,

After seeing the introduction of the national Lecturing by Seniors programme, I signed up for the programme without hesitation. I don't want to let my precious days go wasted. I want to start a new career in teaching in rural areas.

At present, I have been teaching at Huanxi School, a nine-year compulsory education school in Xiaochang County, (at the southern foot of Dabie Mountain), for more than a year. It's like returning to a long-lost homeland after returning to campus. I want to bring the wonderful world outside the mountains to teachers and students here, showing them the new concepts, ideas, methods, tools, and content of educational reform as early as possible.

Source: A Professor Couple Came to the Primary School in the Mountainous area – Retired Teachers Activate Rural Education, available at new.qq.com.

Furthermore, to support the development of higher education in less developed areas, the Ministry of Education of China launched the Lecturing by Seniors Programme for Universities in Western China in 2020. In the first group, more than 140 retired professors and associate professors with high qualifications, experience, ethics, and dedication were selected from reputed universities by the Ministry of Education to teach in western China.

The Ministry of Education has provided sufficient funds to provide subsidies for programme lectures. Meanwhile, with the support of recipient universities, the programme offers multiple benefits to teachers, including pre-service training fees, round-trip travel expenses, accident insurance fees, medical insurance fees, and others.

Specific work of the support programme is a joint responsibility between the universities providing and receiving assistance. The nature of assignment is worked out based on actual needs of recipient universities. The recruitment process includes (1) needs assessment; (2) mobilization; (3) qualification check and selection; (4) public announcement; (5) signing of an agreement; (6) induction. The teacher's personnel relations during the service and retirement benefits remain unchanged.

BOX 3-20   Retired Professors Support Higher Education in Western China

Ma Lihua, head of the department of research and industrial education integration at the West Yunnan University of Applied Technology, a recipient university of the Silver Age Teacher Support Program for Universities in Western China, said, *Our school is fortunate to be one of the first pilots of the program. Despite the challenges of the COVID-19 pandemic and high altitude, the retired professors were able to selflessly pass on their years of teaching experience to young teachers. The grassroots teachers benefited a lot from their precious advice and guidance on the grasp of teaching contents, the improvement of performance competencies in the classrooms, and the use of the case teaching method.*

Source: 12 "Silver-aged" Teachers from Famous Schools Support Teaching and Research at West Yunnan University of Applied Technology, available at wap.peopleapp.com.

3. Strengthening the Quality of Teaching in Disadvantaged Rural Schools by Leveraging the Power of ICT

The application of ICT as a powerful instrument to promote an equitable and quality education has been highly valued by the Chinese government to narrow down the urban-rural gaps in education. The government has implemented a range of projects on the development of ICT infrastructure for education, equipping schools with ICT facilities and its use, especially helping share the quality education resources from developed areas to the disadvantaged rural schools, which has contributed significantly to the improvement of education quality in less developed areas.

The following two cases demonstrate China's good practices in harnessing ICTs in improving teaching and learning in rural schools.

(1) Case: Distance Teaching Support Project Bridging Foshan City in Eastern Guangdong Province and Liangshan Prefecture in Western Sichuan Province

A Distance Teaching Support Project was implemented by Chancheng District, Foshan City, Guangdong Province and Liangshan Autonomous Prefecture of Yi Ethnic Group, Sichuan Province to provide relevant support to education development in impoverished Zhaojue, Puge and Butuo counties of Liangshan by leveraging the power of internet technologies.

In August 2018, Chancheng District and the three counties in Liangshan prefecture kicked off an exchange and discussion on the improvement of ICT infrastructure and the introduction of distance education, and then Chancheng District assigned a task force to have an in-depth survey in the targeted counties regarding the hardware, software, and human resource requirements for distance education. Based on the findings, in September 2018, the Education Bureau of Chancheng District allocated a fund of RMB 960,000 to launch the Chancheng-Liangshan Distance Teaching Support project.

The key achievements of the project include:

- User accounts for online learning have been created for teachers and students for the participating six senior and junior secondary schools, and elementary schools, and the homepages of the benefitting schools built and uploaded online, which has helped promote the exchange between the two parties;
- Working spaces have been established for around 100 outstanding teachers from both parties for facilitating exchange, experience sharing and mentoring;
- More than 150 instructional videos and high-quality coursewares developed

by outstanding teachers in Chancheng District were uploaded to the distance education platform;

- Since October 2018, a total of 41 high-quality courses with a total length of 2,460 minutes were uploaded to the platform, covering pre-primary, primary and secondary education subjects, management and technology, special education, vocational education and other subjects;
- By the end of 2018, a total of 4,351 teachers from both places had joined the online learning;
- Five offline training workshops for 725 teachers were organized in Liangshan by volunteer teachers from Chancheng to enhance the capacity of teachers at recipient schools on practical ICT skills, such as micro-course technology, teaching courseware production and application.

Overall, the Chancheng-Liangshan Distance Teaching Support Project has effectively reduced the cost of time and labor, and it allows students from the two places, who are thousands of miles apart, to jointly enjoy quality educational resources. Meanwhile, teachers and schools have improved their capacities by utilizing the distance education platform for knowledge sharing, and teachers in the recipient area have been trained on advanced educational ideas and practices, and teaching methods. The recipient schools have also established a collective teaching research system, which is essential for teachers' professional development. These supports have helped schools in Liangshan gradually establish a capable team of teachers for further development.

(2) Case: The Demonstration Zone of "Internet Plus Education" in Ningxia Hui Autonomous Region

Since 2018, the Management Centre of ICT in Education of Ningxia Autonomous Region of Hui Ethnic Group has implemented the "Internet plus Education" project to build a demonstration zone of ICT in education and the pilot of "Teaching Force Development through Artificial Intelligence", to enable children in rural schools to have access to quality education resources and promote a balanced development of education in rural and urban areas. It has mainly introduced three practices as follows:

- **Improving the infrastructure and educational technology facilities in schools in poor areas**

In the demonstration zone, remote rural schools have been equipped with computers, interactive teaching screens and other teaching equipment. Promotion campaigns on school networking were organized, through which all schools (including teaching points) have acquired internet access. A "cloud-net-end" architecture was built, so that teachers and students can access educational resources from the "Ningxia Education Cloud" whenever needed.

- **Building Ningxia Education Cloud platform to support quality education resources for all**

The Cloud platform integrates quality courses developed by experts at the national, provincial, and municipal levels, including the local expert teachers. Moreover, in the face of the disruptions caused by the COVID-19 pandemic, the cloud platform was used to set up the air classroom programme, and open up the TV and network synchronous broadcast channels. It ensured learning continuity for every student in Ningxia during school closures caused by the pandemic.

- **Facilitating an urban-rural assistance mechanism through online classrooms on Ningxia Education Cloud**

The twinning of urban and rural schools has been established to improve the teaching of disadvantaged schools by using the online classrooms created on the Ningxia Education Cloud. The four twinning networks are shown as Figure 3-1.

High-quality schools in more developed provinces	⟺	Urban schools in Ningxia
High-quality schools in Ningxia	⟺	Schools in mountainous areas
County schools	⟺	Rural schools
Township (town) center elementary schools	⟺	Teaching points

Figure 3-1   Four Twinning Networks

The Internet plus Education project has achieved satisfactory results, which include:

- In 2020, all 3, 456 schools at all levels in Ningxia had access to the internet. Nearly 63% of schools enjoyed a network bandwidth of 100M or over. About 80% of parents have achieved family-school interconnection.
- The Ningxia Education Cloud has registered 90% of teachers' profiles, recorded learning files of 80% students, and accessed more than 100 applications, such as subject networks and teaching assistants; and provided over 18 million pieces of teaching and learning resources, 100,000 plus micro-lessons, and 5,000 master classes.
- All 1.6 million teachers and students in the region can enjoy quality educational resources from high-quality schools across the country on their mobile devices. All the teachers in the region have registered to use the "Learning Space for All" in Ningxia Education Cloud to carry out hybrid teaching and learning. A total of 1.14 million students and 90,000 teachers have opened online learning spaces in Ningxia Education Cloud. It is estimated that some 28% of primary and secondary schools have online classes.

In a nutshell, the project has effectively solved the problem of unbalanced distribution of quality education resources especially for schools in remote areas,

thus narrowing the gap between rural and urban education. The improvement in infrastructure and connectivity of schools in mountainous areas has laid the foundation of distance learning. In the past, children living in remote areas, such as Baoyu Village in Zhenhu Township, Xiji County, had to travel long distances to township schools for better-quality education. Now children have access to the same quality educational resources through the network at the nearest teaching points.

4. Improving the Quality of Education in Ethnic Group Areas

Improving the quality of education in China's ethnic regions has been a critical part of achieving the goal of poverty reduction. Many ethnic groups in China have their own unique languages. However, as many languages do not have corresponding vocabulary to express terms related to modern science and technology, the children of ethnic groups face challenges in learning relevant subjects. It also poses a challenge in developing the technical skills needed in today's labor market. Additionally, the difficulties in mobility and communication between regions caused by language barriers exacerbate the gaps in development throughout the country. Therefore, a strong foundation of Mandarin, which is China's national language, is necessary for ethnic children to gain subject knowledge and technical skills in the national education system and access employment opportunities in the modern labor market. That said, the acquisition of mother tongues is also equally important as the understanding of local languages is essential for developing a firm foundation for children's cognitive and language abilities, inheriting cultural heritage, and enhancing diversity and inclusivity in society.

To this end, the Chinese government has established different models of bilingual education programmes relevant to the situation of various ethnic groups and the will of the local communities[1]. Furthermore, China continues to implement programmes for collaborative educational development between developed and less developed regions. These efforts have achieved considerable progress in ensuring an inclusive and quality education for people belonging to various ethnic groups.

The following cases show good practices of supporting education for ethnic groups through bilingual education projects and educational collaboration between regions.

---

[1]   After long-term practice, China has developed four modes of bilingual education that include: 1) use the ethnic language as the language of instruction (LoI) and teach Mandarin Chinese as a subject; 2) use Mandarin Chinese as the LoI and teach the ethnic language as a subject; 3) use the ethnic language and Mandarin Chinese as LoI for different subjects; 4) and assist teaching in the ethnic language.

(1) Case: Dong-Mandarin Bilingual Education Project for Zaidang Village in Rongjiang County, Guizhou Province

In the 1950s, few people in Zaidang Village of Dong ethnic group in Guizhou Province could read in the national language, the Mandarin Chinese and most people in the village could only speak some Mandarin. The difference between the mother tongue and the school instruction language has led to a high dropout rate and low level of learning motivation among school-age children in the village. To address this challenge, Guizhou University launched a pilot project on bilingual education in the village in cooperation with the Summer Institute of Linguistics (SIL International). The project aimed to help students from poor families to study modern scientific knowledge, integrate into modern society, and lay a foundation for their future employment and career development.

The project brought together national and international experts and scholars to jointly design a project that utilized local expertise and experiences, provided education responsive to ethnic culture, language and living. Complementary teaching and reading materials were developed. The project recruited teachers locally to draw on their years of experience and suggestions for bilingual teaching in the local communities.

The approach of Dong-Mandarin bilingual education first introduced the Dong language along with elements of local contents and then gradually transitioned to Mandarin. When studying literacy and other courses (mathematics, music, art, sports, etc.) in Mandarin, teachers would demonstrate examples from the Dong indigenous knowledge as much as possible to make students feel that the learning content is relevant to their own lives. Consequently, the pilot project has led to a big decrease in the dropout rate of students in Zaidang Village. It also substantially increased elementary school enrollment and graduation rates reaching almost hundred percent.

(2) Case: The Counterpart Education Assistance from Chengdu City to Ethnic Group Areas in Sichuan Province

The characteristics of vast land area, scattered communities, and limited access to information in areas inhabited by Tibetans in Sichuan province and Liangshan prefecture pose specific challenges in improving the quality of education and accelerating China's efforts in poverty reduction through education. In this regard, the government of Chengdu, the capital city of Sichuan Province, has prioritized the development of education in ethnic areas in its education development plan and annual work plan through the counterpart education assistance scheme. The city government has invested RMB 500 million and implemented 80 counterpart assistance projects. The implementation emphasizes three key aspects:

- Full engagement of schools, teachers, and students;
- The introduction of three types of classes: class with students from ethnic groups, class for students from ethnic groups, and the class for specific plans or programmes.
- Resource mobilization by leveraging the government, schools, and enterprises.

Furthermore, activities of the counterpart assistance for education development in ethnic areas can be categorized into three groups:

- **Twinning programmes among counties and schools**

According to available data, 458 kindergartens and primary schools in 22 districts in Chengdu City and 477 kindergartens and primary schools in 20 counties in prefectures of Ganzi, Aba, and Liangshan, have established "county-to-county" and "school-to-school" twinning/networking programmes. A two-way dialogue session was organized to facilitate the collaborative work, including joint planning and implementation.

Moreover, as part of a strategy to support the development of talented human resource in ethnic areas, *the Special Programme for Teachers* has been implemented to ensure fair benefits to all teachers in ethnic regions and expand the exchange of human resources. So far, the programme has seconded more than 2,000 outstanding teachers from Chengdu City to teach in three less developed prefectures of Ganzi, Liangshan and Aba, while receiving more than 2,000 teachers from the three regions for shadow-learning in Chengdu, which has significantly promoted the professional growth of teachers in poor areas.

- **General education plus vocational education**

High-quality senior secondary schools such as Shuangliu Middle School, Wenjiang Middle School, and Chengdu No.3 Middle School set up enrollment plans to recruit students from poor ethnic groups and offer vocational education courses geared towards the practical needs of ethnic communities. The tailored programme aims to enhance learners' motivation, reduce dropouts, and improve the employability of students from poor ethnic communities.

- **Distance education platform**

By implementing the *Chengdu Development Plan on ICT in Education (2014-2020)* and the *Chengdu "Internet plus Education" Work Plan*, a distance education system covering pre-primary to secondary education and related collaborative working mechanisms have been established, which are currently well working. Now all poor areas in Sichuan province have access to high-quality education resources created by outstanding schools in Chengdu, such as the online school of Chengdu Seventh Middle School and distance education platform of Shishi Middle School.

Over the past few years, more than 10,000 students from poor ethnic group areas have benefited from the counterpart assistance projects, enabling them to enjoy an equal access to quality educational resources (i.e. teachers, learning materials) in Chengdu, and more employment opportunities after graduation.

III. Empowering Poor Families in China through Technical and Vocational Education and Training (TVET) and Skills Development

1. Enhance the Employability for Better Jobs and Better Future through TVET

Many poor rural families in China rely solely on farming for their livelihood and do not have other sources of income or income-generating skills. Enabling these families to acquire technical skills opens the door to more opportunities for employment and entrepreneurship that can alleviate the poverty in the local community.

The following two cases show innovative projects in TVET education in Hainan and Guizhou provinces. The last case demonstrates a national collaborative initiative on TVET between the east and west of China and a practice from the eastern Fujian province.

(1) Case: TVET Pogramme for Girls by Hainan Provincial Economic and Technical School

In 2009, a survey on motivation for access to vocational education in Hainan Province found that around 60% of rural families could not keep their daughters in school after graduating from junior high school, due to the increasing cost and the low motivation of families. These girls were forced to drop out and often engaged in heavy and low-skilled jobs to support their families. Many of them were subject to early marriage, leading to early pregnancy.

To this end, a tailored technical and vocational education programme for girls was launched in July 2009, jointly by Hainan Provincial Economic and Technical School and the Hainan Provincial Women's Federation. Inspired by the vision "educated girls, empowered mothers, and better families", the School developed a ten-year action plan (2009-2018) for the programme, which aimed to train 10,000 students to become skilled personnel to match the needs of building an international tourism island in Hainan Province.

The programme offers 13 specialties, such as hotel service and management, agricultural products processing and inspection, cookery, corporate finance and supermarket cashier, clothing design and production, and golf service and management. The school exempts tuition and accommodation fees for enrolled students and provides

an additional monthly living subsidy of RMB 350 to reduce students' economic burden.

Moreover, the school collaborates with enterprises to provide comprehensive skills development and career services for students. For example, the school partnered with a branded Hainan hairdressing enterprise to organize weekly training on entrepreneurship and employment. Students can acquire solid hands-on experience in skill-set and business management throughout their education and training. Over 30 students per year get jobs in the hairdressing industry upon graduation.

From 2009 to 2016, the programme reached a total of 7,914 adolescent girls, with 5,070 graduates and 2,844 remaining in the school. Many students have become economically productive with their technical skills after graduation and their earning has lifted them out of poverty.

(2) Case: Targeted Poverty Alleviation Programme to Support Libo County, Guizhou Province, by Guizhou Equipment Manufacturing Polytechnic

One of the counties located in the Qiannan Autonomous Prefecture of Buyi and Miao Ethnic Groups, Guizhou Province, Libo is a severely impoverished area. To mitigate the gaps in educational development in Libo County, in 2015, Guizhou Equipment Manufacturing Polytechnic launched a targeted poverty alleviation programme to provide vocational courses in three disciplines with promising job prospects, including machinery manufacturing, elevator installation and maintenance, and automotive maintenance. The programme enables students from poor families to acquire vocational skills matching market demand so that they can obtain a stable income and improve the lives of their families, in a relatively short period of time.

The key features of the programme are:
- **Tailored study plan:** Home visits to the students' families are conducted regularly by the head teachers and government officials assigned to the villages to investigate families' needs and then develop an appropriate and comprehensive study plan that meets the actual needs of each poor student.
- **Mentorship scheme:** The programme adopts the "two-mentor" system to assign a life mentor and a career mentor for each student, giving attention to both students' learning and their wellbeing.
- **Financial support:** The school waives miscellaneous school fees for students from poor families, gives grants to students covered by relevant policies, and provides work-study opportunities for them.

As of 2017, the school has enrolled more than 460 students for the Targeted Poverty Alleviation Programme, of which 56 students have been enrolled from Libo County. By 2020, the graduates reached the goal of full employment.

(3) Case: Action Plan for East-West Cooperation in Vocational Education in China: the Practice of Quanzhou Ocean Institute, Fujian Province

In 2016, the Ministry of Education and the Poverty Alleviation Office of the State Council jointly issued the *Action Plan for East-West Cooperation in Vocational Education (2016-2020)* (hereinafter referred to as the Action Plan), which is a part of the East-West Cooperation in Poverty Alleviation implemented by the Chinese government. The Action Plan is oriented toward the needs of the population in impoverished western regions to promote employment and eradicate poverty, and it includes three major activities:

- The twinning of vocational institutions, including vocational education groups, secondary and higher vocational institutions, between the east and west regions;
- Increasing the enrollment of students from poor families in the western regions to vocational institutions in the east. If they choose to stay and work in the eastern regions after graduation, they will be prioritized for job recommendation;
- Encouraging vocational institutions to contribute to east-west collaboration on labour exchange, through providing free vocational training, such as pre-service training, and training on employability skills, skills upgrading, and entrepreneurship, for the poor population to meet the needs of the labour market.

Following the Action Plan, in April 2017, the Poverty Alleviation Office of the State Council of China set up a National Training Base for Employment and Entrepreneurship for Poverty Alleviation in the Quanzhou Ocean Institute in Quanzhou City, Fujian Province, which is an economically developed province with strong industrial base located in the eastern part of China.

The Quanzhou Ocean Institute gives preference for the admission of students from poor families in five provinces / autonomous regions, including Ningxia, Gansu, Sichuan, Anhui, and Henan, exempting them from tuition and miscellaneous fees, and provides them vocational skills training and entrepreneurship training. The Institute has co-established the Fujian-Ningxia Labor Exchange Centre, the Fujian - Guizhou Labor Exchange and Training Centre, and the Fujian - Guizhou East-West Talent Pool. Besides, in collaboration with logistics and e-commerce companies, the Institute has launched the Zhongjing Hainong Poverty Alleviation E-commerce Platform to facilitate the cold chain logistics to connect the fresh food markets in the east and west of China, inviting rural entrepreneurs and enterprises to join the e-commerce platform and its e-market as partners and promote the development of agricultural plantations, fisheries, and aquaculture in their villages. Relying on the e-commerce platform, students from

the Institute can access training in business development and digital marketing, as well as job opportunities created by the e-market.

The Quanzhou Ocean Institute's innovative practice of the East-West Cooperation in Vocational Education has achieved great results. As of 2020, the training bases and vocational education centre have trained 310 model entrepreneurs, more than 2,200 crew members of various types (all on board, with starting salaries of over RMB 8,000 per month), over 2,000 new employees of enterprises (all on board, with starting salaries of over RMB 4,000 per month). It has benefited 4,200 poor families through vocational education and employment, and equipped farmers in over 300 poverty-stricken villages with technical skills. The training program for crew members, offshore fishermen, entrepreneurs, and new employees of enterprises, have benefited more than 20,000 people, with a total of RMB 2,162,600 training fees reduced and waived. All the trainees were employed by enterprises in Quanzhou City and surrounding areas.

2. Promoting Adult Education and Training for Poverty Alleviation

Many adults in rural areas do not have access to schooling and lacked professional knowledge and skills for employment, which has become one of the leading causes of economic hardship for families in these areas. Therefore, the Chinese government has positioned adult education and training as an effective approach for the rural population to develop practical skills and improve their livelihood.

In January 2013, the Chinese government issued the *Notice on the Establishment of National-level Rural Vocational and Adult Education Demonstration Counties*, aiming to develop model practices of rural vocational and adult education in the demonstration counties and inspire more people from poor communities to learn from the best practices of eradicating poverty through education. Until 2019, 261 demonstration counties / cities / districts have been certified. It serves as a significant part of the work for "San Nong[①]" and rural revitalization in China.

Moreover, in 2016, the Ministry of Education and the All-China Federation of Trade Unions jointly implemented an action plan, namely the *Study for Dream Action* to provide continuous education programmes for migrant workers through a combination of the qualification-oriented education and non-formal education, such as skills training, with an emphasis on the integration of production and education, school-enterprise cooperation, and career-oriented learning. It plays a critical role in supporting the transformation and upgrading of socio-economic development and industrial structure in China, improving the work and living conditions of migrant workers.

---

① The Three Rural Issues, or San Nong, refers to three issues relating to rural development in Chinese mainland: agriculture, rural areas and farmers.

As of 2020, 1.5 million migrant workers who aspire to upgrade their educational qualifications and skill-sets, have been sponsored by the Chinese government to receive continuous education. According to one statistics, by the end of 2020, a total of 710 higher education institutions and 1,796 education and training institutions nationwide had joined the implementation of the action plan. In total, 1.3 million learners have benefited from continuous education for upgrading qualifications, and more than 9.5 million participants have received non-formal skills training. The action plan achieved positive results in migrant workers' skills upgrading and employability.

The following are successful cases in two rural areas in Henan and Zhejiang Provinces on poverty alleviation through adult education and skills development. The success of these two practices can be attributed to a project planning and implementation that corresponds to actual needs of local people and local resources, and partnership between education institutions and government.

(1) Case: Tailored Skills Training for New Farmers in Zhenping County, Nanyang City, Henan Province

Zhenping County is under the jurisdiction of Nanyang City in the southwestern part of Henan Province, with a total area of 1,560 square kilometers and a population of 1.04 million people. Local people have long faced difficulties, such as low employment and income, due to a lack of skills training and insufficient knowledge of new agricultural technologies.

To address this issue, in 2014, the China Adult Education Association (CAEA) launched the second phase of the "Rural Community Learning Centre (CLC) Capacity Building Project" in China. Under the project, 16 pilots have been established, including Yangying Township Adult School in Zhenping County, also named as "Henan Province Rural Adult Education Teaching Reform Experimental School" by Henan Provincial Adult Education and Research Office.

The majority of the CLC trainees are recruited from local poor households. The training combines lectures, including video lectures given by full-time and part-time trainers, and independent learning. A participatory learning model is adopted, which encourages regular interactions between learners and trainers. In response to the local needs, the CLC and the county's craft vocational college co-organized a 25-day summer course on jade carving in 2018, for a total of 54 trainees. In addition, the CLC and the township government jointly provided technical training for new farmers for targeted poverty reduction in 2018, reaching 60 learners. Besides, experts are invited by the CLC to deliver lectures on family education and raise people's awareness on the importance of family education, including effective approaches.

These activities have equipped local farmers with practical and easy-to-follow skills,

improving their confidence in acquiring new means of income generation for better life. Moreover, the CLC capacity-building project promoted the benefits of lifelong learning and practices that are context-specific for people in Zhenping County in order to make a sustainable impact.

(2) Case: Skills Training in Tourism Resource Development for Poverty Alleviation: the Case of Datian Village, Lishui City, Zhejiang Province

Some poor villages in developed areas have high potential for promoting tourism, thanks to their natural beauty and abundant organic agricultural products. However, the local people lack relevant skills to translate the available tourism resources into income generation for better life. For instance, Datian Village in Dazhe Township, Suichang County, Lishui City, Zhejiang Province, is widely known for its tea production and beautiful scenery. Ten years ago, although every household in Datian planted tea, their standard of living was still low. Additionally, Datian Village did not fully utilize its advantages in tourism and convenient transportation, though it was located on the only way to the national AAAA scenic site Qianfo Mountain and Nanjiangyan, Jiulongshan National Nature Reserve, and on the way to the ten townships in the west of Suichang County.

In 2010, the Dazhe township government worked out a development strategy for the development of tea industry, tourism and leisure industry, following the principle of green, sustainable and harmonious development. After nearly a decade of efforts, villages like Datian and Cheqian have become specialized villages[①] and demonstration villages of new rural construction, for their integrative development of agriculture and tourism, and they have become a highlight of tourism and leisure industry in Zhejiang Province.

The Dazhe Centre Adult Technical School in Dazhe Township has played a crucial role in this process. The school organized skills training for local villagers on agricultural and leisure tourism, tea culture, catering service, and hospitality, in order to leverage the advantages of local natural and agricultural resources. It also delivered projects and information on tourism resource development for local communities. With the support of the school, Datian village has built a comprehensive visitor centre that integrates catering, accommodation, parking, and customer service. It is now known for its tea culture and agri-tourism, attracting tourists nationwide.

The farmers' life has been greatly improved, thanks to the growing income generated from the tea industry and agri-tourism. In 2018, there were only 600 households but more than 50 rural leisure resorts in the village. The per capita income of villagers was

---

① "Specialized villages in China" refers to the villages in rural China that are engaged in a certain industry with specialized production skills according to professional division of labour.

RMB 22,135, ranking first in all the villages of the county. This small village received 118,000 visitors and earned an income of more than RMB 12.1 million. The case of Datian village is a successful practice of utilizing skills training to transform local resources into economic growth and eradicate rural poverty.

3. Leveraging Local Traditional Skills for Poverty Alleviation

Each rural community has its unique traditional cultural resources, especially the Intangible Cultural Heritage (ICH), such as embroidery, paper cutting, shadow making, lantern making, gourd carving and so on. Developing the commercial values contained in local cultural resources not only ensures the inheritance of cultural heritages in rural communities, but also generates income for poor rural families.

The first case demonstrates how Xi'an Shiyou University combines research and teaching programmes to identify and safeguard the local ICH and develop creative entrepreneurial initiatives for tourism in Yongshou County, Shaanxi Province. The second case is a successful example of alleviating rural poverty through skills training and small business on Zhuang textile skills, an intangible heritage in Guangxi Autonomous Region.

(1) Case: Xi'an Shiyou University Supports the Development of Cultural Tourism in Yongshou County by Harnessing Local Intangible Cultural Heritage [1]

Yongshou County, Shaanxi Province, is blessed with a long history and splendid traditional culture. Its arts of war drums, paper cutting, and Tuliang oil making have been included into the list of ICH at the provincial level. However, for a long time, the value of preserving their cultural heritage in poverty reduction and sustainable development have not been realized due to lack of systematic planning and development.

To this end, under the national policy of pairing-up assistance for poverty alleviation, Xi'an Shiyou University, the counterpart of Yongshou County for paring, initiated a project "discovering ICH and building a brand of cultural tourism in Yongshou County". The project aims to combine the university's research and human resources, with the unique cultural resources of Yongshou County to promote cultural products with core competitiveness, create a distinctive cultural brand, and boost the development of local industries and the local economy.

The project includes three interlinked components: intangible culture brand

---

[1]　Research Group of Renmin University of China, Summary of Poverty Reduction through Education Since the 18th Party Congress (Collection of Good Practices), 2020.

building, marketing and promotion, and registration of identified intangible cultures in the ICH list. It sought to build cultural brand mainly through the following four steps:

- Discover and identify local ICH.
- Design touristic services and products in response to market demands.
- Create a product line of identified and designed handicrafts.
- Develop e-commerce of cultural products in Yongshou County.

The Department of Design in the College of Humanities, Xi'an Shiyou University arranged practice sessions for students to develop business plans and design packaging for Yongshou County's arts and cultural products. Besides, the university jointly organized two exhibitions of packaging design for arts and cultural products in Yongshou, in collaboration with the County Government. The exhibitions showcased the beauty of the ICH of Yongshou County, which has significantly contributed to its branding.

In addition, the University set up a dedicated task force to assist the County on the identification of cultural programmes and their inclusion in the list of ICH. The task force conducted an in-depth field survey on the potential ICHs and established close contact with local communities. In addition, the task force also helped complete 11 proposals for ICH registration.

Following the launch of the ICH project, local cultural and creative entrepreneurship initiatives in Yongshou County have been rising, promoting the development of local cultural tourism, and providing a new path for impoverished communities to get out of poverty.

(2) Case: Indigenous Craft Skills Training to Alleviate Poverty: the Practice of Moli Village, Leye County, Guangxi Zhuang Autonomous Region

Moli Village, Leye County, was a deprived rural community in Guangxi Zhuang Autonomous Region. It has sparse and poor land with a per capita cultivated area of 0.65 mu[①], and farmers' income is mainly dependent on farming and labour exports. This situation has been changed in recent years. Leye County has been leading the development of the cultural and tourism industries in the area to promote the village's "Bulong" culture, which has led to the development of both the traditional culture and farmers' income in Moli Village.

Leye County government has emphasized developing localized industries as a means to reduce poverty and inheriting indigenous culture and skills from generation

---

① Mu: a unit of area used in China, and 1 mu equals to 666 square metres.

to generation. Since 2008, Leye County has been organizing an annual tourism-related handicraft competition, aiming to safeguard and inherit the traditional Zhuang textile skills with a history of over 400 years. Moreover, the county supports representative inheritors of Zhuang textile skills at the county level to attend skills development sessions organized by the Baise city and the Guangxi Minzu University.

The handicraft market of Moli Village is thriving, thanks to the strategic support from the County government in cultural tourism and increasing efforts in skills training in this regard, which has largely changed impoverished state of many local households. So far, the Moli village has 464 households and 2, 270 people, of which 427 households and 2, 045 people are engaged in Zhuang textile making, which can earn an average of RMB 50 per person per day by weaving. The textile households can bring in more than RMB 10,000 per year by weaving. From 2014 to 2019, the households registered for targeted poverty reduction has reduced from 165 to 10, and from 742 people to 36 people.

BOX 3-21　Luo Meilie's Story: Women Stand out and Lead the Way to Wealth with Zhuang Traditional Textiles Skills

Although the Zhuang traditional textile skills have a history of more than 400 years in the village of Moli, the younger generation in recent years has been reluctant to acquire the skills because of the complexity, low efficiency, and high cost of production. Therefore, the Zhuang cloth textile is at risk of being lost for posterity.

Luo Meilie, born in 1955, is a native Bulong descendant who learned Zhuang native cloth weaving from her mother at the age of 12. She was diligent and studied hard, and her work in Bulong Zhuang textiles was exquisite. Luo Meilie continues her efforts to learn various Zhuang textile techniques. She also leads other people to learn together, often holding free training sessions on Zhuang textile techniques at her home or the training centre to teach young and middle-aged women in her village. She has become a renowned Zhuang weaver in the area and was awarded the title of Model Inheritor of the Autonomous Region's ICH (Zhuang Weaving Technique) in November 2017. She can now make a decent living through the business of Zhuang cloth textiles.

Inspired by Luo Meilie, more women in the community are joining traditional weaving and starting a business. The products made by Zhuang textile techniques, such as Zhuang clothing and Zhuang quilts, straps, cloth shoes, insoles, door curtains, window curtains, mosquito net curtains, satchels, pillowcases, and other products, are popular among Zhuang communities and tourists and make considerable profits for the households.

Source: The Leader of "Intangible Heritage + Poverty Alleviation" in Leye County: Luo Meilie: Women Stand Out and Lead the Way to Wealth with Intangible Cultural Heritage, available at www. gxcounty.com.

Ⅳ. Boosting Rural Industrial and Economic Development by Higher Education Institutions and Vocational Schools

1. Cultivating Entrepreneurial Leaders for Poverty Alleviation in Rural Areas

Many rural communities stagnate in poverty because of a lack of rural entrepreneurial leaders or role models that can transform local resources into profitable industries. The training of rural entrepreneurial leaders is a key measure to address this gap, through education and skills training in agriculture and relevant skills.

The first case demonstrates a distance education programme that has improved the capacity of learners from remote rural areas to become local entrepreneurial leaders. The second case highlights the story of Professor Li Baoguo from Hebei Agricultural University, who brought his expertise in agriculture and management to Gangdi Village.

(1) Case: "One College Student Per Village" Programme Provides Higher Education for Selected Villagers: a Case from Hu'Nan Province

In 2004, the Open University of China initiated the "One College Student Per Village" Programme which aims to train village leaders and local entrepreneurial leaders in management, entrepreneurship, and agricultural technologies for rural areas through long-distance education. Since 2017, the programme has been integrating artificial intelligence technology into education and teaching, delivering higher education and high-quality educational resources to rural areas while providing tailored learning programmes for grassroots officials or farmers. Until 2021, the programme has trained more than 600,000 rural learners who have become a strong force for poverty reduction and local development. The Programme was awarded the UNESCO ICT Education Prize in 2020.

Hunan Open University, a branch of the Open University of China has successfully implemented the programme in the Province. It has provided tailored training programmes on rural administration, agricultural economic management, animal husbandry, and veterinary medicine, and included some compulsory courses such as rural policies and regulations, village financial management, and information technology application.

The programme combines online lectures delivered by expert teachers nationwide with onsite practical training offered by local experts. Teachers can develop tailored educational resources, adjust their teaching methods relevant to the different groups of learners, and provide individualized guidance through an e-platform. Furthermore, offline teaching is provided in each city and prefecture-level branch of Hunan Open

University, and county teaching sites close to the learners' place of residence, based on the needs of learners and local contexts. It includes inductions, face-to-face tutoring, and practical training. Technical specialists and skilled practitioners have been employed to provide hands-on guidance for rural learners.

The use of ICT in learning is also highly promoted. Students can log into the Farmer Student Learning Network through computers, smartphones, or iPads, study in their individual learning space, participate in collective learning activities, and take exams on the public platform.

According to available statistics, 85% of the rural learners trained by Hunan Open University have served in administration teams for the villages, over 60% have become local role models for income generation, and 7% have been recruited as civil servants. The programme has successfully developed the talents contributing to new rural reconstruction.

BOX 3-22 Long Siqing, a Graduate from Hunan Open University, Leads the Local Business in Citrus Production and Lifelong Learning in Guchong Village, Huaihua City, Hunan Province

Guchong Village in Zhijiang Dong Autonomous County, Huaihua City, Hunan Province, which was in extreme poverty for decades, was able to change this scenario drastically, thanks to the work of Long Siqing, a graduate from Hunan Open University.

Long Siqing acquired her adult higher education diploma from "One College Student Per Village" programme implemented by the Hunan Open University. Harnessing her knowledge and skills learned from the programme, she developed a successful business in citrus production and e-commerce. She said,

The theory and practice of rural administration and management that I learned from the Open University has greatly improved my capacity in managing village's affairs and opened up my views for seeking new opportunities and solutions to problems. I have also improved and expanded the sales outlets a lot.

Inspired by Long Siqing, many villagers participated in this adult education programme and became college students. Meanwhile, more than 200 villagers in Guchong have joined the citrus production industry, with around 6,000 mu of citrus planted and an annual output value of nearly RMB 80 million. It has also helped drive the development of other agriculture-related industries. For example, Guchong Village has enclosed more than 300 mu of land for farming chickens that breed green-shelled eggs. The village has built a standardized pig farm with an annual output of 10,000 pigs.

Long Siqing became the head of the Village Committee, and the elected representative of the 17th and 18th National Congress of the Communist Party of China. She has won the honorary title of "National Model Worker" in recognition of her inspiring story of lifelong learning and achievements in lifting people in Guchong Village out of poverty.

Source: Distributing High-Quality Educational Resources to the Grassroots - "One College Student Per Village" Programme to Help Cultivate Practical Talents in Rural Areas, available at www.gov.cn/xinwen.

(2) Case: Professor LI Baoguo Helps Fruit Tree Cultivation in Gangdi Village

Gangdi is an impoverished village in Houjiazhuang Township, Neiqiu County, Hebei Province. In the 1980s, there were 160 households with 690 people in Gangdi Village with a per capita income of only RMB 50. The village covered some 8,000 mu of barren mountains and around 250 mu of farmland in the mountains. In 1996, the entire 250 mu of arable land was destroyed by a flash flood. The village's few remaining dozens of orchards became the only hope of the whole village. However, the apples produced in the village were of low quality and unsalable, as people called them "small black eggs".

With over 35 years of his career, Li Baoguo, a well-known forestry expert and a professor from Hebei Agricultural University, was committed to the ecological improvement of the Taihang Mountains and helping the masses to get rid of poverty. Having observed such a situation in Gangdi Village, Professor Li Baoguo and his wife, Guo Suping, who also taught at Hebei Agricultural University, moved to Gangdi Village and lived there for nine years to help the villagers through training and hands-on guidance on agricultural technologies.

Li Baoguo designed and implemented a plan for apple production to help lift the villagers of Gangdi out of poverty based on his research and analysis of local soil and geomorphology. He gave a first-hand demonstration to villagers in the fields, explaining fruit tree cultivation and management techniques. As Li Baoguo found that learners had difficulties with techniques especially bud notching, he developed a standardized process of orchard management based on field research, analysis, evaluation, and revision in consultation with community leaders, to support farmers to grasp the techniques. A handbook for orchard management and apple farming, which describes the complete and precise process of 128 technical control points for the whole year, was developed in a scientific and easy-to-read manner and distributed to every villager. Thanks to his training and the handbook, Gangdi fruit farmers can now produce high-quality organic apples.

Today, the Fugang apple cultivated by Li Baoguo has become a well-known brand in China. Apples weighing over 400g are sold at RMB 50 each and RMB 100 at the most. Chain production bases were established in 369 villages in the Taihang Mountains, with a planting area of 58,000 mu and an annual output of more than 100 million kilograms. Gangdi Village has now flourished as a model of poverty alleviation, with a total asset of RMB 105.53 million, an annual output value of RMB 68 million, a per capita income of RMB 10,300, including a per capita fruit income of RMB 9,000, and vegetation coverage of 82%.

Credit goes to Professor Li Baoguo for all these achievements that people made. His expertise and dedication made this change possible. Over the past 30 years, Professor

Li Baoguo has demonstrated and promoted 36 standardized forestry techniques, which have been applied to a total area of 18.26 million mu and increased the value of agricultural output by RMB 3.5 billion. He held more than 800 training courses at different levels and trained more than 90,000 fruit farmers. His work has nurtured many rural entrepreneurial leaders in the Taihang Mountains and the farmers who have been grubbing for a life in the barren mountains for generations were finally lifted out of poverty.

2. Utilizing Research of Higher Education Institutions to Facilitate Industrial Development

Higher education and its researches can play a role in driving industrial development that leads to economic growth, poverty reduction and an improved quality of life in impoverished areas. Since 2012, with a view to advancing the industrial development of the poorest areas, the Chinese government has arranged 44 national universities to provide paired-up support for poverty alleviation in 44 targeted counties that were on top of the agenda for national poverty alleviation and development. In 2019, additional 20 national universities joined this programme for poverty alleviation adopting the "1+1" model, which means one newly-joined university would work together with one of the first group of 44 universities to provide paired-up support to the targeted counties. Meanwhile, the programme is also supported by provincial universities under the guidance of the provincial government.

The following cases are two successful practices showcasing how higher education institutions can leverage experts and research capacities to develop local industries and businesses in poor counties in Yunnan and Shanxi Province, lifting local people out of poverty.

(1) Case: Seconded Zhejiang University's Associate Professor Helping Develop Local Business in Chicken Breeding in Jingdong County

Jingdong Autonomous County of Yi Ethnic Group, Pu'er City, Yunnan Province, is located in the centre of southwest Yunnan and the northernmost part of Pu'er City. The poor population in the county is huge, with seven out of 13 townships being in poverty, of which four townships have been registered with a portfolio in the national poverty alleviation information system. Most local poor households belong to ethnic groups and reside in hardship conditions in mountainous areas, arid and water-scarce areas, and geological disaster-hidden areas around Ailao Mountain and Wuliang Mountain.

In Jingdong, the income of over 90% of the poor households highly depends on breeding black-bone chickens. Jingdong Wuliang Mountain Black-bone Chicken is

famous for its good quality and taste, and it has been listed in the China National Livestock Genetic Resources in 2010. However, the traditional form of chicken farming didn't help raise the of income of local people because of the low egg production rate, low survival rate of chicks, and a lack of relevant techniques.

since 2013, Zhejiang University has started paired-up support to Jingdong County. Dr. Yin Zhaozheng, an associate professor from the Agricultural Technology Extension Centre of the University with expertise in livestock and poultry breeding, was deployed to Jingdong as a seconded expert to implement poverty alleviation programmes.

Upon his arrival in Jingdong, Dr. Yin Zhaozheng immediately started a survey by visiting the households to investigate their chicken farming. He observed the traditional techniques closely used in raising chicks. He noted that the chicks were kept in the small coops in front of the house, under the woodpile or in the sheep pen. He also found that the so-called chicken coops were poorly built, and the day-old chicks were mostly not healthy. In addition, a Jingdong black-bone hen could only produce around 40-60 eggs per year, while in Zhejiang province, some of the selected black-bone hens could have an annual egg production of up to 100 or more.

After a comprehensive investigation, Dr. Yin Zhaozheng and his team designed a programme to cultivate the best quality of Jingdong black-bone chicken and prepared for industrialized operations of the Jingdong chicken farming. He emphasized the need to improve villagers' skills and techniques in chicken farming and to increase the investment in facilities. Under his guidance, the programme has introduced relevant measures and yielded productive outputs:

- Training on standardized chicken farming in local markets and farms were conducted at least twice a year.
- In collaboration with the Jingdong County Agricultural Science Bureau, the *Comprehensive Technical Specification for Breeding Black-bone Chickens in Wuliang Mountain, Jingdong* was developed, which is handy for every villager to breed high-quality black-bone chicken on their own.
- Apprentices in Jingdong who can timely solve technical problems in the field and deliver the skills to wider communities were trained by Dr. Yin Zhaozheng.
- Technical guidance and services for enterprises and large farmers regarding local farm construction, quality testing, breeder selection, artificial insemination, machine hatching, marketing, and other processes of chicken production were provided.
- Alumni and funding of Zhejiang University were mobilized to build the Jingdong black-bone chicken genetic resources protection base.
- A large breeding farm that applies mechanical and three-dimensional cage

breeding mode was built in Jingdong.

- A high-yielding breed with different feather colors was developed. The breeding performance and chicken breeding survival rate were significantly improved.

The sales of high-quality chickens produced by the modern breeding farms of Jingdong black-bone chickens have achieved considerable growth. The number of black-bone chickens sold in Jingdong reached 4.388 million in 2018, which was over 200% higher than the sales in 2012 when Zhejiang University's paired-up support started, achieving an output value of RMB 365 million. As a result, 19, 000 poor households for targeted poverty reduction and 65,000 people have been lifted out of poverty. The featured black-bone chicken industry in Jingdong has become a "golden phoenix" that brings wealth and prosperity to the county.

(2) Case: Targeted Poverty Alleviation Action of China Pharmaceutical University: Cultivate a Unique Brand of "Bashan—the Pharmacy City"

Zhenping County, Ankang City, Shaanxi Province, is located at the southernmost tip of Shaanxi, and at the junction of Shaanxi, Chongqing, and Sichuan provinces (cities). It belongs to the Qinba Ecological Function Area of Biodiversity under the National Main Functional Area Plan, with a forest coverage rate of 86.4%. It boasts of its rich Chinese herbal resources, with over 420 kinds of herbs and more than 400,000 mu of land suitable for growing Chinese herbs. However, for a long time, due to the lack of relevant technology, talent, and other supports, Zhenping County has not been able to make a substantial breakthrough in the utilization of Chinese herbal resources.

To leverage the potential of Chinese herbal resources in Zhenping County, China Pharmaceutical University was assigned by the central government in 2012 to provide designated paired-up support in research and business development in pharmaceuticals to the County in accordance with the national strategy of targeted poverty alleviation. Since then, the University has been harnessing its research capacity and experts to address the root causes of poverty in Zhenping County. The specific objectives of the paired-up support are to improve the capacities of professionals and technicians in Chinese herbal medicine, develop the County's Chinese herbal medicine industry, facilitate its social development, and provide consultation to local decision-making.

The key activities of paired-up support from the China Pharmaceutical University include:

- **Financing**

An amount of RMB 500,000 was allocated from the research fund of the university to set up research projects on the development of local Chinese herbal medicine industry in Zhenping. The university also coordinated with

the local government to support the herbal development projects in Zhenping, establishing a scientific research support platform and brands for the local herbal industry.

- **Sustainable industrial chain**

    An interlinked industrial chain has been established, covering herbal food, health care products, cosmetics, organic chemicals, fertilizers, feeds, and others. The university also provided technical assistance to develop ecological tourism commodities, such as health care, and medicinal food, and to promote the sustainable use of biodiversity and environmentally friendly tourism in Zhenping County.

- **Partnerships**

    The university introduced more than 10 famous pharmaceutical enterprises, such as China Sciences Group (Holding) Co., Ltd., Guangzhou Pharmaceuticals Corporation, Jinling Pharmaceutical Company Limited, and Chia Tai-Tianqing Pharmaceutical Holdings Co., Ltd., to invest and establish production bases, herbal medicine plantations, and herbarium in Zhenping. It also organized visits to famous pharmaceutical enterprises in Jiangsu, Chongqing, Chengdu, and other places for professionals in Chinese medicine in Zhenping, to exchange experiences on developing pharmaceuticals and related industries.

The paired-up support from the China Pharmaceutical University has achieved remarkable results.

- Zhenping County Pharmaceutical Factory, which had been shut down for 8 years, reactivated the production, and expanded its product line with an annual output of 5,000 tons of Chinese medicine tablets, and renovated its production plant and temporary storage space by 4,000 square meters.
- 14 herbal medicine planting and breeding bases have been built, 200 large plantation households and over 4,000 herb farmers have been trained, with the total herbal medicine plantation area reaching 181,000 mu.

In 2015, Zhenping County achieved a total production value of RMB 1.36 billion. The herbal medicine industry increased the average household income of poor households by more than RMB 1,000. The per capita disposable income of urban residents reached RMB 26,941. The Per capita net income of rural residents reached RMB 8,088. Its economic growth ranked at the forefront of Ankang City.

3. Professional Skills Training to Drive Industrial Development in Poor Areas

The Chinese government values vocational and skills training in poor areas in

supporting local industrial development and poverty reduction. In 2019, the Ministry of Education and 14 other departments jointly launched the "Action Plan for Vocational Training to Promote Employment and Entrepreneurship in Vocational Colleges and Universities," which aims to encourage vocational colleges and universities to provide employment and entrepreneurship training for people, such as migrant workers, laborers with poverty portfolios, and people with disabilities. The Action Plan focuses on agriculture-related vocational colleges to carry out skills training, to cultivate high-quality farmers and contribute towards poverty elimination and rural revitalization.

The following cases presented below demonstrate effective practices of leveraging vocational education to improve local employment and nurture talents needed for industrial transformation in rural areas in Jingning County, Gansu Province, and Wuling Mountainous Area, Hunan Province.

(1) Case: Vocational Education Centre in Jingning County, Gansu Province

Jingning County, located in the western part of the Liupan Mountains, is one of the 23 severely impoverished counties in Gansu Province and a key target county for national poverty alleviation. In recent years, many people have left their homes in search of jobs, but not all are able to find decent jobs. Many of them end up in unstable employment and income insecurity due to insufficient skills and qualifications. Meanwhile, local industries such as apple production and construction business are in shortage of qualified human resources but it is hard to recruit laborers from other areas. Therefore, improving the employment and entrepreneurship of people in Jingning County is much needed to improve their livelihood and reduce poverty.

Jingning County Government regards vocational education as a driver of economic development. The county government invested RMB 260 million to construct a new campus for the Jingning County Vocational Education Centre. In the centre, there are 76 training rooms, one simulated training room for construction professionals, 16 bases for industry-training-research alliance; and off-campus training bases for the Jingning apple industry. Some 58 training rooms and 10 on-campus practical training bases (training centres) are open 24/7 for students. The County Vocational Education Centre offers 16 programmes, such as numerical control techniques, construction, automotive operation and maintenance.

To promote the employment of the graduates, especially those from poor households, the Jingning County Vocational Education Centre has built partnerships with more than 30 enterprises nationwide and established an employment assistance mechanism for students from poor families. These measures have effectively ensured quality employment after graduation, reaching 99% in total and 100% for students living in poverty.

BOX 3-23   The Stories of Students from Jingning County Vocational Education Centre

Song Jingpeng is a student from Jieshipu, Jingning County, Gansu Province, and is studying construction at the Jingning County Vocational Education Centre. He recently won the third prize in the National Vocational College Student Entrepreneurship and Innovation Skills Competition, which would lead him to secure a good job. He deeply feels the power of education to change his life, when he thinks of experiences of his hometown peers who left for work after graduating from lower secondary school and now are facing the difficulties of low income and unstable employment.

Cattle breeding has been the dominant livelihood for Zhang Liancheng's family. However, they could not make profits due to the low quality of the breeding and lack of modern techniques. The cattle are now sold for RMB 5,000, which is higher than the price in previous years. The skills of animal husbandry he learned from the Centre played a big part in raising in earning.

Wang Fushuai studies horticulture at the Centre. Under her guidance, her family built greenhouses and developed a variety of fruit trees such as nectarines and apricots, which were marketed one month earlier through low-temperature induction technology. *Thanks to my daughter, now we can make a living from technology.* Her father, Wang Wu, said happily.

Source: Gansu Education Reform Helps Poverty Alleviation, available at www.gov.cn.

(2) Case: On-Site Training by Huaihua Vocational and Technical College in the Wuling Mountains, Huaihua City, Hunan Province

Huaihua Vocational and Technical College has achieved remarkable results in supporting poverty alleviation in the Wuling Mountainous Area, a contiguous poverty area identified by the Chinese government. It is partly located in Huaihua City, Hunan Province.

The College selects the best teachers to participate in poverty alleviation in the fields. The college assigns more than 40 expert teachers from its provincial first-class programmes, to provide relevant training for rural learners, aiming to help them get rid of poverty. The college has also established a team of external experts consisting of experienced and skillful technicians from higher education institutions, city and county agricultural bureaus, and animal husbandry bureaus to jointly undertake the training.

Moreover, every year the College deploys more than 20 excellent agricultural science and technology teachers to the townships and villages in Wuling Mountainous Area to provide technical guidance and skills training on farming. Over the past five years, the college has guided more than 100 households in planting and animal raising, helping lift at least 500 households out of poverty.

BOX 3-24   Outstanding Teacher Hu Hui to Provide Guidance on Animal Feeding in Wuling

Hu Hui, an award-winning professor and senior veterinarian in the Department of Animal Science and Technology, is a beloved teacher at Huaihua Polytechnic College.

She believes that, to solve the real problems rural learners encounter, the teaching should be linked with the daily practice of learners. She uses local language and terminologies when communicating with students and encourages them to participate in on-site and practice-oriented training in the fields. Hu Hui has shared her WeChat, QQ, and mobile phone number with the trainees so that they can reach out to her whenever they have questions or need some guidance. For example, in 2018, a trainee contacted Hu Hui regarding issues concerning chicken raising through WeChat. She diagnosed that it was mild bird flu and guided the trainee to take an emergency vaccination, and effectively controlled the spread of the flu.

Hu Hui's professional guidance and her dedication to supporting every learner makes her well respected among her trainees and local communities.

Source: Stories of Huaihua Vocational and Technical College's Support to Poverty Alleviation in Wuling Mountainous Area, available at www.huaihua.gov.cn.

BOX 3-25   Trainees of Huaihua Vocational and Technical College Established Agricultural Enterprises

Yang Shiqian is a trainee who studied cattle breeding and forage grass planting at the 20th rural science and technology backbone training course organized by Huaihua Vocational and Technical College, and the training was initiated by the Provincial Poverty Alleviation Office.

In 2016, he established Xinghuang Huihuang Herding Company, which is a leading enterprise of agricultural industrialization in Huaihua City with 12 large-scale farms and more than 100 beef cattle for each farm. The company has set up 22 cooperatives distributed in 8 townships in Xinhuang County, benefiting over 1,250 farmers and 5,000 plus people, with an annual per capita income of more than RMB 2,000. He also launched one-to-one poverty alleviation programme for staffs of subordinated cooperatives, lifted a total of 600 households and more than 2,130 people out of poverty.

Yao Maosheng, head of Songjiawan Village Commission, Tanjiazhai Township, Mayang County, is also a trainee of the institute. In 2009 and 2017, Yao Maosheng attended trainings at the Anjiang Campus of the College to study freshwater aquaculture and poultry farming. He then led the villagers to establish the "National Entrepreneurial Innovation Park" in Songjiawan Village to facilitate the local agricultural development.

Source: Huaihua Vocational and Technical College: Cultivating Entrepreneur Pioneers for the Wuling Mountainous Area, available at new.qq.com.

Huaihua Vocational and Technical College has organized 54 training sessions, including basic training on rural science and technology, grassroots agricultural technicians training, local entrepreneurship training for rural industry development and income generation and others, reaching a total of more than 17,000 trainees, and 500 plus village cadres, who have acquired a diploma from three-year high education programmes. The trainees have well utilized the newly acquired skills to drive local economic and social development.

Ⅴ. Cross-Sector Collaboration for Poverty Alleviation through Education

1. Mobilizing Enterprises and Social Organizations for Poverty Alleviation through Education

Addressing poverty is a collective responsibility. China mobilizes resources from various enterprises and social organizations in its efforts for poverty alleviation. The cross-sector cooperation and multi-stakeholder participation has brought significant results in educational development and poverty alleviation in rural areas.

The first case provides an example of how China's social organizations have contributed to the teachers' professional development in rural areas through collaboration with higher education institutions and other enterprises. The second case shows how a Chinese corporation supports education and poverty alleviation in impoverished areas in Henan, Sichuan, and Shanxi Provinces.

(1) Case: Youchange China Social Entrepreneur Foundation and Green Pepper Project Support Young Rural Teachers

In 2017, YouChange China Social Entrepreneur Foundation, Beijing Normal University and Hujiang Net in collaboration with more than 30 social organizations, academic institutions, and enterprises, jointly launched the "Green Pepper Project" to support rural teachers' development, addressing the issues of inadequate capacity and high turnover of rural teachers. It aimed to improve the capacities of young rural teachers and enhance their motivation through developing Massive Open Online Courses (MOOCs) that respond to their needs, providing online training and encouraging the establishment of learning communities of teachers. The project includes following activities:

- **Curriculum design**

  Beijing Normal University, the country's top teacher education institution,

developed courses on pedagogy to address the challenges faced by young rural teachers in teaching and learning.

The project developed 18 elective courses in four modules: early childhood education, elementary education, secondary education, and general education, to help young rural teachers improve their teaching skills and introduce new teaching methods.

- **Learning community of teachers**

The project has established an online learning community of teachers, encouraging experience sharing and peer support among teachers. It also assigned a facilitator to moderate discussions on issues relating to the training curriculum.

- **Incentives**

To conclude each year's training, the project selected 100 outstanding young teachers to attend a one-week summer training programme at Beijing Normal University. The programme provided face-to-face learning opportunities with education experts, training instructors, and experienced peers from across the country.

In September 2018, YouChange Foundation joined hands with enterprises to raise incentive funds to reward outstanding rural teachers who participate in the project,"Green Pepper Project" Summer Research and Training Camp in 2018.

The Project has achieved significant outcomes:

- A tailored curriculum for the young rural teachers participating in the project has been developed, including 50 core professional courses for teacher training, 144 sub-courses, and 60 thematic training courses.
- Around 20,000 rural teachers have benefited from the training, online experience-sharing and peer support.
- Nearly 200 liaison WeChat groups have been established for experience-sharing. Relying on these groups, the participants have created hundreds of themes or columns on Jianshu[①] to publish articles on the training courses and teaching practices.

(2) Case: Poverty Alleviation through Education: the Practice of China National Machinery Industry Corporation

China National Machinery Industry Corporation (hereafter referred to as Sinomach) is one of the world's top 500 enterprises and has been supporting the development of

---

① Jianshu is a website and mobile application that allows users to read and write Chinese and English articles.

primary, secondary, and vocational education in four poor counties (districts): Gushi County and Huaibin County of Henan Province; the Chaotian District of Guangyuan City, Sichuan Province; and Pinglu County of Shanxi Province. Sinomach has made impressive achievements in improving school conditions, retention of students, teaching, and employment in these targeted areas. Its support ranges from financial support to teachers training, employment and skills training.

- **Financial support**

  Sinomach has invested considerable amount of funds to support primary and secondary schools in poor areas to improve school conditions. From 2016 to 2019, the company invested more than RMB 14.76 million in the four poor counties (districts) to improve teaching facilities and school living conditions in primary and secondary schools. For example, in the Chaotian District, Guangyuan City, Sinomach contributed nearly RMB 3 million to systematically renovate the original Yudong Township Primary School and transform it into a Happy Sinomach Primary School, which has become the "most beautiful rural school" in Guangyuan City. The number of students returning to the mountainous areas and the quality of teaching has been increasing year by year.

- **Teacher training**

  Since 2017, Sinomach has provided funds for the training of primary and secondary school teachers in its paired-up assistance counties (districts). Every year, more than 500 people, including teachers of Mandarin, mathematics, English, and other subjects, and school principals at the grassroots level, attended a week-long training at Beijing Normal University to improve their capacities in subject knowledge, pedagogy, and school management.

- **Employment**

  Sinomach has supported poor students to learn skills and obtain employment by utilizing the resources of its affiliated vocational schools. The schools in the Chaotian District has set up a targeted enrollment strategy to expand access to vocational education for the high school graduates from poor households with poverty portfolios and the junior and senior high school graduates under 30 years old. The accepted students receive a 3-year vocational education. The tuition fees are borne by the government, and Sinomach bears the cost of accommodation, management, books, internship, and other expenses during the school years. The vocational schools provide comprehensive career services for students who have completed their studies and obtained vocational qualifications, and they will be prioritized to be hired in the subsidiary companies of Sinomach.

- **Skills training**

The Training Centre of Sinomach's affiliated Deyang Installation Technician College provides free skills training with a duration ranging from 15 days to 6 months, covering more than 30 types of work and job opportunities for people in need aged 18-45 in poor households with poverty portfolios in Chaotian District. From 2016 to 2018, Sinomach invested over RMB 1.2 million in skills and entrepreneurship training, reaching around 3,500 people in the district.

The practice of Sinomach showcases the significant role of corporations' engagement in poverty alleviation and educational development in poverty-stricken areas.

2. Advancing Poverty Alleviation through Education in Collaboration with International Organizations

Following the reform and opening-up policy in China, the Chinese government has been enhancing cooperation with international organizations to advance the work of poverty reduction through education in underdeveloped areas in western China. The following cases show two successful partnerships with United Nations Children's Fund (UNICEF) and United Nations Educational, Scientific and Cultural Organization (UNESCO).

(1) Case: Unicef's Child-Friendly Schools Programme: Towards Equitable, Inclusive and Quality Rural Education

In 2001, UNICEF and the Department of Teacher Education, Ministry of Education of China, jointly launched a pilot project on Child-Friendly Schools in 72 county-level centre schools and village primary schools in seven counties from three western provinces of China. The project developed and implemented the China's Child-Friendly School Standards, which has integrated the national policies and international best practices, aiming to improve the quality of schooling in terms of access, school environment, learning content, learning process, and learning outcomes, to ensure the all-round development of students and their healthy growth.

In accordance with the new national curriculum reform in basic education, the project integrated the values of child-friendly schools into the teacher training curriculum, such as equality, inclusion, participation, and effective learning. It aimed to promote a student-centered approach in schooling, improve the relationship between teaching and learning, enhance the interaction between school, family, and the community, create a supportive atmosphere for students' physical and mental health, and ensure the quality of education in the western rural areas.

By the end of 2005, the project had organized more than 500 training sessions benefiting about 13,000 plus teachers, many of whom later became grassroots trainers and backbone teachers to cascade the training among their colleagues. The project laid a solid foundation to expand it on a larger scale in the western region. In addition, 85% of the programme schools have been improved by implementing the child-friendly school standards, with significant achievements in school environment, student participation and performance, teaching methods, and school management.

The Project has contributed to the universalization of nine-year compulsory education in western China, especially in remote and poor areas. It has trained a group of experts and trainers at the national and provincial levels who have acquired knowledge and skills for building child-friendly schools. These trainers can further organize participatory training sessions in their positions in different institutions to support others.

(2) Case: UNESCO Promotes Community Learning Centres in Ethnic Rural Areas in Yunnan Province

Promoting rural community education in Yunnan Province has many difficulties due to its unique natural setting, ethnic diversity and multiple cultures. Different ethnic peoples inhabit together in ethnically mixed vast areas while some live in individual compact communities within their own group, which poses challenges when gathering residents from different ethnic groups to engage in community development initiatives.

Since 2005, the Chinese National Commission for UNESCO, the UNESCO Beijing Office, and the China Adult Education Association have jointly implemented the Rural Community Learning Centre (CLC) Capacity Building Project and have established five CLCs in Yunnan. Considering the development scenario of the communities where the CLCs are based, the five CLCs have implemented a range of activities, including capacity building for the villagers. The project has played a vital role in creating a harmonious relationship between and/or among different communities, improving the quality of local people's life, protecting the cultural heritage of ethnic groups, and promoting rural economic and social development.

The five CLCs established by the project have gradually evolved into three development models in response to different needs of the communities: government-led CLC, community-centered CLC, and school-centered CLC.

● Government-led CLC

Shilin Nanmen CLC and the Kaiyuan Xiaolongtan CLC are led by township government and the residential district commissions. They aim to support the

government to provide social services, adult educational activities, women's employment, policy advocacy, skills training, and community's self-governance. It serves as an extra hand of the government to function at the grassroots level, enriching residents' lives, and maintaining a harmonious community.

- **Community-centered CLC**

   Lancang Mangjing Village CLC takes into account the unique culture of an ethnic group, Bulang, and provides services and activities that promote productive capacity and protect local environment. Leveraging the prestige and resources of Bulang's community head, also known as Bulang's "last prince", the CLC has built an ethnic museum and cultural buildings to preserve the local heritage. Moreover, the CLC has integrated the local thousand-year tea culture and industry into its training for income generation and promoted the ecological harmony and sustainability in the community.

- **School-centered CLC**

   The Xundian Liushao Township CLC is housed in the local centre primary school, dedicated to building a harmonious relationship between the school and the community for joint development. It unifies the school's educational resources with those of the community to promote community development. The CLC has established a community library, built an experimental base for breeding detoxified potatoes, and carried out a training on agricultural science and technology, and organized various ethnic cultural activities.

   The Shangri-La Ren'an CLC was established based on a free kindergarten built by local residents. The CLC supports formal preschool education and encourages the participation of students and parents in learning, community services, and preservation of ethnic cultural heritage.

The five CLCs have showcased effective models of rural community education in different villages and multicultural contexts. They have conducted educational activities while considering the economic and social development needs of the communities, and taken great efforts to preserve the traditions and cultures of ethnic communities. The CLCs value sustainable development, the preservation and inheritance of ethnic culture, contributing to the harmonious coexistence of different ethnic groups in targeted communities in Yunnan.

Conclusion

Over the decades, especially since 2012, impressive achievements have been made in education development in China, particularly in the less developed areas. Essentially, investment in education is an investment for poverty reduction. China has successfully positioned education as a key factor for alleviating poverty. Persistent educational issues such as drop-out of students from poor families, inequitable access to education resources in poor and hardship areas and among minority and vulnerable communities, unbalanced urban-rural development, and others have been significantly solved. This can be attributed to the systematic, holistic and contextualized educational support through social protection, human resource development, capacity building, employment, entrepreneurship, industrial development, and others.

As a result, all of China's 770 million poor population in rural areas, including those living in contiguous special hardship areas, have been lifted out of poverty according to current poverty lines. China has achieved the SDG 1 on poverty reduction 10 years ahead of schedule, while actively promoting international cooperation on poverty reduction.

The above 38 good practices of poverty alleviation through education in China exemplify programmes and actions of China's targeted poverty alleviation through education from five aspects including access to education, quality improvement, skills development, localized industrial development, and cross-sector collaboration. These diversified cases demonstrate successful and innovative practices at different levels and initiated by different stakeholders, with solid evidence from various sources. The experiences and lessons underpinning the success can be summarized as follows:

- **Strong political will and sustained policy commitments of the government** towards ensuring inclusive, equitable and quality education for all have been a critical factor. Furthermore, poverty reduction has always been on top of

the policy agenda of government at different levels, including the national commitment to translate relevant goals of SDGs into concrete actions.

- **Substantial financial support** from the government in particular has always guaranteed the implementation of relevant policies, programmes and activities in China. Funding assurance ensures the completion of projects and helps achieve expected outcomes and impacts.
- **Central local policy alignment** ensures a coherent and harmonized approach towards poverty alleviation through education. This approach stakeholders at sub-national levels to adapt policies and programmes to local context, needs and resources.
- **Strong social mobilization and active public participation** encourages diversified organizations including enterprises, social organizations, foundations and individuals like experts, teachers, village heads and relevant stakeholders to come together to support and innovate the practice of poverty alleviation through education.
- **Cross-sectoral and multiple partnerships** have been crucial in China's actions of poverty alleviation through education. The selected cases illustrate how corporates, civil societies, higher education institutions and international organizations mobilize their resources and expertise to advance the planning and implementation of programmes and activities at all levels.
- **Bridging the gap between education and employment** to promote the income generation of poor households and lift them out of poverty, through skills development, entrepreneurship training, and local industrial development and so on.
- **Reaching the most disadvantaged**, especially households in extreme poverty, girls and women, children with disabilities, ethnic groups, etc. to ensure that no one is left behind.
- **ICT-related measures**, such as the provision of multimedia equipment at schools and distance learning programmes, have been effective in reducing the inequitable distribution of educational resources and creating a more open and interactive space for learning and experience sharing among learners.
- **An accurate and reliable information system** enables the identification of people in need, especially the poor and marginal groups living in hard-to-reach areas. It also increases the availability, range, and quality of support and services for poverty alleviation through education; and facilitates effective monitoring and evaluation of the progress and results of programmes.
- **Paired-up support** provided by the advanced eastern regions, higher education institutions and schools in cities has played a key role in promoting poverty

alleviation through education in remote rural areas. It functions as a mechanism of "development aid" in China.

In the final analysis, it is necessary to stress that the achievements in poverty alleviation through education cannot be reached without strong political commitment, sufficient resource inputs, active participation and genuine dialogue among all stakeholders, and documentation of progress and challenges. Meanwhile, it is worth noting that there is no one-size-fits-all approach, as each practice needs to be responsive to the unique local contexts and needs, including socio-economical, cultural and geographical factors. In this regard, we hope the selected cases and lessons drawn from them can be a reference for future practice in China. These experiences can be insightful for advancing the cause of poverty reduction through education in other countries around the world on the way towards 2030.

References

Refer to the Chinese part of the references.

Acknowledgement

At the completion of this report, we should first pay our great tribute to the grassroots educators and community workers who have been fighting on the frontier of poverty alleviation over the years. Their wisdom and hardworking have made the stories in this report more fruitful.

We greatly appreciate the guidance, support and contributions from the Secretariat of the Chinese National Commission for UNESCO, thanks are also given to Beijing Normal University which is the host organization for UNESCO International Research and Training Centre for Rural Education (INRULED). We would also like to express our gratitude to the Department of Development Planning, Department of Finance, Department of Basic Education, Department of Vocational and Adult Education, Department of Teacher Education, Ministry of Education; National Institute of Education Sciences, China National Center for Student Financial Aid, the Open University of China, UNESCO Beijing Office, UNICEF China, and other institutions for their valuable suggestions.

The preparation of the Chinese version was led by Mr. Wang Li, with support from a group of experts and INRULED's staff. They are: Li Xingzhou, Zhang Tiedao, Meng Hongwei, Dong Jianhong, Tan Yanqing, Min Bista, Robert Parua, Fang Yuan'an, Qi Zhiyong, Li Xiaoping, Hou Xiaoyu, Pan Kunfeng, Wang Di, Cui Jianmin, Li Lei, Lu Yifan, Huang Linjia, Wang Yawen, Yao Jikun, Ren Chao, Qi Xinjian, and Li Yang. The cases in this report were provided by Shen Peng, Lu Huijie, Li Jinsong, Jiang Genxing, Zheng Gangqiang, Liu Fenglei, Yang Wenming, Jin Yan, Wu Yanlei etc. The outline preparation and final check on Chinese version was done by Mr. Qin Changwei, Mr. Wang Li, Ms. Jia Nan, Mr. Zhang Songyun, Mr. Guo Zhijun, Mr. Wang Yongqian, Mr. Shen Kaiwen, and Mr. Xia Jingxuan.

The English version was finalized by a working team led by Dr. Zhao Yuchi, Deputy Director of INRULED, with Dr. Liu Jing (Director, Office of International Exchange

and Cooperation, Faculty of Education, Beijing Normal University), Ms. Liu Ruixi, and Ms. Jiang Zhujun as team members. Mr. Wang Li and some colleagues have also contributed to the translation from Chinese into English. Mr. Min Bista, former Professor of Education Tribhuwan University Nepal and Education Specialist of UNESCO, has helped review and polish the report.

This report wouldn't have been finalized without the strong support from Professor Huang Ronghuai, Director, and Professor Zeng Xiaodong, Executive Director of UNESCO INRULED.

UNESCO International Research and Training Centre for Rural Education

November 2022